BLACK
IN FASHION

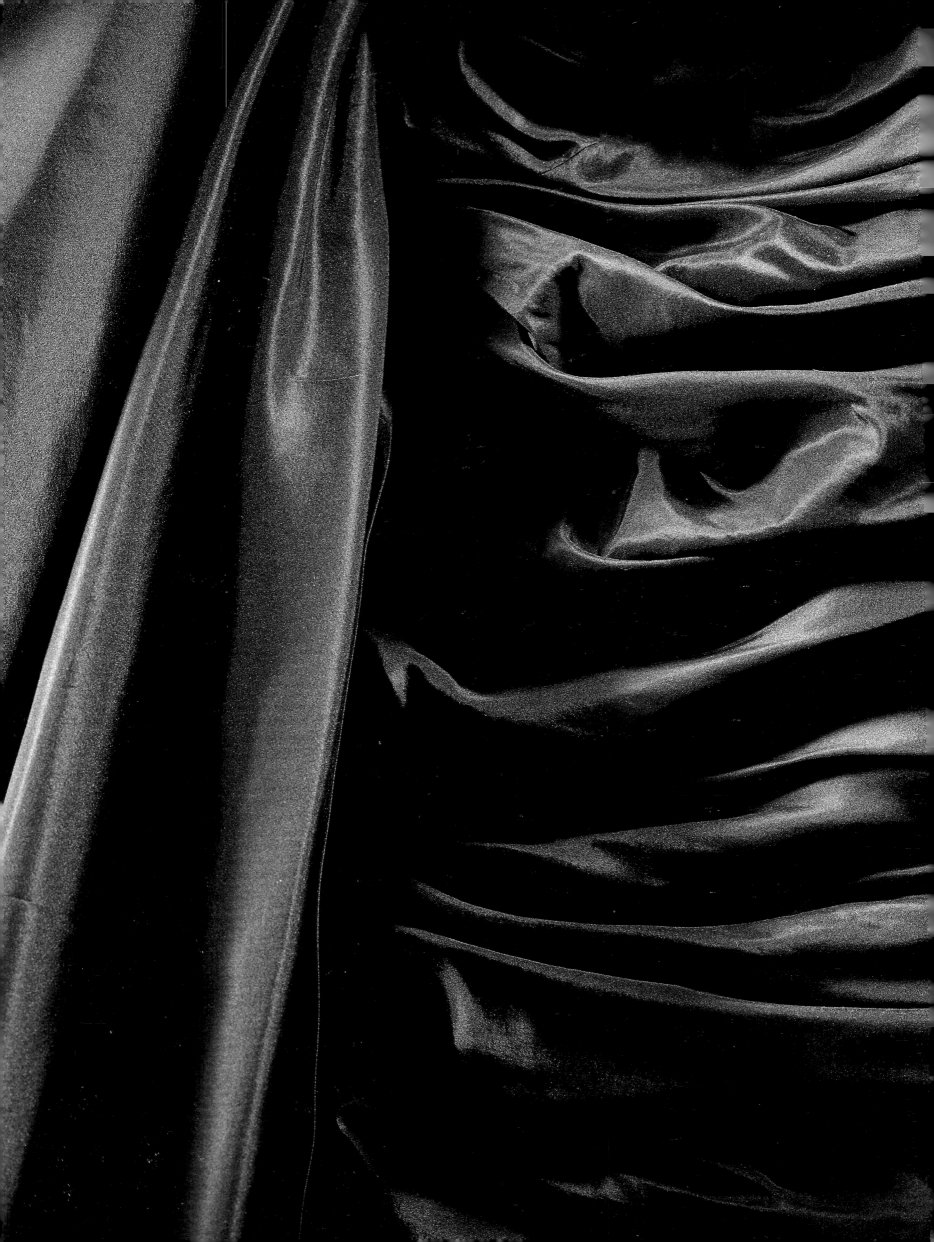

BLACK IN FASHION

VALERIE MENDES

PHOTOGRAPHY BY RICHARD DAVIS

V&A PUBLICATIONS

British Library

Designed by johnson banks
Photgrahy by Richard Davis,
V&A Photographic Studio
Photographs styled by Sue Milner
Line Drawings by Leonie Davis
Originated and printed in Singapore, by C. S. Graphics

Frontispiece:
Detail of evening gown, ruched silk taffeta
Christian Dior, Paris c. 1950
Worn and given by Lady Joan Black

Jacket illustrations:
Front: Evening gown, Christian Dior,
Paris, 1955, front view
Back: Evening gown, Christian Dior,
Paris, 1955, back view

YOU CAN WEAR BLACK
AT ANY TIME
YOU CAN WEAR IT
AT ANY AGE
YOU MAY WEAR IT ON
ALMOST ANY
OCCASION
A LITTLE BLACK FROCK
IS ESSENTIAL TO
A WOMAN'S WARDROBE
I COULD WRITE
A BOOK ABOUT
BLACK

CHRISTIAN DIOR 1954

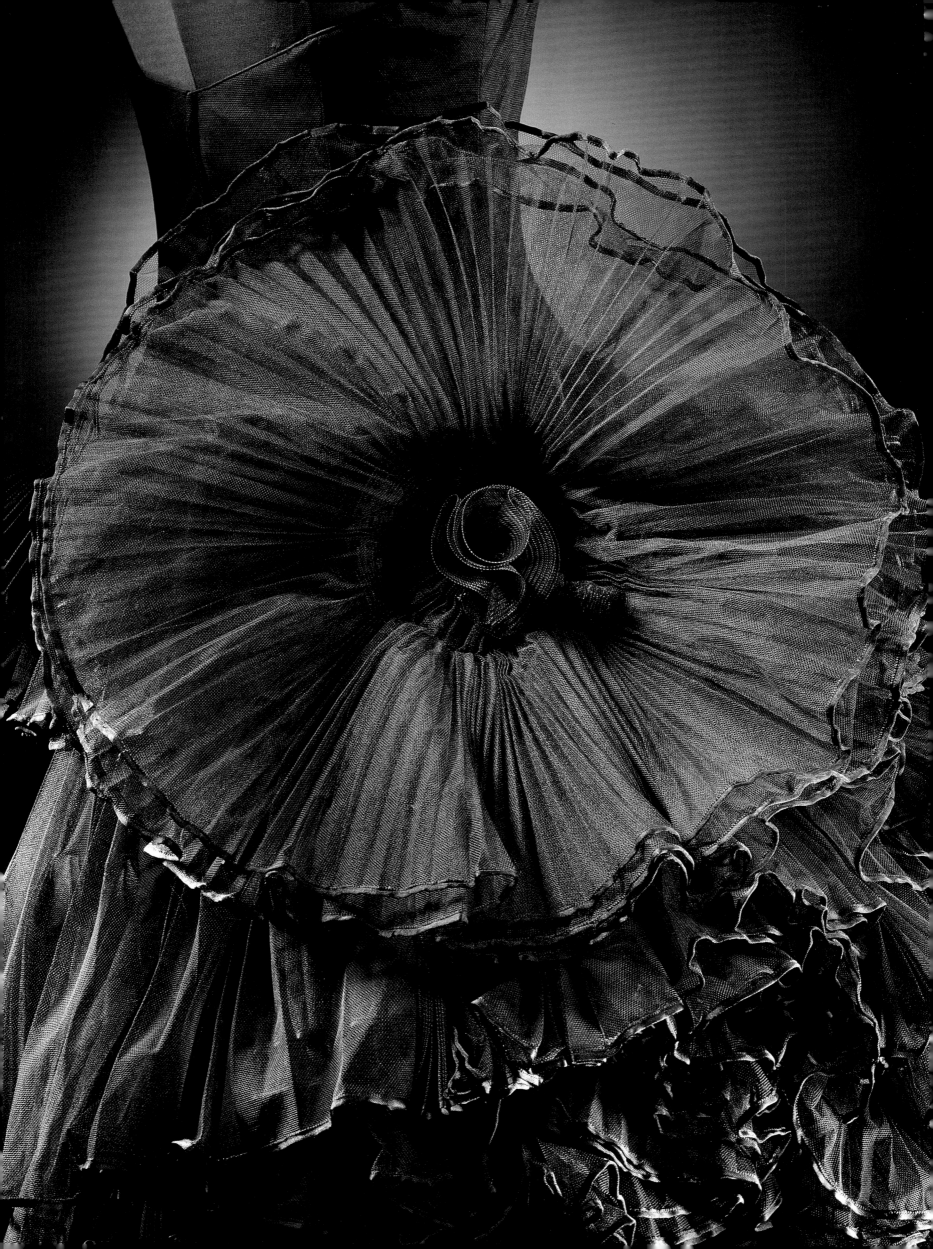

Introduction

You can wear black at any time
You can wear it at any age.
You may wear it on almost any occasion.
A 'little black frock' is essential to a
woman's wardrobe.
I could write a book about black…
Christian Dior, 1954

Black in fashion, particularly in the guise of the little black dress, became an indispensable feature of cosmopolitan style after World War I. Designers harnessed the power of black, drawn irresistibly to its innate qualities of drama and strength of line. With their keen appreciation of dress history, these designers have always been aware of the black bloodline in fashion and alert to their role in its continuum. For the past five hundred years, aside from the use of black for mourning as well as for religious, academic, legal and ceremonial dress, black with a greater or lesser dominance has been a fashion constant. In the fifteenth century it was favoured by Philip the Good, Duke of Burgundy (ruled 1419-67), who made deliberate and effective appearances (ostensibly in mourning) clad from head to toe in stylish black. Henceforward black became a significant player in fashion; as Max von Boehn stated: 'Black now entered the lists, and its dusky trail may be followed throughout the succeeding centuries. It spread like a pool of spilt ink, staining as it ran' (*Modes and Manners*, translation 1932). Black (for both men and women) asserted itself in the dress of sixteenth- and seventeenth-century Spanish aristocrats; it was favoured by the *haute bourgeoisie* of seventeenth-century Holland and, in the late nineteenth to early twentieth centuries, was the not-so-secret weapon of a few daringly elegant women of the *Belle Epoque* in Europe and America. By the early 1900s, the stage was set for designers to consolidate the position of black in the realms of high fashion.

A panoply of associations attends achromatic black. *The Oxford English Dictionary* warns that it is 'a word of difficult history', its origins being complex and multi-stranded. In the West it signifies 'the garb of mourning and woe and the emblem of death and destruction' (GA Audsley, *Colour in Dress*, 1912). To many this 'non-colour' is perceived as the very nadir of negativity. Hostile and threatening, black has come to represent disaster, evil and wickedness. It is the antithesis of its unsullied sister, the chaste and pure white. As a prefix it bodes ill, as in black magic, black witch, black Sabbath, black sheep, black mass, blackmail, Black Maria, black mark, Black Death and black hearted. It has become the convention to brand financial catastrophes with this indelible word; thus the first disastrous day of the Wall Street crash in 1929 is forever Black Thursday. Derek Jarman, in his staccato insights into black, pinpointed indisputable links with sex: 'Is their underwear black?/Sexy Soho Black?/Do they lie on black sheets?' (*Chroma*, 1994). Paradoxically, the black leather and lace of S&M means vice and sex, while the black of religious orders signifies piety. In the course of their work, psychologists, psychiatrists, colour consultants, dyers and printers, designers, artists and craftspeople regularly confront and utilize black. Even in its most fashionable phases, black is not favoured in colour preference tests; its intimations of oblivion and death trigger anxiety and many find it utterly repellent. The black of high fashion carries hints of all these connotative properties, and those who choose to wear black and onlookers alike take on a heavy symbolic burden.

Fashion is determined by its raw materials — first and foremost by fabrics. Though black textiles have a long history, examples of pre eighteenth-century black clothes are rare due to the destructive characteristics of the natural dyes and fixing agents required to achieve a true black. Synthetic dyes (introduced in the 1850s) replaced corrosive natural dyes, dramatically improving the survival rate of black dresses. The twentieth-century plethora of dyeing methods and recipes resulted in a wide range of black, a diversity increased by the fact that every fibre and fabric responds to dye and reflects light in varying ways. Techniques, such as pleating, ruching and quilting (pages 24, 48 and 52), add to this abundance. Nomenclature is a minefield. Without a universally observed colour code, the industry continues to give fanciful names to black samples, and the use of handy compound terms such as blue-black, green-black and purple-black is unscientifically widespread. Black fabrics age and deteriorate at various rates according to dye, fibre, fabric, wear, tear and owner care: an expensive cashmere gown of 1910-12 (page 20) appears fresher than a dress thirty years younger in a budget-priced rayon (page 44). Etiquette manuals warn women to beware of tired, badly maintained black clothes. A black achieved in Japan by repeated dyeing with indigo proved to have hidden assets. Yohji Yamamoto explained:

It wasn't exactly black but an indigo blue dyed so many times it is close to black. The Samurai spirit is black. The Samurai must be able to throw his body into nothingness, the colour and image of which is black. But the farmers like black or dark, dark indigo, because the indigo plant was easy to grow, and the dye was good for the body and kept insects away (Leonard Koren, *New Fashion Japan*, 1984).

In the early years of the twentieth century, designers in Paris and London provided elegant and wealthy clients with a vast array of extravagant clothes to meet their every need. The black of mourning was inevitably among these accoutrements and the more adventurous added day wear and sophisticated evening gowns in eye-catching black. Notable antecedents included the audacious black satin evening gown in the 1884 portrait of *Madame X* (Virginie Gautreau) by John Singer Sargent. Lady Troubridge's memoirs describe Lady Feversham's daughters in Edwardian England: they 'had to be seen to be believed, for it was a unique combination of perfect features and almost miraculous complexions. They were dressed quite simply, often in black, but everyone used to stare at them as they came into a ballroom' (*Memories and Reflections*, 1925).

Upholding tradition, late nineteenth-century women had cut a dash, tightly corseted and compressed into black riding habits (the best were provided by London tailors). The *demi-mondaine* 'Skittles' (Catherine Walters, 1839-1920) was noted for her faultless appearance (in riding clothes by Creed and Henry Poole) on horseback in London's Rotten Row, while Queen Alexandra's tiny-waisted form was often photographed in immaculate black habits. Flora Thompson, remembering English country life before World War I, wrote of 'women sitting their side-saddles with hour-glass figures encased in skin-tight black habits. "*Looks for all the world as if she'd been melted and poured into it, now don't she?*"' (*Over to Candleford*, 1941). Later in the century fashion-alert equestriennes from Coco Chanel to Jackie Onassis continued the custom of riding in chic black.

The 'little black dress' was born some time in the early 1900s. For the main part, clothes worn by the *beau monde* at this time were far too elaborate, with their yards of over-decorated fabrics and attendant frou-frou, to have been accurately termed 'little', though in 1902 Henry James wrote: 'She might have been dressed tonight in the little black frock...'(*The Wings of the Dove*). In July 1903 *The Lady's Magazine* mentioned a 'pretty black afternoon frock' and asserted that 'The black gown is, of course, the stay-by of the woman with a limited income; it is such a particularly useful garment and can be worn on so very many occasions.' Illuminating a way through the complexities of the manners and rules of polite society pre-World War I, etiquette handbooks describe the black of mourning weeds, invariably adding comments about black's further sartorial potential. The anonymous author of *Comments of a Countess* mused in 1901 that: '...my garments invariably reflect the colour of my moods. Black imparts a feeling of

dignity, pathos and unapproachableness.'

Traditional mourning attire blazed a trail for the march of fashionable black and the little black dress. Until the custom for lengthy periods of mourning lapsed after 1918, Western society grieved in orthodox black. However, in metropolitan centres the convention of self-effacement in unflattering clothes of undistinguished cut was gradually abandoned. Most unusually, in 1910, with Britain still in mourning for Edward VII's death, a highlight of the season, the Ascot race meeting, was not abandoned and it became the legendary 'Black Ascot'. As usual, society paraded in its finery, though on this unique occasion it was all black. The fashion side of mourning was openly debated, and readers of the *Evening Standard and St James's Gazette* (26 May 1910) were advised that: 'One of the chief features of Ascot this year will be the numbers and the beauty of the black net and lace coats. These will soften the rigour of mourning attire, and will bring a distinctly decorative note into the scheme.' In her *Modes of Mayfair* column for *The Play Pictorial* (June 1910), Rita Detmold granted that the entire world was lamenting its terrible loss but then noted almost petulantly: 'Black, mourning black, is but an outward semblance after all, and with the advent of summer, white, greys and purples, etc., will gradually be substituted, and the mournful and depressing sight of black and nothing but black will be alleviated...'. While observing the protocol of bereavement black, young women were no longer castigated for pursuing fashionable mourning. They ordered the very latest styles to be made in the universally accepted Courtauld crape and undemonstrative fabrics with the correct matt finish. Paris designers led and journals published their modish creations. *Les Modes* in March 1911 described two especially chic mourning toilettes as '*ravissantes*' in spite of their sad overtones, asserting that, even in the depth of sorrow, women's coquettish instincts prevailed as they made themselves appealing clad in exquisite black. Lucile (Lady Duff Gordon) ensured that her fashion parades included mourning-ready black 'gowns of emotion' (page 22) to which she gave evocative names such as 'A Lament', *Chagrin d'Amour* and 'Let Us Forget'.

As with so many other aspects of cultural evolution, World War I marked a turning point. Although it plunged many women into deep mourning, new attitudes towards black became evident. Some, on grounds of morale ('a universal wearing of black as an expression of sorrow would have been unthinkably depressing to the public', *Vogue*, 15 July 1927) eschewed black altogether, adopting black or purple armbands while others flaunted ultra-fashionable attire in black. Fashion magazines barely mentioned the effects of hostilities until 1916 when the ravages started to bite. Then, appeals for economy suggested that readers 'Use just the necessary and not the fashionable number of yards of material for new dresses' (*The Queen*, 7 October 1916). Clothes became smaller as skirts were dramatically shortened, allowing women increased mobility for their war-linked tasks. It was within this historical context that the adjectives 'small', 'simple' and 'little' began to invade the language of fashion journalism. Thus, out of necessity, the concept of the little dress emerged and was accepted. One page in *The Queen* (7 October 1916) contains no less than four references to the 'little dress', including a tantalizing 'charming little black satin dress'. Sound advice was given to the working woman in 1917: 'The busy woman who has to take the metro, the tram or to go on foot, does well to indulge in one of the many little models in black…'(*The Queen*, 9 June 1917). Black was obligatory for those in mourning but it was also sensible wear for those who struggled daily with the grime of city travel and office, shop or workroom routine. The passage of black from the rites of mourning to its eventual unassailable and widespread position as a fashion classic was virtually complete.

In 1919 Chanel set a seal upon the fashionable validity of black, though the notion that she was the inventor of the little black dress must be treated with caution. Black threaded through Chanel's life. Friends even relied on it to describe her: Jean Cocteau wrote that she had the head of a 'little black swan', to which Colette added, and the heart 'of a little black bull'. Chanel's biographers recorded a variety of sources (some of them apocryphal) for her discovery of the potency of black and agreed that it became a central plank in her oeuvre. Edmonde Charles-Roux (*Chanel*, 1975) stated that Chanel made black 'the instrument of her success', an endorsement that meant black 'ceased to be seen as a passing accessory in the eyes of posterity and became the expression of an age'. Marcel Haedrich (*Coco Chanel*, 1972) asserted that she 'made black mandatory'. Chanel had told him that it all stemmed from a charity ball for the *Petits Lits Blancs*, when she perceived that '… the colours are too awful, they make the women ugly. I think they ought to be dressed in black.' Then, 'For four or five years I made only black. My dresses sold like mad, with little touches — a little white collar, or cuffs. Everyone wore them — actresses, society women, housemaids.' She was incensed when her pared-down designs in black were dubbed 'poverty *de luxe*', 'soup kitchen style' and 'poor girl fashion', retorting that these impeccably made clothes in the finest materials (especially when combined with her costume jewellery) allowed women 'to walk around like millionaires'. Claims that she decided to plunge the entire world into mourning at the loss of her lover Captain Arthur Capel in 1919 infuriated Chanel, though the depth of her grief is well documented. Edmonde Charles-Roux described an all-black bedroom that was so tomb-like that Chanel never slept in it and her subsequent decision to have the shutters of her weekend villa lacquered black. Throughout her long career, she frequently dressed in black and accorded it pride of place in her collections. In 1939 she closed her house, but, typically, in her come-back collection in 1954 she commenced with a black suit.

Though they were arch rivals throughout the 1930s, Chanel and Schiaparelli, often depicted as the classicist versus the entertainer, had in common an understanding of the value and longevity of the simple black dress. In self-awareness, Schiaparelli wrote: 'in spite of Schiap's apparent craziness and love of fun and gags, her greatest fans were the ultra-smart and conservative women, wives of diplomats and bankers, millionaires and artists, who like severe suits and plain black dresses' (*Shocking Life*, 1954). The originals were confined to her rich clientele but illicit copies made them widely available — not something Schiaparelli worried about. Copying to her signalled that she was newsworthy and in fashion's vanguard. So compelling was the sensual black spread by the Hollywood films, *noir* and otherwise, of the 1930s (pages 34, 36 and 38) that, to enhance its 'fathomless lure', Weil created the perfume 'Noir'. Schiaparelli's fantasies, such as the famous shoe hat, were often black, and black served as a background for her witty embroideries (page 42). In appreciation of the significance and versatility of black, she noted '…I had designed a very plain black dress typically "Schiap", a dress that was high in the neck and could be worn both at the office and at the theatre, the sort of dress I wear all day myself'. In 1937 she outlined the contents of a capsule wardrobe including an essential black suit and black dress. Emphatically adding the stamp of her own opinions to the authoritative views of her grandmother, the model and actress Marisa Berenson wrote: 'Schiap was just as famous, however, for black. Basic black. As in *little black suit*. As in *little black dress*. The most important thing for a woman to have in her wardrobe, she said, and so do I' (*Dressing Up*, 1984).

During World War II women were chiefly confined to uniforms, the overalls of war-related occupations or remodelled pre-war clothes, while fashion (including black in fashion) marked time. The black of mourning was dreaded though on occasion when fabrics became scarce women ran up little numbers in black-out material and were tempted by the fashion offerings of black marketeers. Graphic black has recorded shifts in style perfectly; it caught the bullishness of the squared-off, war-time silhouette (page 44) and then, five years later, brought the rounded contours of the conquering New Look into sharp focus (page 50). Christian Dior was a lead player in one of the most active decades for black in fashion, the 1950s. He developed a special alliance with black:

> I have no wish to deprive fashion of the added allure and charm of colour, but I could perfectly well design a whole collection simply in black or white and express all my ideas to my complete satisfaction. Colour cannot transform a failure of a dress into a success: it merely plays a supporting role in the cast where the cut is the star performer
> (*Dior by Dior*, 1957).

Black prevailed; he used it to emphasize particularly elaborate structures (pages 50 and 66); employing long-forgotten techniques, he invariably stiffened and lined clothes with an assortment of horsehair, cambric and taffeta. He enjoyed the challenge of black and outlined the dilemma of choosing exactly the right black to make just one little black dress from thirty black woollen fabric samples. Not averse to a touch of black humour, he told of a charming client who viewed a whole collection of black suits and murmured, as she made her choice, 'It's such a pity that mourning is so common at funerals'.

Balenciaga found black the perfect vehicle for his unsurpassed works that straddled the boundary between fashion and the fine arts. From the 1930s to the closure of his establishment in 1968, black heightened the line and volume of designs that were sophisticated and wearable but at the same time resembled powerful abstract sculptures. While he confined his most exaggerated concepts to evening wear, classic dresses and suits for daytime were distinguished by their sculpted minimal forms. *Harper's Bazaar* (October 1938) applauded his particular brand of black: 'Here the black is so black that it hits you like a blow. Thick Spanish black, almost velvety, a night without stars.' At Balenciaga's first collection in Paris in 1937, fashion editor Bettina Ballard decided that the 'black day dresses were exactly what I needed' and ordered one immediately. A timeless design, in 1960 she still had the pattern which had been copied many times (*In My Fashion*, 1960). Thirty years later the socialite Tina Chow, a Balenciaga devotee, treasured a number of his severe black designs in her notable collection of twentieth-century couture. Like Chanel, whose sorrow in 1919 confirmed the place of black in her work, Balenciaga, grief striken at the death of his friend Vladzio d'Attainville in 1948, did homage in a resolutely black collection. Balenciaga championed semi-fitted clothes and (for day wear) worked towards stark simplicity by paring away decoration and superfluous details – simplicity made all the more effective in black (page 70). It further empowered the extraordinary shapes he achieved, from cocoon-shaped dresses to conical ball gowns. Célia Bertin declared that Balenciaga's formal evening dresses 'are always striking; they are meant to be looked at as one looks at a work of art' (*Paris à la Mode*, 1956). In this spirit he created masterpieces ranging from the double-tiered 'balloon' ensemble of 1950 to the tapered, four-sided dress of 1967, all in 'the ever present black' (Marie-Andrée Jouve, *Balenciaga*, 1989).

The late 1940s heralded a period of boom for the little black dress and suit. One London-based gown manufacturer, Dalton Fashion Ltd, even changed its name to the more enticing 'Lady in Black Fashions', organized an effective advertising campaign and ran its wholesale and export operation solely to answer the demand for smart black clothes. Copywriters rose to the challenge as they charted the progress of good taste in fashionable black: 'The little black suit that starts out in the afternoon and continues on to dinner' (*Harper's Bazaar*, November 1946); 'Invest your all in one good little black dress' (*Woman and Beauty*, 1951); 'Many tones of black – one sure allure. Black on black for little evenings' (*Vogue*, November 1951); and 'It's no secret what black can be when all the elements are right: worldly, elegant, plainly alluring – indispensable' (*Vogue*, September 1957). The smartly tailored black suit (page 62) had every requirement for success at work or at play in its natural habitat – the city. It was not marred by metropolitan dirt. It looked efficient and neat around the clock and could be dressed up for evening engagements. Dior pronounced that 'the little black suit cannot be beaten for elegance and usefulness'. In a predominantly male environment it gave its wearer authority, being the nearest female equivalent of the businessman's suit and the predecessor of the 1980s power suit. The preferred combination was a fitted jacket with peplum and matching pencil-slim skirt. A similarly versatile relative was a little black dress with a trim woollen top attached to a pleated skirt (page 64). Jean Dessès and Jacques Fath (among many other couturiers) created variations on this theme. A copy of a Fath original was described as 'The sweater idea attached to a short skirt of knife pleated nylon marquisette. A dress to go on into winter evenings. The whole thing, black, black' (*USA Vogue*, May 1951).

Both suit and little black sweater-dress would not have been out of place at smart 1950s cocktail parties. At these early-evening gatherings the little black dress reigned supreme. Competitive ladies changed for cocktails (pages 58 and 82), and the most assured wore modish little black cocktail hats (tiny confections of decorated silk and tulle) perched on their heads. Dresses specifically for the taking of cocktails were designed in the 1920s and 1930s and the tradition gained a new lease of life in the 1950s. Throughout these semi-formal occasions (of about two hours duration) participants usually stood and mingled and for this endeavour, according to etiquette manuals, every guest required correct attire, top-to-toe grooming and charm. Dior decided that cocktail dresses were 'elaborate and dressy afternoon frocks'. In the preferred black, he counselled that materials such as taffeta, satin, chiffon and wool were cocktail-worthy but that elaborate embroidery and brocade should be confined to evening gowns (*Christian Dior's Little Dictionary of Fashion*, 1954). Such formality extended into the next decade when Geneviève Antoine Dariaux (formerly directrice at Nina Ricci) advised that 'from 6pm on, the dress comes into its own again, in the form of a cocktail or dinner dress. This is the moment of triumph for the famous "little black dress", somewhat *décolleté*, made of sheer wool or silk crêpe, and with all of its chic concentrated in its cut and line' (*Elegance*, 1964).

The 1960s youth revolution that affected all levels of the fashion industry in Europe and America also revised the notion of the little black dress. Formerly it had been monopolized by women aged perhaps twenty-five and over; though the young might have yearned for 'slinky, shiny black dresses' they were cautioned to wait until they were 'matured, when it will give you dignity and poise' (Betty Page, *On Fair Vanity*, 1954). However, in the hands of a new wave of young designers creating for their own generation, black lost its smart, older woman appeal, being translated into teenager wear (pages 86 and 88). With her finger on the pulse, Mary Quant spearheaded the movement rejecting 1950s mannered sophistication (the New Look legacy) by initiating short-skirted, body-skimming, easy-to-wear styles. Black in the 1960s had to vie with trendy 'little girl' pastel colours and the bright zingy hues of Pop Art, but it survived and, teamed with white, became an Op Art inspired adjunct. Four little black dresses appeared in the value-for-money searchlights of the consumer magazine *Which* (January 1965). A panel of experts compared the qualities and stylistic impact of garments ranging from exclusive *haute couture* to a mass-produced line. 'To make the comparison as simple as possible, we chose "the little black dress" to which fashion journalists – and their readers – are devoted'. The critical assessment took place at a party – 'the natural habitat of the "little black dress"', and the verdict was inconclusive: 'the right dress can do

something for its wearer. And that "right dress" is as likely to cost six pounds as it is to cost sixty'. *Time* magazine christened London 'the swinging city' (April 1966), praising it as the colourful mecca for the teens and twenties with money to spend. In this kaleidoscope black quietly held its own. Customers had to rush before stocks of 'groovy' black dresses sold out in Barbara Hulanicki's Biba boutique. Cecil Beaton for *Vogue* (April 1967) photographed top mannequin Twiggy as a 'high drama girl' in Biba's 'deep black tragedy' mini dress. Biba eye make-up in its little black pots offered dark purples and sludge greys – perfect companions for black.

At the beginning of the 1970s, the brewers of Guinness exploited the success of the little black dress in an ingenious publicity campaign targeting young women. Alongside a photograph of a mannequin about to sip Guinness, the advertising copy ran:

Every girl should have a little black drink. Paris, some say is dead. Carnaby Street was where it used to be at. Then the King's Road. Then Kensington Church

Street. Mini. Maxis. Minis. Midis. Minis. Madness. About the only thing a girl could confidently slip into recently is our little black drink. It hasn't been out of style since 1759. It looks well at any season and at any hour permitted by law. It's clean, dry and long lasting. And, being black and white, it subtly complements whatever happens to the trendy tomorrow. In fact, the most accessible accessory of all is our little black beer. Try it on, tomorrow.

The fashionable lure of black was not lost elsewhere, from the glossy black pack of John Player Special cigarettes to the 'diminutive' car, the Fiat 126 'Black'.

Other arts made gainful use of black attire. Authors manipulated it to enhance the cunning of a spy, the wickedness of a witch, the evil of a murderess, the wiles of a seductress and the piety of a widow. Perhaps the most famous black dress quote is Masha's opening response to the question asking why she always wears black in Chekhov's *The Seagull* (1896): 'I am in mourning for my life. I am unhappy.'

Gaston Leroux's detective story *The Perfume of the Lady in Black* (1908) is on a more popular literary plane, while the fashionably successful Gothic novel *The Woman in Black* by Susan Hill was published in 1983. In the 1940s and 1950s black clothing was affected by those who aspired to be 'Beat'. On Paris's Left Bank, Juliette Greco was an existentialist heroine who dressed entirely in black and sang soulful ballads. Black became the visual interpretation of the basically pessimistic existentialist philosophy. Edith Piaf also had a penchant for simple black dresses. They did not distract her audience from her expressive face and gestures, nor from the content of her plangent refrains. American modern dancer Martha Graham frequently clothed her lithe form in black.

The black of black-and-white movies became a powerful fashion tool in the hands of costume designers and great directors. Marlene Dietrich was glamorously dressed in costly black (by Travis Banton) as Shanghai Lily in Josef von Sternberg's *Shanghai Express* (1932). Possibly the most

notorious black dress in cinema history is the glistening satin sheath (by Jean Louis) worn by Rita Hayworth for her solo 'Put the Blame on Mame' in *Gilda* (1946), and Audrey Hepburn was the epitome of elegance in svelte black dresses in *Breakfast at Tiffany's* (1961). Givenchy redesigned one of these dresses for the New York department store Barney's in 1993; they were so popular that they 'flew off the rack'. Images of other black-clad film actresses come to mind – director Antonioni used the ruse frequently. One of the most compelling little black dresses (by Chanel and Bernard Evein) on film was worn by Delphine Seyrig in Alain Renais' elegiac *L'Année dernière à Marienbad* (1961). Twentieth Century Fox's horror musical *Shock Treatment* (1981) featured a memorable song 'Little Black Dress' (by Richard O'Brien and Richard Harley): 'When its time to be discreet, there's just one thing you can't beat, that's the backless, strapless classical little black dress…That minimal, criminal, sinable little black dress…let's face it Mac that basic black is coming back.'

All black can be too severe but black with a touch of white has long been a designer ploy. The permutations are infinite, and details have been borrowed from a spectrum of clothing. The dress of barristers, priests, nuns, puritans, pierrots and schoolgirls has proved inspirational. Black (with or without colour highlights) has been a constant in etiquette and 'how to dress' manuals. American arbiter of taste Emily Post reported: 'It is tiresome everlastingly to wear black, but nothing is so serviceable, nothing so unrecognizable, nothing looks so well on every occasion' (*Etiquette*, 1922). Nevertheless, her contemporary the Honourable Mrs Forester warned, 'Black is unbecoming at any age if worn with a muddy complexion' (*Success Through Dress*, 1925). In the 1950s it was recommended that black (with the one exception of black linen) should not be seen in the country or by the sea, but the take-over of black in the 1980s brought little black swimsuits into prominence and summer travellers were encouraged to 'pack black'.

Annexed by mainstream fashion and analysed by dress historians, the anti-fashion black clothes of rebellion and anti-establishment culture lost something of their outsider status and power to shock. An achromatic subcultural line can be tracked from the all-black leotards and skirts of American beats through the black leathers of bikers (immortalized by Marlon Brando in *The Wild One*, 1954) to the black cherished by punks and goths. Vivienne Westwood and Malcolm McLaren harnessed black to heighten the self-conscious venom and destructive message of the iconic punk rock band the Sex Pistols. Locked into and steering a coterie of disaffected youth, Westwood and McLaren, under the Seditionaries label, created an ideal vehicle for the lead singer Johnny Rotten (John Lydon) – the black sateen bondage suit of 1976 (page 98). Along with body piercing and spiked hair, it became part of the punk 'uniform' for either gender. In later years Vivienne Westwood discarded cheap black cotton and made up-market versions of the bondage suit in costly, bright worsteds and tartans. At the end of the 1990s, ageing punks, true to their subversive adolescence and accompanied by new recruits, were still to be found in black bondage gear. The black of early 1980s goths was an altogether more refined and knowingly fashionable black. Dave Vanian, lead singer of the goth band The Damned, was the ultimate goth dandy. Impeccably dressed from the London shop Symphony of Shadows (run by his wife), he wore well-cut clothes in black and purple with touches of white indicating the goth's preoccupation with the rituals of death and mourning.

Body-conscious black came into its own in the disco-loving 1970s. Sexy black evening sheaths for the dance floor went hand-in-hand with a continuing vogue for exercise and the adulation of a taut, slender body. The elasticity of fine, jersey-knitted synthetics as well as Lycra encouraged designers to experiment with garments that became second skins and clung to bodies like wet swimming costumes. Zandra Rhodes's 1977 'Conceptual Chic' collection (page 100) recognized and adapted the brutal inventiveness of British punks, whereas the streamlined Swanky Modes disco sheath (page 102) may be seen as a precursor of 1980s minimalism. Both were forerunners of the revealing 'safety pin' dress by Gianni Versace made notorious by Elizabeth Hurley at the London premiere of *Four Weddings and a Funeral* (1994). In the 1980s Azzedine Alaïa brought another dimension to ultra-tight clothes by employing a knitted technique with constructional lines that followed the body's contours with great erotic effect (page 112). Spanning seventeen years, all these four designs are remarkable for their predetermined cut-outs and holes positioned suggestively (even in Zandra Rhodes's apparently random rips) to reveal the skin beneath.

A counter-movement to tight black garb commenced in the mid-1970s. Far from glorifying the body, the 'Big Look' was to swamp and deny the physique and ultimately to forge a partnership with black. Few were prepared for the momentous surge of black at the beginning of the 1980s, nor its subsequent monopoly of fashion. Its champions (each creating highly individual pathways) were avant-garde Japanese designers Issey Miyake (page 130), Rei Kawakubo (page 106) and Yohji Yamamoto (page 118). Exploring the complexities of their beliefs and radical output, Dorinne Kondo identified ideas that linked their work: 'loose architectural shapes, uneven hemlines, unusual textures, sombre colours' (JJ Tobin (ed), *Re-Made in Japan*, 1992). The full force of this movement and the status of black were apparent when Rei Kawakubo first showed in Paris in 1981, and the message was reinforced the following year when the work of twelve Japanese designers was seen in the capital of fashion. Huge, wrapped, layered and asymmetrical clothes astonished an audience of journalists and buyers normally difficult to shock. By a relentless combination of black and revolutionary constructional methods divorced from pattern-cutting conventions of Western couture, these designer-innovators thrilled many and alarmed a few. Henceforth Rei Kawakubo was identified with black as 'the woman who took the colour out of fashion'. Deyan Sudjic reported: 'her clothes are behind the wave of monochrome minimalism that has turned every fashionable gathering in London, New York, Paris and Tokyo into a solid, all-black wall' (*The Sunday Times*, 20 April 1986). The consensus was that this revolution offered a new direction for women's clothing, a direction that was serious, intellectual and usually black. The impact was enormous and far-reaching.

Black dominated the realms of high fashion in 1981-82 and swiftly spread to all market levels. Dress rails at home and in shops were crammed with black – it outsold everything else. The fashion press (Tish Jett, *The International Herald Tribune*, 16 December 1982), keen to account for the phenomenon that 'on both sides of the Atlantic, day and night, black is the fashion color of the moment' turned to the medical profession for comment. Professor of Psychiatry Nathan Kline linked it with world recession: 'Black is a conservative color and in view of the current economic insecurities, people look for outward signs of stability and security'. Associate Professor Ruth Westheimer of Cornell University Medical School perceived inner meanings in the adoption of black and the rejection of 'frivolous' jewels and colours: 'You can be somebody in a black dress and it says to a man, don't just look at the glitter, look at me as a personality, a human being – look under the skin'. With metropolitan centres

inundated by modish black, Suzy Menkes highlighted Yves Saint Laurent's role in the dissemination of this fashion classic. Considering his retrospective exhibition at the Metropolitan Museum in *The Times* (6 December 1983), she wrote, 'little black dressing says it all: simplicity of line, perfection of cut and a dash of wit'. He 're-invented the art of black magic' and in the mid-1960s had made a key intervention bringing the black tuxedo suit into women's domain. Twenty years later, in the 1980s women who found the all-enveloping black of Japanese designers too overwhelming turned to Yves Saint Laurent's body-aware, Parisian black. Black was inescapable and headline capturing – 'Basic Black is Back', 'Black Nights', 'Stay in Black this Christmas', 'Black and Soft as Sin', 'Black Economy', 'Hats Off to Black', 'Black Looks', 'le mystère de la dame en noir' and 'That Old Black Magic'.

Leaders of an inevitable reaction to black had an uphill task. Fashion editors made a stand, many arriving to take front seats at the fashion collections in bright red jackets (over black). Sarah Mower reported her rejection of black in favour of red (*The Guardian*, 22 January 1987) under the headline: 'Wearing black as outward proof of an inward superiority'. She owned up to the inexorably black contents of her wardrobe, pondering on the 1980s creed 'that one cannot take oneself seriously unless one wears black, carries a black Filofax, drives a black car and, preferably lives in a home with black Italian furniture and white walls'. The struggle to escape the tyranny of black was valiant but doomed, the fate of a similar backlash in 1963. Opposing black with the claim that 'It encourages women to stop trying – they just sink into their Little Black and think they're home and dry', *The Evening Standard* (26 August 1963) continued 'It's so OBVIOUS. Aren't you bored with it too?' The answer was 'no' and a resounding vote for perennially versatile black. Twenty-five years later Rei Kawakubo joined the 1980s revisionist campaign when she declared (March 1988) that red is black.

All was in vain, however, and black remained in the ascendant throughout the 1990s. Age was no deterrent: for her *Frock of Ages* piece, Lucinda Alford put three generations of women (from eighty-two to twenty-seven years old) into little black dresses (*The Observer Life*, 5 December 1993). In her Barbara Vine persona, Ruth Rendell observed that 'most London girls dress entirely in black, as if in mourning for the lost freedom of colour' (*The Chimney Sweeper's Boy*, 1998). *Vanity Fair* profiled the saviour of Gucci's fortunes: 'Tom Ford wants you in black ... As long as what you wear from head to toe, sunglasses to shoes, is Gucci' (*Vanity Fair*, March 1998). Ford linked the 'black everything in the '80s and '90s' to

the coming of AIDS and 'a general grimness in urban life'. From the late 1980s until her death in August 1997, black was a regular choice for Diana, Princess of Wales. Possibly emulating a couple of low-necked black gowns worn (most unusually) by her mother-in-law in 1953 and 1956, she riveted the world's press in an infamous *décolleté* black dress by the Emanuels on her first public engagement with Prince Charles (9 March 1981). The Princess was much photographed looking *soignée* in black by her favourite designers, and the sale of formal gowns from her collection (Christie's, New York, June 1997) featured some black numbers that had raised many eyebrows with their audacity.

Attempts to sound the death knell of black in fashion failed. Lowri Turner documented its stranglehold on women:

'Black is dead, long live black...the little black dress may be this season's fashion *faux pas*, but that won't stop women wearing it' (*The Evening Standard*, 30 October 1995). Two years later in the same newspaper Mimi Spencer decided that, 'It's time to bid a fond farewell to the little black dress...wear any little number as long as it's not black'. In turn red, white, chocolate-brown then grey were heralded as the new black but only black had staying power. It made a sensational appearance as a little black tennis dress (by Nike) worn by Mary Pierce at the French Open Tennis Tournament in 1996. So deeply ingrained is this icon that Gerald Scarfe titled his cartoon for *The Sunday Times* (2 August 1998) 'The Little Black Dress'. The drawing showed President Clinton hitching up his trousers on the run from a flying little black dress (the garment referred to was in fact blue-black). In 1998 the press conceded that 'The little black dress is still the crucial item in any modern, elegant wardrobe ...And it's as chic and suggestive as ever it was' (*The Guardian Weekend*, 5 December 1998). These characteristics no doubt encouraged Camilla Parker Bowles to select a classic little black dress by Tomasz Starzewski for her first appearance in public with the Prince of Wales (at the London Ritz, 28 January 1999).

Early in 1999 Channel 4 promoted the UK launch of the raunchy American TV series *Sex in the City* with billboards of the four main protagonists in sexy little black dresses. In London the Publishing Publicity Circle Awards were accepted by six young women dressed in black, prompting an aspiring publicist to plead 'I never wear black. Will I ever win one of the awards?' (*Publishing News*, 5 February 1999). In the same month, an episode of the British soap *Eastenders* included a telling line, 'you can't go wrong with black'. Architect and designer Philippe Starck's first venture into fashion in 1998 was to design the ultimate minimalist little black dress for Wolford – 'Starcknaked' being an 80-denier, one-piece synthesis of stockings and a long, narrow tube offering variations on three themes: skirt, tube dress and strap dress. At the beginning of 1999, as Chanel announced that their last collection of the twentieth century was to be without a hint of black, an expectant fashion world still awaited the 'revolution away from the shade of eternal security' (*The Observer Life*, 28 February 1999).

It seems that dressed in black a woman can be pious, slender, seductive or witchlike; she can stand out in a crowd or vanish into the background. Some think that the little black dress is a soft and tedious option while others agree that black is the 'invariable choice of the elegant and well dressed' (advertising slogan, Lady in Black Fashions, 1949). Sonia Rykiel confirmed her addiction to black in fashion with this eulogy: 'They kiss your hand, they worship you, woman become Queen, enrobed in black, possessed by black, submerged in black, with a white face of ecstasy' (*Et je la voudrais nue*, 1979).

REDFERN

Afternoon dress
(half mourning), Redfern
London 1910-1912

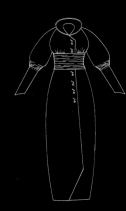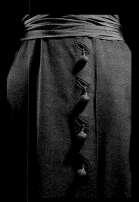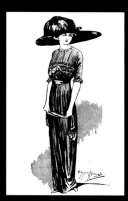

Left to right:
Line drawing, front of gown
Detail, centre front of gown
Bessie Ascough sketch of
'a toilette of black charmeuse'
Evening Standard and St James's
Gazette, May 25, 1910

It is likely that Heather Firbank (1888-1954) wore this gown while in the later stages of mourning, possibly for a member of her family. Immediately after the death of a close relative it was the convention to wear clothing in an unrelieved black, which eventually gave way to half mourning, when black could be enlivened with touches of purple, grey or white. Miss Firbank, daughter of the wealthy MP Sir Thomas Firbank and sister of the coterie novelist Ronald Firbank, dressed in a refined yet distinctive manner, buying her clothes from leading London designers. She adored fashion, spending hours collecting and sometimes annotating cuttings of her favourite styles

snipped out of newspapers and magazines. Miss Firbank avoided blatantly avant-garde designs and selected colours with care – though it announced her state of mourning, the purple crêpe bow fitted her love of heathery colours, which complemented her name. Even her tiny silk monogrammed handkerchiefs were in shades of mauve and purple.

This kimono-like gown is a fine illustration of the high-waisted, long-skirted style known variously as Empire, Directoire or Madame Récamier, which prevailed in cosmopolitan centres by 1910. In soft-to-the-touch, expensive cashmere with a lustrous sheen, it has an unusual

bodice (without a centre back seam) incorporating batwing sleeves with long, tapered cuffs. The bodice is gathered into the waist, from which falls a slender columnar skirt; the flat plane at the back is created by a pair of deep inverted pleats. The gown wraps over and fastens along the left front with tiny press-studs under a line of blind buttonholes with pendant buttons. Black is dominant, punctuated with striking notes of purple – the deep cummerbund, the line of buttons and, with its touch of historicism, the wired 'Tudor'-style, heart-shaped collar.

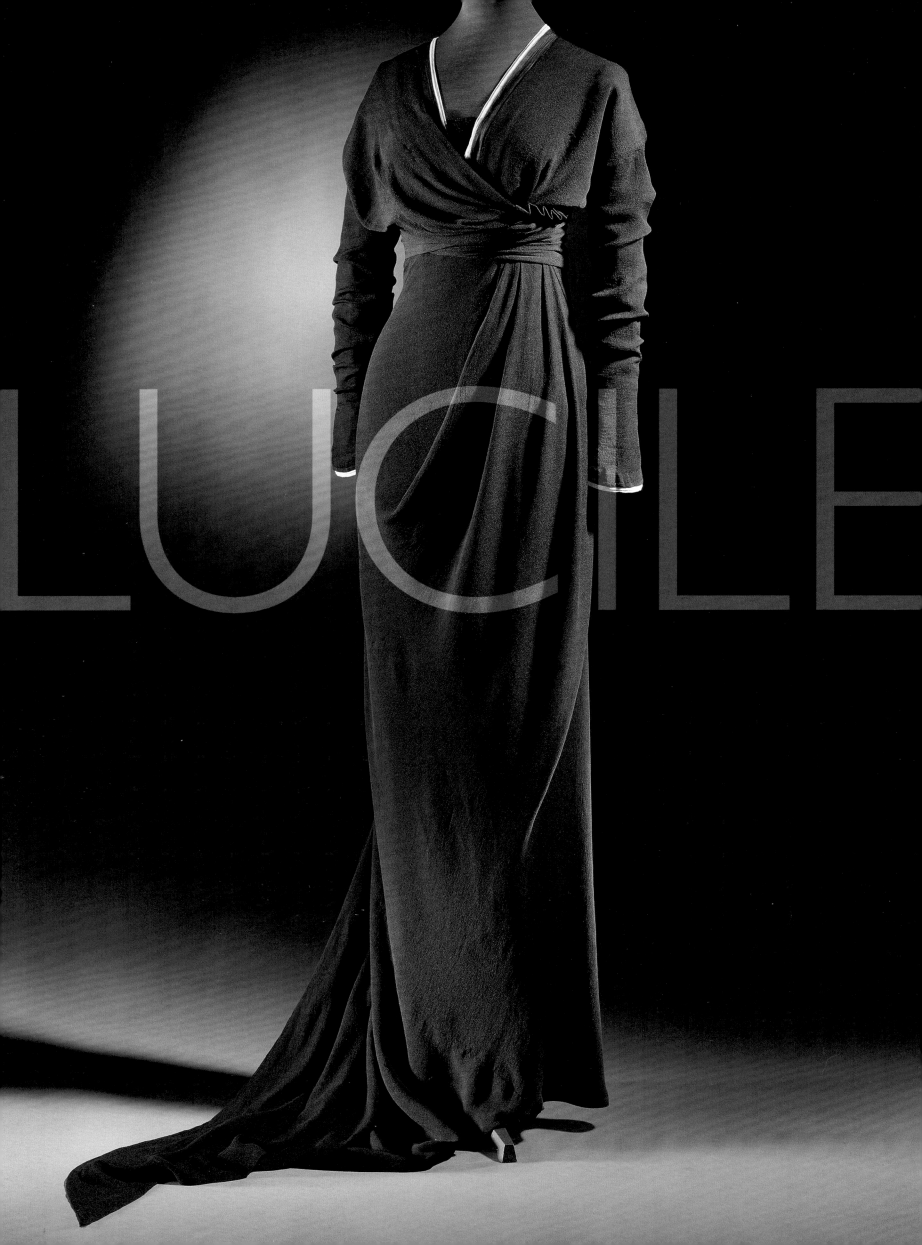

Dinner gown, Lucile
London 1910-1912

Heather Firbank ordered this elegant gown from the London fashion house Lucile. Masquerading as a demure (possibly half mourning) gown, it is in fact a highly seductive creation in matt black crêpe. Founded by Mrs Wallace (1862-1935, later Lady Duff Gordon) in 1895, Lucile was such a success that by 1915 there were branches in Paris, New York and Chicago. After her first marriage foundered, Lucy Wallace was penniless with a child to support and, having made clothes for herself and her sister, the popular novelist Elinor Glyn, she decided to forge a career as a fashion designer. She built up her business from modest beginnings, eventually offering clients the most luxurious premises in which to view and order the latest Lucile models. The

stage was an outlet for her most lavish concepts, including costumes for the triumphant operetta *The Merry Widow* (1907). A huge, broad-brimmed hat in black with bird-of-paradise feathers for the star Lily Elsie was an instant hit. Meredith Etherington-Smith recorded that it made a fortune for Lucile as 'women in Europe and America clamoured for exact copies' (*The IT Girls*, 1986).

The house was renowned for its asymmetrical styles of which this gown is a perfect example. It was constructed directly on a dressmaker's dummy, a technique that demands considerable expertise and dexterity. Set into a high waist, the bias-cut skirt is softly swathed over the left hip but in contrast is drawn sexily tight over the

right hip, while the hem is extended into a triangular train. The subtly draped, crossover bodice has a plunging V neck made respectable by a lace modesty concealing the cleavage, while touches of cream silk brighten the neck and cuffs. Long, clinging sleeves were worn slightly ruched to echo the theme of bodice and skirt. In 1932 Lady Duff Gordon gave a testament to the durability of black in fashion: 'I had one dress of which I was especially fond. It was black velvet, which fell in soft folds to the feet, and there was a deep belt. It could be easily worn today, which shows how little clothes change in their essentials from one generation to another' (*Discretions and Indiscretions*, 1932).

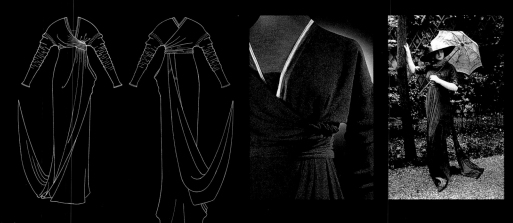

From left to right:
Line drawing, front of gown
Line drawing, back of gown
Detail of bodice front
Photograph of Lucile model, 1911

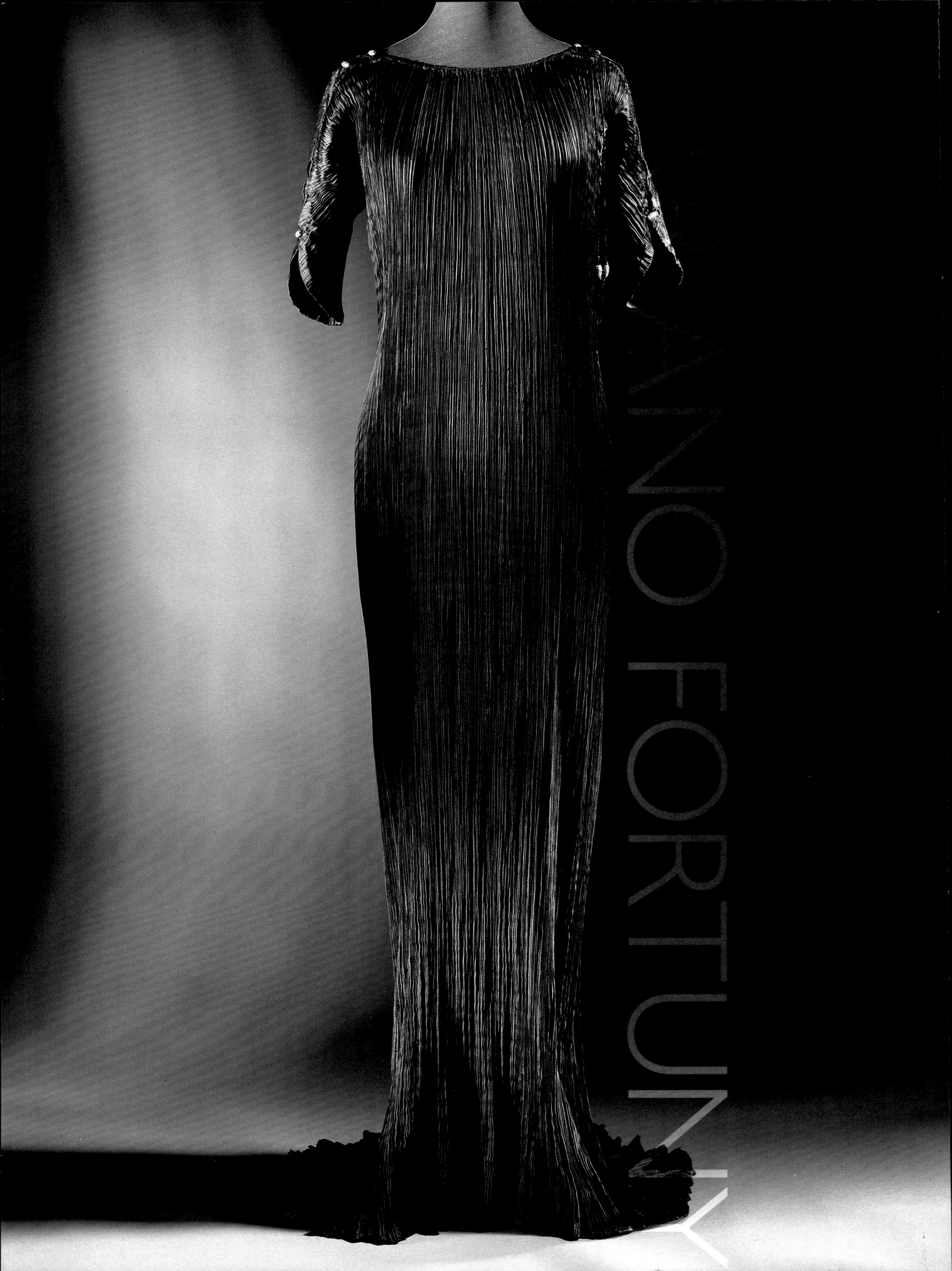
ANO FORTUNY

Evening gown, Mariano Fortuny

Venice about 1920

Given by Mrs Hollond

The multi-talented Mariano Fortuny (1871-1949) was, at times, a painter, theatre designer, photographer, inventor and scientist, though he is best known as a creator of extraordinary fabrics and clothes. Resonant colours characterized his output, but black was ever present and much used as a background for exotic prints in gold and silver pigments. Based in the Palazzo Orfei, Venice, Fortuny operated outside the mainstream of fashion, taking inspiration from classical Greek costume and historical textiles (especially those of the Renaissance). By adhering to simple, dramatic shapes in sumptuous materials, he achieved clothes that did not date and appealed to women in artistic and bohemian circles eager to resist the dictates of Paris couture with its quick-moving trends and complexities of cut and construction. Famous customers included the dancer Isadora Duncan, film star Lilian Gish and art collector Peggy Guggenheim. A revival of interest in Mariano Fortuny's work began in the 1960s, generating exhibitions, publications and a boom in auction prices for shimmering silk and velvet garments with his distinctive circular label. Fashion designers were entranced by his inventions and a number started to experiment with pleating.

In 1909 Fortuny registered his design (based on the Ionic chiton) for the 'Delphos' gown, which formed the basis for subsequent variations on the style until production finally ceased in 1952. Typical of this genre, this glistening black columnar gown consists of five narrow widths of pleated silk hand sewn into a tube just 47 cm (18.6 ins) wide. Neck and sleeves are adjusted to fit by concealed drawstrings, while a slender black rouleau, threaded with light-catching Venetian glass beads, laces the outer sleeves. Light as a feather, extremely flattering and easy to wear, 'Delphos' gowns simply pulled on over the head and glissaded over the body's contours.

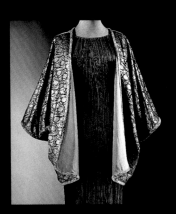

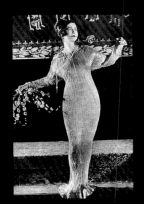

From left to right:
Line drawing,
front of gown
Gown with its printed
velvet jacket
Dorothy Gish wearing
Fortuny, *Photoplay*,
December, 1924

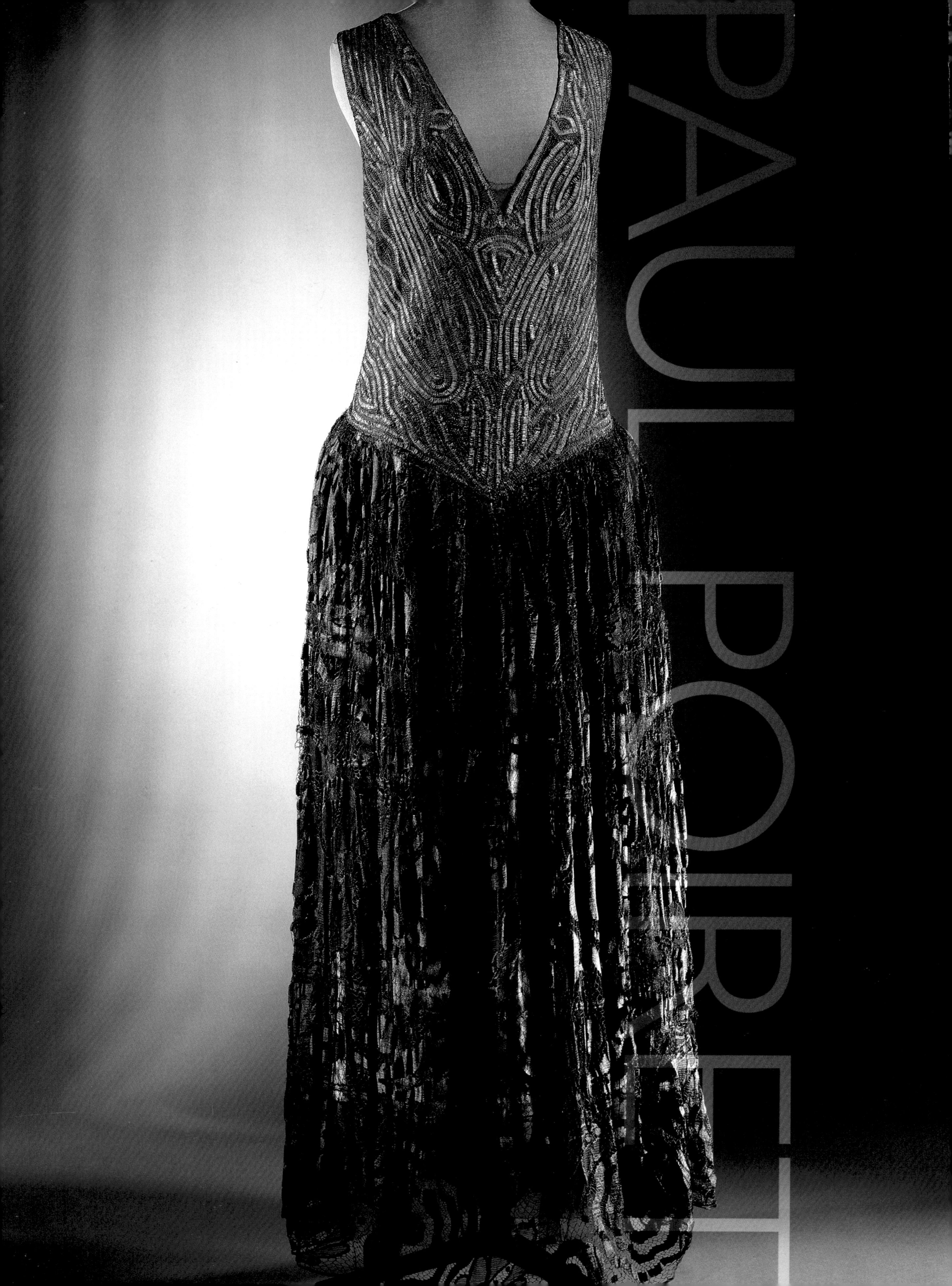
PAUL POIRET

Evening gown, 'Samovar', Paul Poiret

Paris 1919-20

Given by Mr Vern Lambert

Paul Poiret (1879-1944) was a superb colourist who handled vivid hues and sumptuous fabrics with panache, and though he possessed an ambivalent attitude towards black it was a recurring feature in his collections. In his autobiography (*My First Fifty Years*, 1931) he extolled the chic nature of black, describing how he had attired an erstwhile mistress: '... with great elegance and piquancy. I remember a costume of black cloth with a little black pelerine that stopped at the shoulders, she wore it with a little black tricorne hat surmounted by a white cock's head with a red comb. It was a delight.'

Exploring the tension between black and gold in this long evening gown, he composed a figure-hugging, low-waisted bodice attached to a gathered lace skirt. Texture and pattern are skilfully juxtaposed in an opulent mixture. Embroidered meanders of gilt strip on glistening black rayon ornament the entire bodice, while the skirt (over a double petticoat of gilt tissue and black tulle) is of machine-made lace with a bold, stylized floral pattern probably based on a design from Martine, the school of design he established in 1911. In common with a group of works produced from about 1919 to 1922, he exaggerated the curve of the hips by means of short, stiffened flounces set into the petticoat. Though at his zenith in pre-war years, Poiret remained a creative force in the 1920s, drawing upon his considerable experience and spirited approach to style. In her monograph *Paul Poiret* (1987), Yvonne Deslandres reported his lack of synergy with the times, noting that 'it was with secret despair that Paul Poiret saw the swarms of emaciated "telegraph poles", the blasé college girls wearing the black dresses that he so thoroughly deplored'.

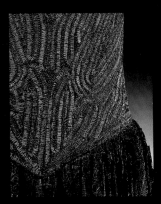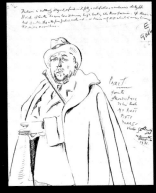

From left to right:
Detail of bodice and skirt
Cecil Beaton sketch of
Paul Poiret from a
photograph by Lipnitzi
(frontispiece, *My First Fifty Years*, 1931)

CHANEL

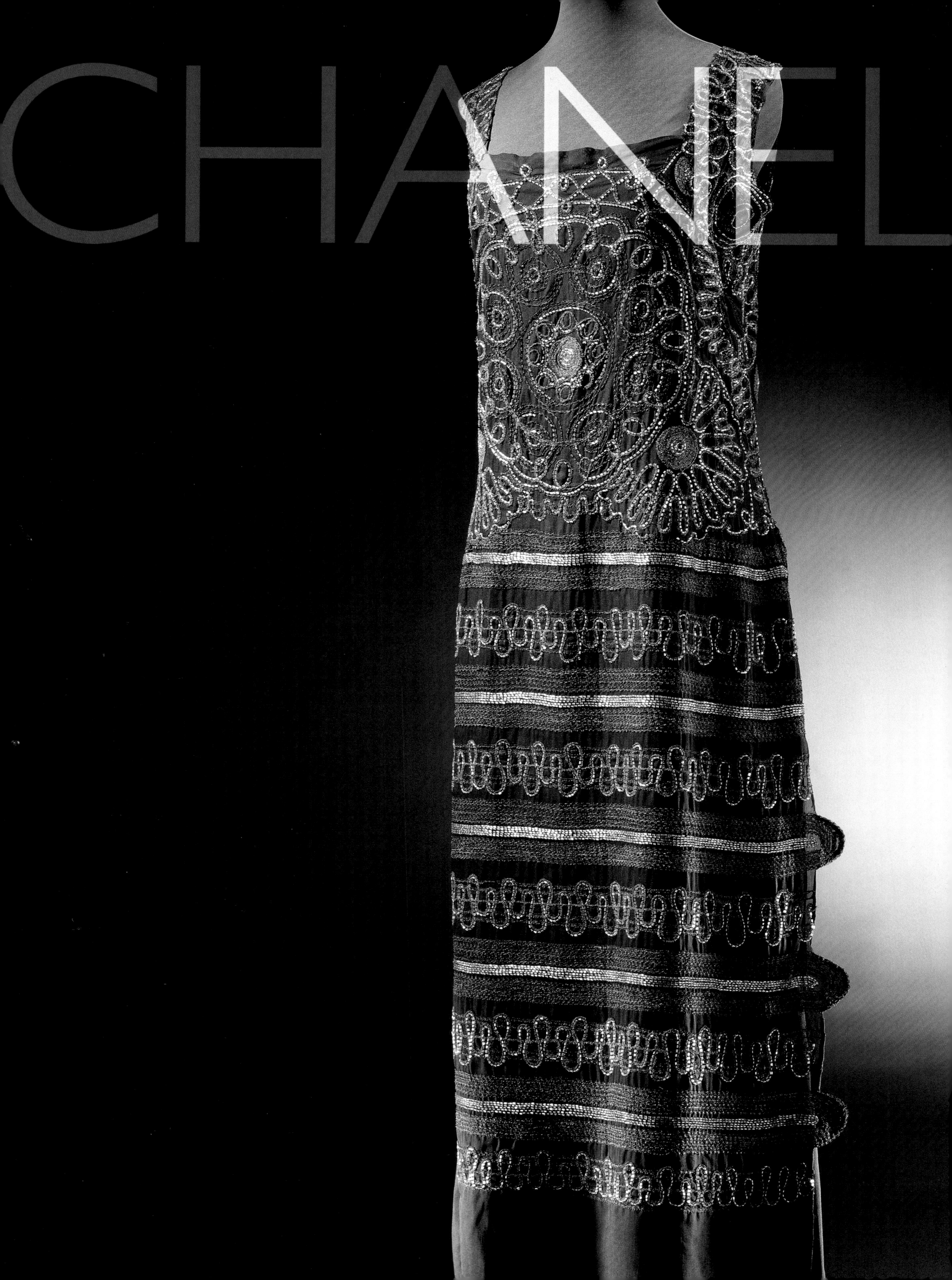

Evening dress, Chanel

Paris about 1922
Worn and given by
the Hon. Mrs Anthony Henley

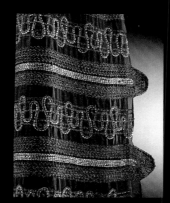

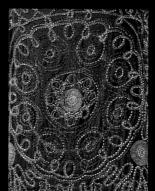

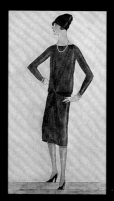

From left to right:

Detail. lower side skirt

Detail of bodice

Chanel day dress 'the
frock that all the world
will wear', USA *Vogue*.
1 October 1926.
Copyright *Vogue*, Condé
Nast Publications Inc

It is possible that the first professional dress design by Chanel (1883-1971), of 1913, was in black; according to Edmonde Charles-Roux (*Chanel and her World*, 1981) it was a demure velvet day gown with a white petal collar for Chanel's friend Suzanne Orlandi. Black clothes held a special appeal for Chanel – the black of children's uniforms, the strict black of tailored riding habits and the sometimes dusty black of peasant attire. Apparently this fascination grew after the death in 1919 of her lover and patron Arthur ('Boy') Capel.

In 1920 Chanel used delicate embroideries, and *Vogue* illustrated a long gown adorned with rows of decorative beadwork much resembling the linear motifs enlivening this black dress. Tubular and long waisted, it is a precursor of her 1922-23 designs inspired by the exotic embroideries of Russia, China, India and Romania. Chanel employed rhythmic patterns – an embellished shield-like circle on the bodice and horizontal bands of meanders and stripes in glistening bugle beads – to break the dress's dominant vertical line and relieve its blackness. In a decorative touch that signals the time and money that an *haute couture* establishment can lavish on details, the bands are extended to form protruding side tabs over floating chiffon panels that drift below the hemline.

Black in fashion had a long history pre-Chanel, but the myth arose that she invented the first ever little black dress and subsequently the claim proved excellent publicity for the house. Her penchant for black was highlighted by the fashion press in 1919, but black and Chanel became synonymous during the boom year for black fashion, 1926. A perceptive copywriter in the October 1 issue of 1926 in American *Vogue* described a classic day dress as 'The Chanel "Ford" – the frock that all the world will wear – is model "817" of black crêpe de Chine'. The dress was copied and recommended for the business woman who was assured that, though it was tucked and pleated, it did not 'muss easily'.

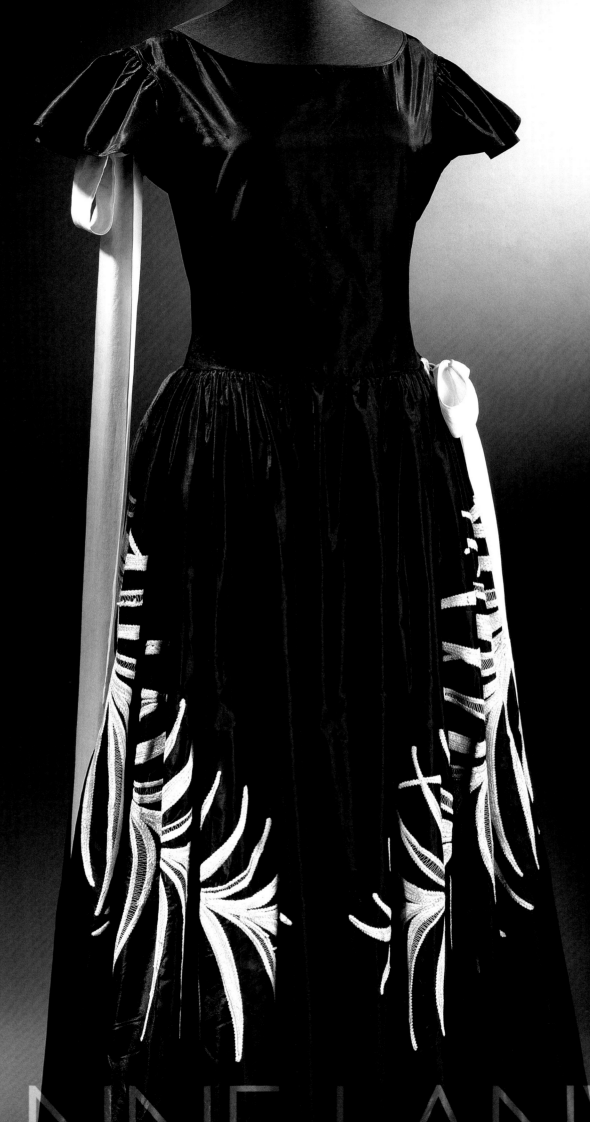

JEANNE LANVIN

Evening dress, Jeanne Lanvin

Paris winter 1922-23

Throughout the 1920s Jeanne Lanvin (1867-1946) excelled in the creation of ultra-feminine dresses with fitted bodices and long, full skirts known as *robes de style*. Her designs, often in virginal white and sugar almond colours, were among the prettiest available, with a *jeune fille* appeal and a delicate touch based on her experience of designing special occasion dresses for children. Lanvin had made clothes for her adored daughter Marguerite Marie-Blanche, who was born in 1897, which were so much admired that she began a business producing clothes for youngsters. Subsequently she introduced designs for adults, but dainty outfits for little girls continued to play a key role in her collections. By adding black to the formula, Lanvin immediately replaced the innocent aura of such 'picture' dresses with a sophisticated gloss that appealed to a more knowing clientele. Fashion editors and illustrators in the early 1920s were captivated. For the *Gazette du Bon Ton*, Georges Lepape and Pierre Brissaud portrayed mothers and daughters (in their Lanvin finery) at play in idyllic garden settings, while other glossy magazines (especially *Les Modes*) featured photographs of chic interiors peopled with similarly attired groups in loving poses.

To relieve the impact of all black and add texture to this *robe de style*, Lanvin had a pair of immense fern-like fronds embroidered in furry cream chenille on the skirt. Cream is echoed in floating bands caught in bows at the right sleeve and left waist. The romantic mood was enhanced by setting these streamers in soft, matt georgette against glistening crisp taffeta, which with the slightest movement made seductive rustling sounds. Immaculately realized details reveal Lanvin the perfectionist: neck and sleeve edges are finished with the narrowest possible bindings; the skirt is attached to the low waistline with the most minute gathers; and inside the customary Lanvin label is helpfully stamped with the gown's date, season and model number.

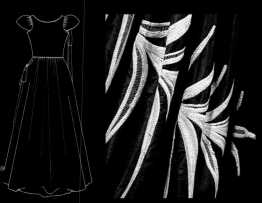

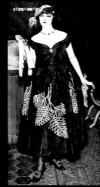

From left to right:
Line drawing, back of gown
Detail of side skirt
Mlle Jane Renouardt in a
robe de diner by Lanvin,
Les Modes, 1920

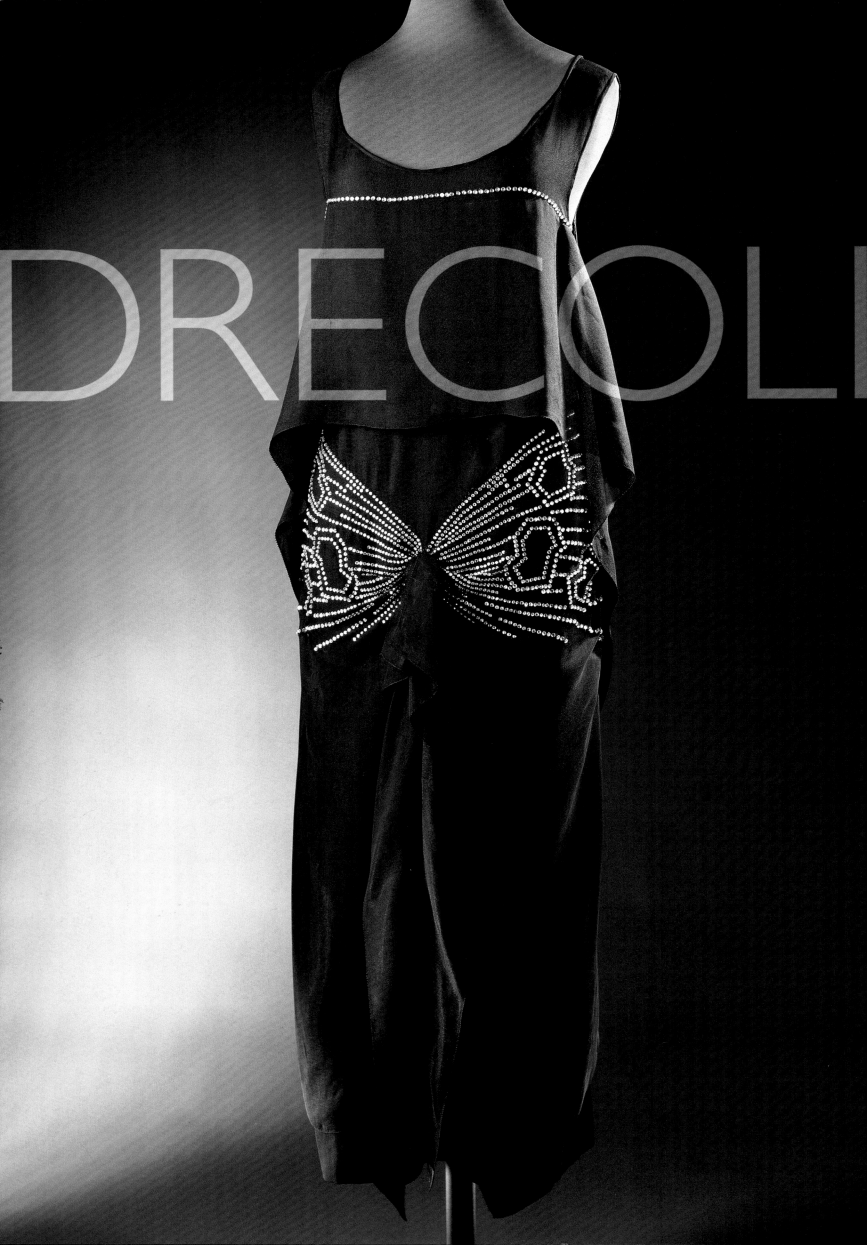

'Minuit Sonne' evening dress, Drecoll

Paris, imported by Lord and Taylor
New York 1926
Given by Miss N Moyer

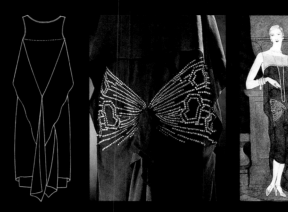

At Lord and Taylor (established in 1826), the prestigious New York department store on Fifth Avenue, discerning clients in the late 1920s could select from up-to-the-minute fashions, including imported Paris originals and excellent copies of French models as well as American-designed but unnamed ready-to-wear. Many trading links with Paris were severed during World War I, leading to the increasing importance of home-grown US high fashion, and Lord and Taylor were among the first to champion American talents. In the late 1920s they proclaimed the availability of evening clothes by an anonymous 'famous American designer', and

by 1932 their advertising campaigns and in-store promotions prominently featured the names of young American designers.

Tantalizingly, the label in this little black dress simply reads 'Lord and Taylor', but an illustration in American *Vogue* of 15 April 1926 identifies it as a Drecoll, 'one of the many black chiffon gowns that are included in the collections' with 'strass embroidery outlining the yoke and emphasizing the tied-in effect at the hips'. It was the height of 1926 night-time chic, when volants and floating panels had been introduced to soften the harsh cylindrical silhouette of mid-1920s styles. Being in fine black voile,

it was completely in tune with the cosmopolitan craze for black. The Paris Exposition des Arts Décoratifs (1925) inspired designers to explore what became known as art deco style, and the *diamanté* butterfly burst over the hips is a perfect example of this trend. Sleeveless, with a low, scooped neck, the garment allowed its owner to remain cool when performing the latest, frenetic 1920s dances. In movement, the drifting tunic top and the skirt's central fluted drapery would flutter in a gently beguiling manner.

MADELEINE VIONNET

Evening gown,
Madeleine Vionnet

Paris about 1934

Worn by Mrs Opal Holt and given by
Mrs DM Haynes and Mrs M Clark

Acknowledging her to be a dressmaking genius, Cecil Beaton drew a vivid pen picture of Madeleine Vionnet (1876-1975), describing her as 'a parrot-like little woman with a shock of white hair' (*Glass of Fashion*, 1954). Not an inspired colourist, her palette in the 1930s tended to be subdued, with an inclination towards dull pastels in her favourite matt crêpe romain, though she achieved many dramatic gestures in bright hues and black.

In this case softly pliant silk velvet in black makes a slip of a dress that weighs a mere 380 gms (13.4 oz). Considered to be one of the finest technicians in couture (Dior also called her a technical genius), Vionnet's approach to structure was founded on an innovatory use of fabric cut on the cross or bias (against the straight grain of the material). Garments made according to this technique (which demands absolute mathematical precision) are supple and anatomically revealing.

Glossy black pile conceals the construction of this seductive gown, which employs only four panels in its crossover, slightly bloused, sleeveless bodice and svelte skirt that ripples on to the floor. Vionnet disliked the artificiality of shape-making foundations involving cumbersome interlinings, linings and padding and also kept applied decoration and trimmings to a minimum. Adding spice to this black velvet sheath, she attached a pair of asymmetric georgette streamers to the shoulder back – toffee pink on the left and, slightly shorter in length, royal purple on the right. Interviewed by Anny Latour in 1956, Madame Vionnet voiced her opinions about the ideal dress that should 'bring the body and its movements into harmony' and she declared poetically (and famously) that 'when a woman smiles the dress must smile with her' (Anny Latour, *Kings of Fashion*, 1958).

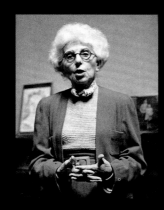

From left to right:
Line drawing, front of gown
Line drawing, back of gown
Portrait of Madeleine Vionnet
by Cecil Beaton, 1953

ANONYMOUS

Evening gown

London or Paris 1935-37

Given by Joanna Wellington

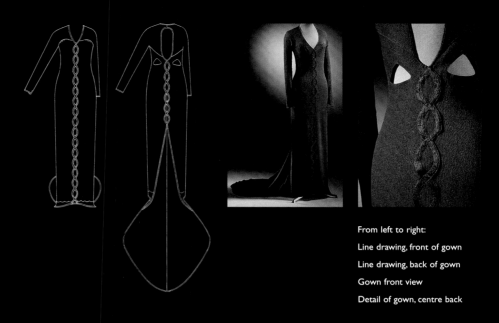

From left to right:
Line drawing, front of gown
Line drawing, back of gown
Gown front view
Detail of gown, centre back

Matt crêpe was an enormously popular fashion fabric in the last half of the 1930s, as its stretch-and-cling characteristics were perfect for dresses that, to be chic, had to be shaped close to the body's contours. Black crêpe added a note of adventure and sexiness to evening wear, becoming a focal point in crowds dressed in the prevailing pastel coloured, bias-cut gowns.

This dress lacks a recorded history. Though it is unlabelled and has no known designer, the careful cut and meticulous finish indicate that it was professionally made. Labels were often cut off garments for aesthetic or physical reasons – they were sewn in obtrusive positions or irritated the skin; or to avoid paying duty, labels were sometimes removed from Paris fashions, since without identification customs officers found it difficult to enforce fines. Some owners hated to flaunt the names of their couturiers and so dispensed with the offending tags.

The long scalloped train identifies this as a gown designed for special occasions – in white or a pale colour it might have been a wedding dress. Almost Hollywood-like in its daring and body-skimming glamour, the back plunges nearly to the waist and is provided with extra cut-outs allowing tantalizing glimpses of the flesh beneath. Like many gowns of this period, the sleeves are extremely narrow and tapered, fastening at the wrists with rows of minute buttons and loops. Emphasizing the fluid lines, interlaced bands of tree bark satin run suggestively down the centre front and back. Underwear became softer to accommodate the fitted flow of crêpe and satins that often revealed the lines of undergarments and unwanted bulges. The fashion conscious followed fitness and slimming regimes to achieve a svelte shape, and gossip magazines speculated that some body conscious film stars wore nothing beneath their second-skin gowns.

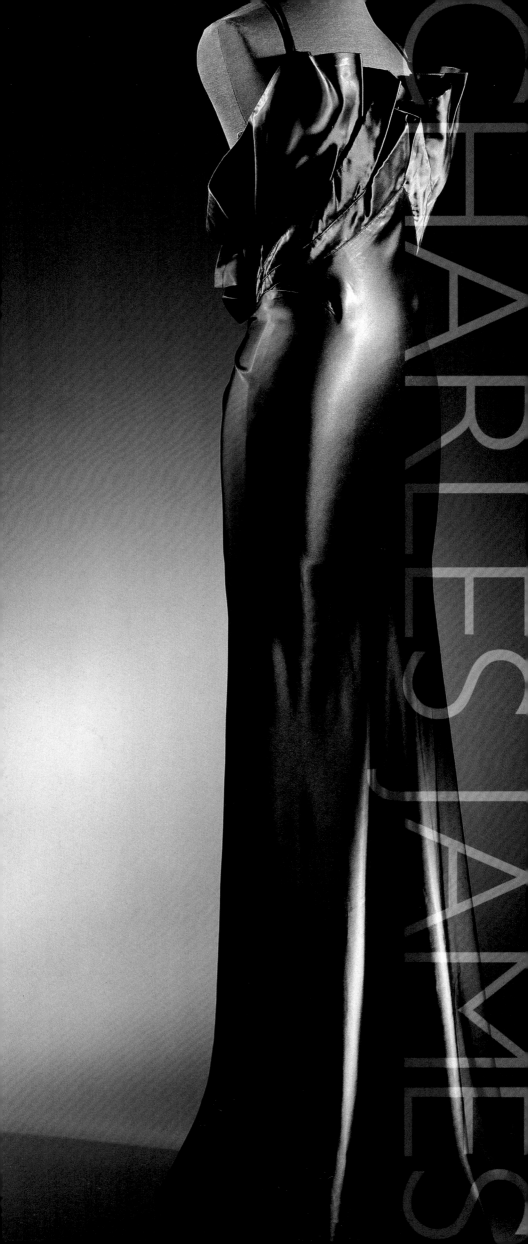

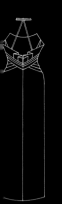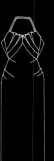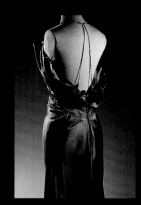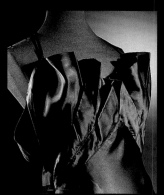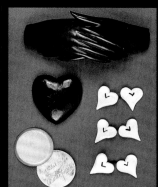

From left to right:
Line drawing, back of gown
Line drawing, front of gown
Gown back view
Detail of bodice front
Photo of buttons and clasps
designed by Charles James,
mid-late 1930s

Evening gown, Charles James
Paris 1936-37
Bequeathed by Miss Philippa Barnes

In 1928 the Anglo-American designer Charles James (1906-78) brought a non-conformist vision to fashion that won him the ardent support of an elegant coterie of women with the courage to wear his adventurous and, at times, demanding creations. Working in London, Paris, Chicago and eventually settling in New York, he made valiant attempts to become part of the conventional fashion world, but his quixotic temperament alienated many and he never found a permanent niche to accommodate his untoward talents. Bettina Ballard (fashion editor at *Vogue* from the 1930s to 1950s) identified his skill: 'Charlie was much more than a designer or dressmaker; he was fascinated with construction, the kind of construction that makes a bridge a thing of beauty' (*In My Fashion*, 1960). In agreement with her, Madge Garland (founding professor of the Fashion Department at London's Royal College of Art) praised his 'dazzling virtuosity of cut' which endowed his work with a 'timelessness of real worth' (*The Indecisive Decade*, 1968). A restless spirit, he constantly reworked ideas and his precious toiles – this black slither of a dress in shiny slipper satin was the culmination of months of experiments with pleating wide ribbons (from the French silk weavers Colcombet) to create bodices which

opened around the torso like petals. Ann Coleman recorded the 1937 success of the ribbon garments in Paris (*The Genius of Charles James*, 1982). On viewing them Paul Poiret is reported to have told James: 'I pass you my crown, wear it well'.

Miss Barnes had been James's loyal assistant in London and Paris and bequeathed this vampish gown to the V&A, together with sample swatches of heavy French silks which held the architectural lines of James's designs for spectacular evening coats and ball gowns. The plunging back neckline, insubstantial rouleau straps and the all-revealing cut were features shared with modish 1930s evening wear, but the pleated bodice is unique and gives this alluring gown the Charles James stamp of originality.

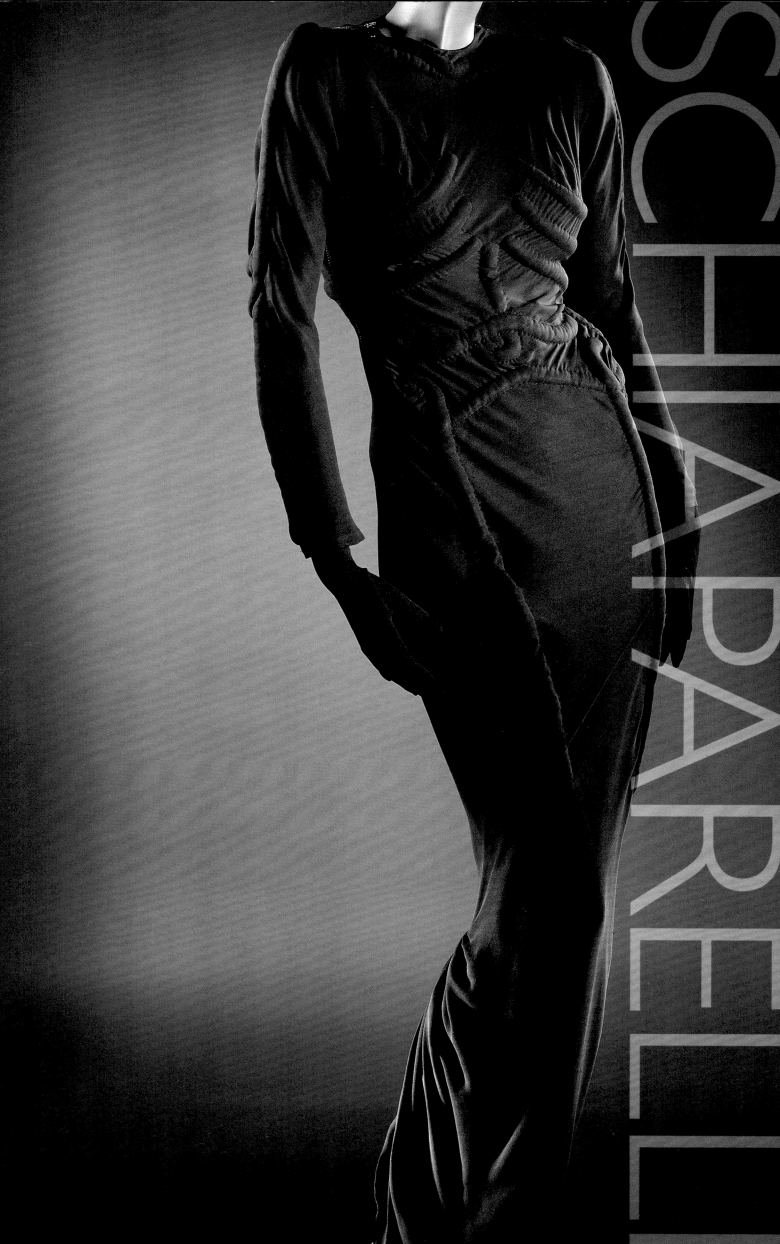

SCHIAPARELLI

From left to right:
Line drawing, front of gown
Detail of bodice front
Detail of bodice back
Detail of lower back skirt

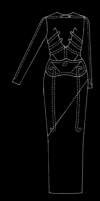 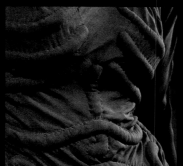 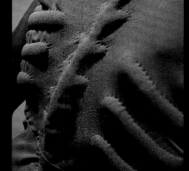 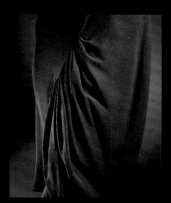

Evening dress, Schiaparelli

Paris 1938

Worn and given by Miss Ruth Ford

To Schiaparelli (1890-1973) dress designing was 'not a profession but an art', and as a fantasist she accomplished her most outstanding work in a milieu that included such artists as Salvador Dali, Jean Cocteau and Christian Bérard. While shocking pink is the colour immediately associated with Schiaparelli, black was always a central factor in her output. Her very first evening dress (of about 1928) was 'a plain black sheath of crêpe de Chine down to the ground. This proved to be the most successful dress of my career. It was reproduced all over the world' (*Shocking Life*, 1954).

To many contemporaries the sinister black skeleton evening gown of 1938 with its padded representation of human bones was an outrage – an offence against good

taste. Schiaparelli was returning to a theme of 1927-28, when she had created a white on black skeleton sweater 'that shocked the bourgeois' and gave the women who wore it the appearance of being seen through an X-ray machine. Though otherwise in elegant harmony with the prevailing lines of late-1930s evening wear, the skeleton dress is so constricted that it became a second skin and the *faux* anatomy sat defiantly proud of the fine matt silk surface. Schiaparelli exaggerated the usually delicate trapunto quilting technique to make enormous 'bones' filled with cotton wadding. The skill of concealing where and how a garment actually fastened was normally sacrosanct; visible buttons were acceptable but zips were definitely not, until Schiaparelli decided to make a feature of them. In a 1930s publicity campaign, she endorsed Lightning's brightly coloured plastic zips; here, however, the shoulder seams and right side are closed by Eclair's bold black plastic zips. An extraordinary concept for its time, this eerie black gown is in complete accord with Schiaparelli's quest for 'an absolute freedom of expression, and a daredevil approach, with no fear'.

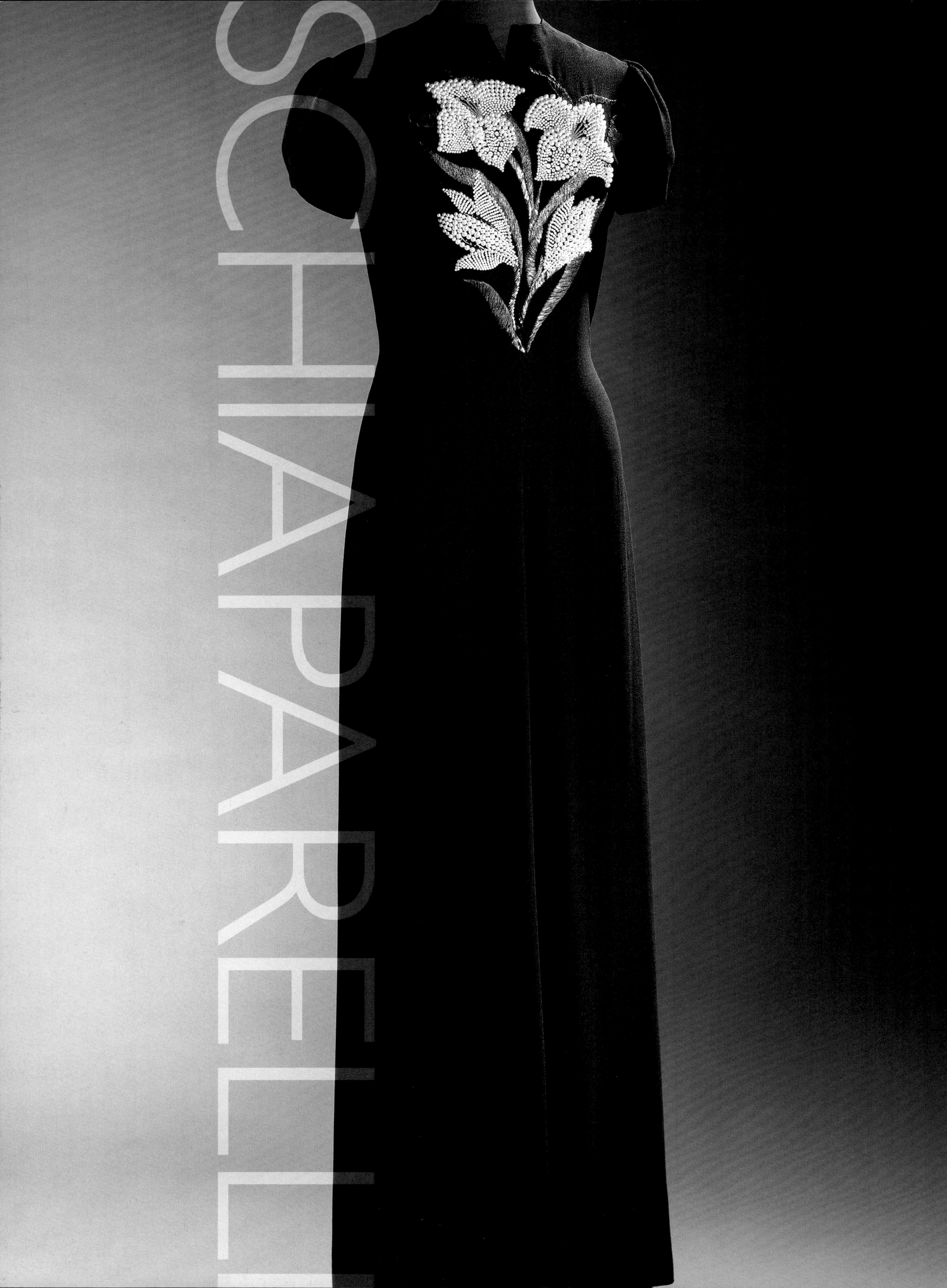
SCHIAPARELLI

Evening gown, Schiaparelli

Paris autumn 1940
Worn and given by
Madame Elsa Schiaparelli

Elsa Schiaparelli enjoyed the enormous publicity generated by her bizarre designs, from black hats shaped like shoes or lamb chops to buttons in the form of miniature carrots. The fashion press throughout the 1930s, and dress historians subsequently, emphasized this gift for the extraordinary. Her less provocative designs rarely caused a furore and have been somewhat neglected. While indicating her attachment to black, the skeleton dress and the lily evening gown reveal the two faces of Schiaparelli – the inventive daredevil and the refined traditionalist. She frequently used black as a background for her witty ideas or allowed it to stand alone, stark and undecorated. She often referred to her simple black dresses and their versatility, and regularly wore black herself. The black-and-white sign identifying her premises at 4 rue de la Paix read 'Schiaparelli pour le Sport', and in 1930 and 1932 she challenged convention when she introduced black towels and black beach pyjamas for the seaside. In the catalogue of the exhibition, 'Hommage à Schiaparelli', 1984, at the Musée de la Mode, Ville de Paris, Billy Boy highlighted Vogue's coverage in February 1940 of Schiaparelli's predominantly black wardrobe for her journey to New York. Practical and versatile, it revolved around three black dresses, three slim, black evening dresses, a black wool suit and two black jackets, one with passementerie, the other with gold embroidery.

It is tempting to speculate that this gown, given to the V&A by Elsa Schiaparelli in her retirement, was one of these very dresses. In matt black crêpe, Schiaparelli composed a short-sleeved gown with an extremely simple, fluid shape relieved by a slashed neckline and a bold embroidered spray of lilies (by the specialist embroidery company Lesage) in various sizes of pearls, sequins and metallic strip.

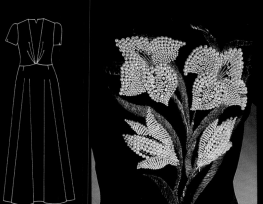
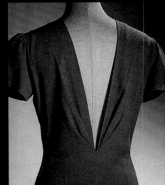
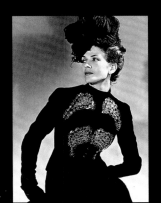

From left to right:
Line drawing, back of gown
Detail, embroidery by Lesage
Detail of bodice back
Photograph of 'mutton chop'
jacket (embroidery by Lesage)
Schiaparelli, 1938

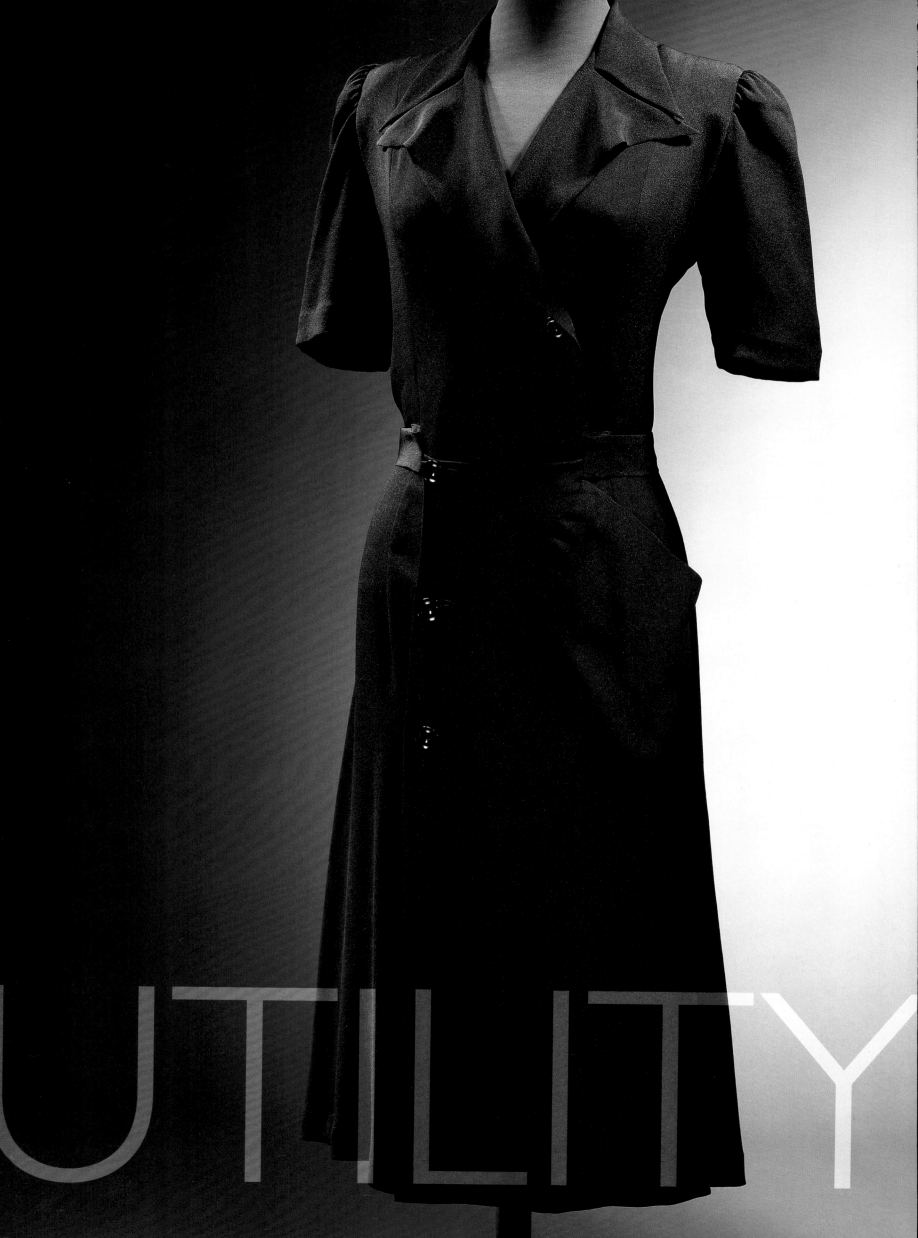

UTILITY

Proposals to standardize civilian clothing during World War I proved unsuccessful, but this did not deter the British Board of Trade in 1942, when it commissioned ten members of the recently formed Incorporated Society of London Designers to create a collection of regulation day wear under the auspices of the Utility scheme. At a time when resources were limited and the war effort was a priority, the participants were instructed to observe strict regulations governing yardage allowance, numbers of buttons and the sizes of hems and seams. Eminent designers, including Hardy Amies, Digby Morton and Charles Creed, attempted to keep their work anonymous and devised a collection that British *Vogue* (October, 1942) praised for 'the clean elegance of a style stripped of all superfluities'. Patterns of each design were made available for manufacturers after the Board's press view of the collection (3 September 1942) when, in order to avoid accusations of frivolity, it was announced that '…it may be of interest to observe that their shoes – and stockings when they are worn – are Utility. The mannequins are all engaged in war work, and have given up their spare time to help today.' Curators at the Brooklyn Museum, New York, were so impressed that they asked for the prototypes, but the President of the Board of Trade decided that it was more appropriate for them to remain in a British institution.

Smart yet practical, this shirtwaister was the only black garment in the designer Utility collection. Though applied decoration was forbidden, the designers devised eye-catching details, such as bold lapels and a roomy pocket set diagonally on the left hip. In a low grade, difficult to handle slippery rayon, the frock has all the characteristics of wartime clothing – broad shoulders (shaped by heavy flock pads), a skirt length just below the knee and a square silhouette – features that five years later Dior was to banish with his New Look revolution.

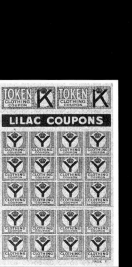

From left to right:
Line drawing, front of dress
Detail of sleeve and collar
Page of clothing coupons
from Board of Trade ration
book, 1946-47

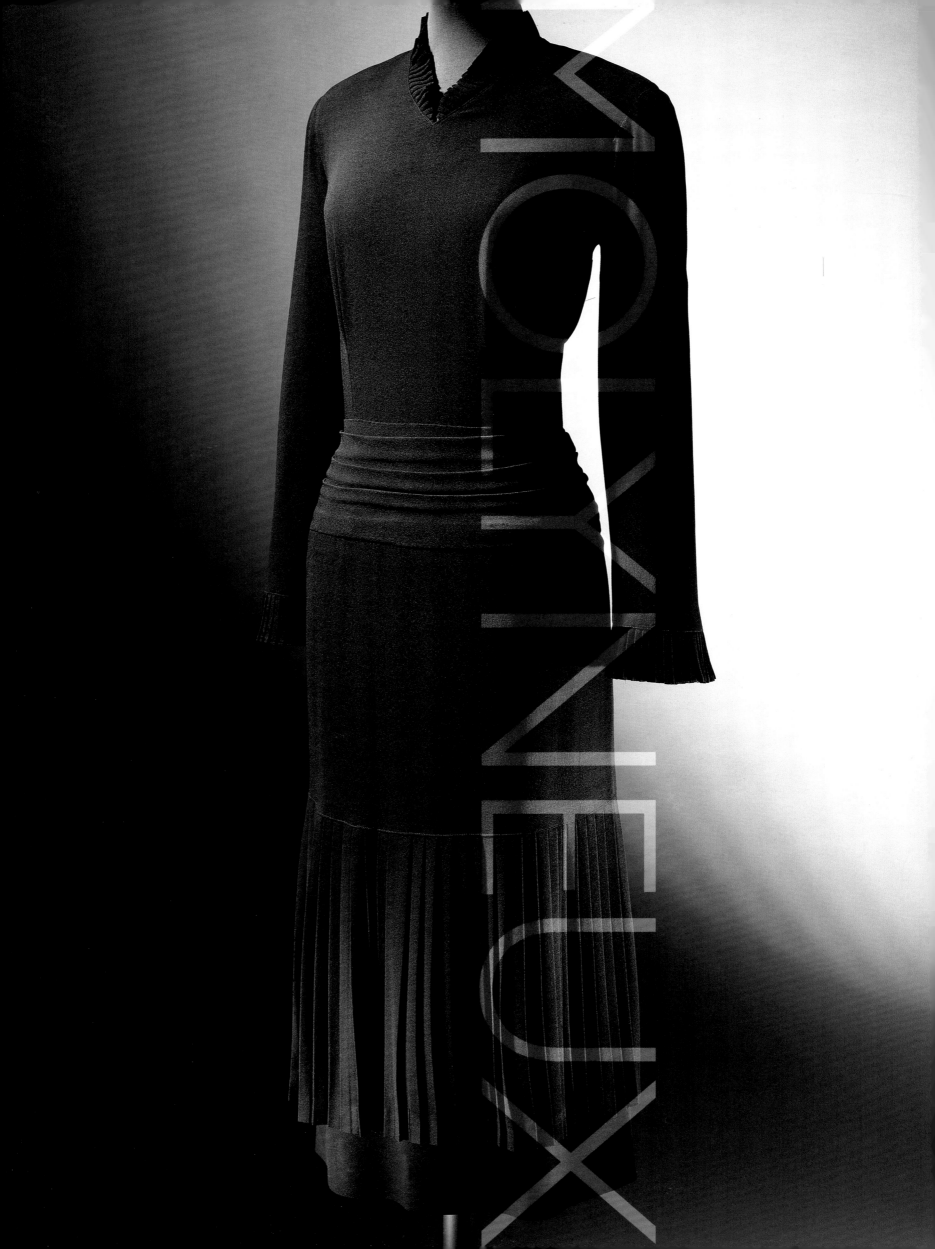

Afternoon dress, Molyneux

London 1946
Worn by Mrs Opal Holt and given by
Mrs DM Haynes and Mrs M Clark

A black afternoon dress with a good label was at once a chic and sensible choice, and Edward Molyneux (1891-1974) could be relied upon to provide streamlined distinction. After training with Lucile (Lady Duff Gordon), who described him as 'a pale, delicate boy, with a passion for drawing', he opened his own house in 1919. He had a rigorous attitude towards colour; his premises in the rue Royale were decorated in Quaker grey throughout, with touches of gold, and his staff wore grey to match – even their shoes were grey. E F Benson captured the designer's essence in 1939 in the phrase 'reeking of Moylneux and simplicity' (Trouble for Lucia, 1939). Captain Molyneux appreciated the geometric precision of pleats and the fact that, without being overly decorative, they added interest to an otherwise unadorned garment.

One of Molyneux's earliest independent designs to be featured in the fashion press was a suit with a knife-pleated skirt. Nearly thirty years later, he gave a day time dress a schoolmistress-like authority and propriety; its covered-up look features a demure high neck, long sleeves and a safe, calf-length skirt. However, he transformed it into a little black dress with attitude by cutting the matt crêpe to skim sensuously over the body's curves and by introducing pleats at salient points. A wide sash arranged in folds

below the waist emphasized the slenderness of the wearer; circling to the centre back, it tied and cascaded suggestively over the derrière. A long panel, pleated from thigh level, forms an overskirt, breaking the uniformity of the otherwise plain straight-line skirt, and the theme recurs at cuffs and collar to complete the composition. In Balmain's words, the dress typifies the 'supreme international elegance of Molyneux' (My Years and Seasons, 1964).

From left to right:
Line drawing, front of dress
Detail of collar
Detail of sleeve and side skirt
Detail, back of skirt

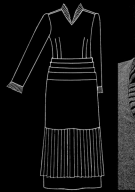
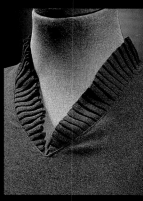
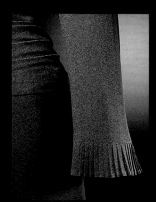
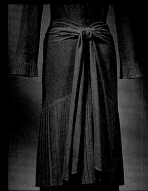

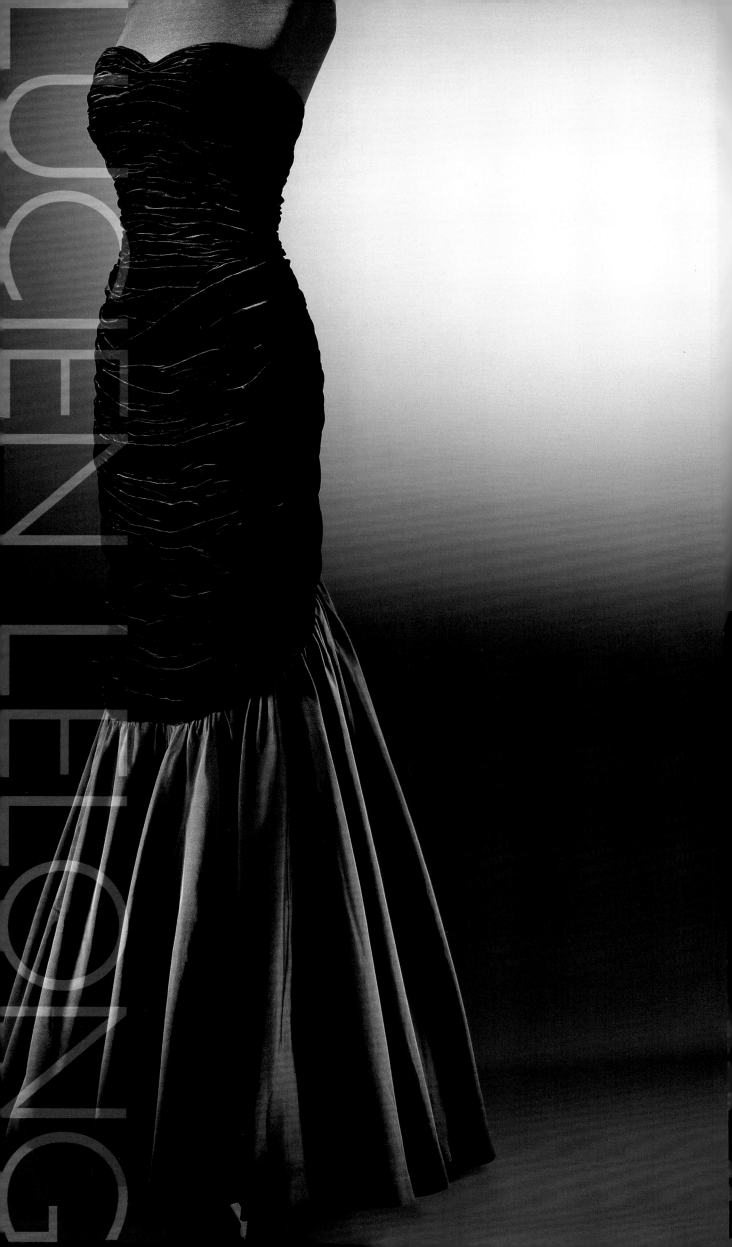

LUCIEN LELONG

Evening gown, Lucien Lelong

Paris 1946

Worn and given by Stella Lady Ednam

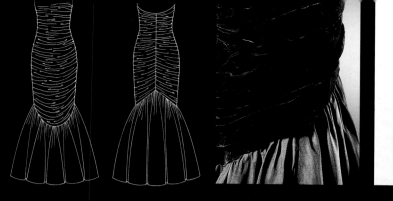

Though Lucien Lelong could design, cut and stitch, he saw himself as the *animateur* of his collections, 'the one who imposes his taste and thus brings about artistic unity' (USA *Vogue*, December, 1925). Harry Yoxall (head of British *Vogue* for forty years) described Lelong (1889-1958) as 'an inspirer of designers rather than a designer himself' (*A Fashion of Life*, 1966). Throughout his long career he spotted and employed new talents, including Pierre Balmain and Christian Dior, who both designed for him over the war years. Lelong had an excellent eye and maintained tight control over the look and content of each collection.

Dior wrote of his happy days at Lelong, but Balmain documented a difficult relationship, including a tussle over a black dress. Balmain had an idea for a tunic dress in black crêpe de Chine, whereupon Lelong reminded him that on joining the house he had been instructed never to use black crêpe. However the toile was so impressive that, with considerable reluctance, Lelong accepted it. Balmain christened the dress 'Little Profit', which became 'big profit' as three hundred and sixty copies were sold (an amazing number in wartime), giving Balmain enormous satisfaction. As Président of the Chambre Syndicale de la Couture during the occupation of Paris, Lelong was largely responsible for preventing the Germans transferring Paris couture to Berlin and Vienna.

Lelong's house was known for supremely elegant clothes, such as this all-black, trumpet-line evening gown. Glossy silk velvet is finely ruched around the body from a provocatively low neckline to knee level, where a seam curving upwards at the sides joins it to a flared skirt of silk taffeta. A halter strap once passed around the neck but has been removed to achieve a more tantalizing strapless neckline.

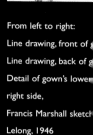

From left to right:
Line drawing, front of g
Line drawing, back of g
Detail of gown's lower
right side,
Francis Marshall sketch
Lelong, 1946

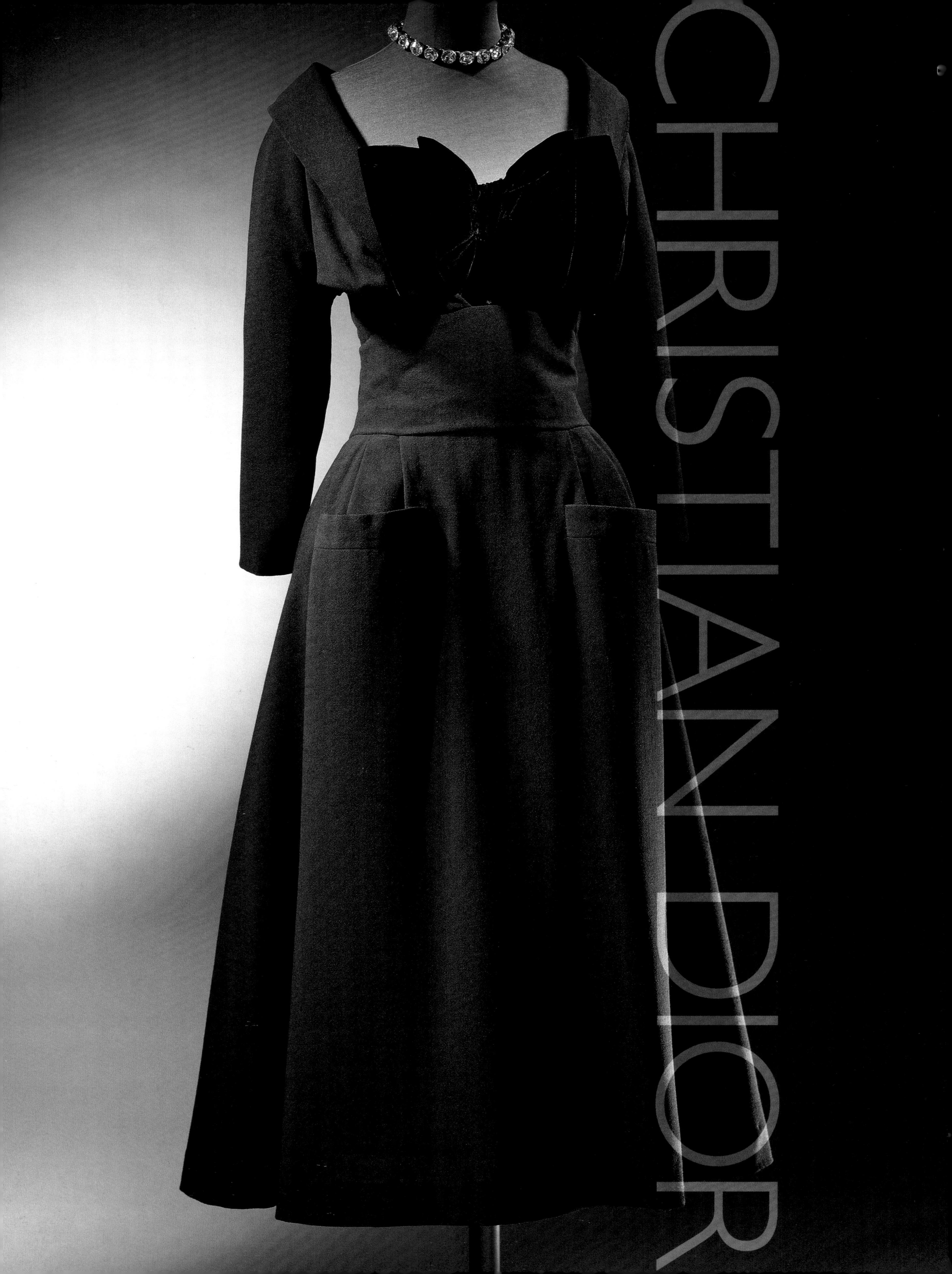
CHRISTIAN DIOR

Afternoon dress, 'Maxim's' Christian Dior

Paris spring-summer 1947

Worn and given by Mrs David Bruce

Christian Dior's inaugural collection for spring 1947 featured two themes, *La Ligne Corolle* and the *En Huit silhouette*; the show caused a sensation and was christened 'The New Look' (by Carmel Snow of *Harper's Bazaar*). Dior (1905-57) offered the glamour and romance of full skirts and nipped-in waists to women who were tired of the skimpy, utilitarian clothes with boxy silhouettes, mannish square shoulders and practical short skirts necessitated by war and its aftermath. He wrote, 'as a result of the war and uniforms, women still looked and dressed like Amazons. But I designed clothes for flower-like women, with rounded shoulders, full feminine busts and hand-span waists above enormous spreading skirts' (*Dior by Dior*, 1957).

A favourite with fashion editors, 'Maxim's' was categorized by the house as a '*robe d'après-midi habillée*' and was worn with a black tulle cartwheel hat, long black gloves and simple black court shoes. Dior became the master of ultra-sophisticated black fashion, perfecting the technique of assembling in one design various opulent black fabrics with different reflective characteristics. Setting glistening silk velvet against matt, light-absorbing wool, 'Maxim's' was elaborately constructed to enhance the natural female curves. Emphasizing the bust, a large bow was set into the low, square neckline; the waist was compressed to a tiny 51.5 cms (21 ins) by a

cummerbund-style lower bodice. Stiff, frilled underpinnings rounded out the hips, and unpressed pleats fell into stand-away pockets. Special undergarments were designed to achieve the desired curvaceous contours, including a corset with *en suite* ruffles to fill out the bosom and hips as well as a short, boned corselet (*guêpière*) to constrict the waist. The substructure of a garment was always of primary importance to Dior, and this intricately cut dress made out of many yards of wool is supported, and its form defined, by an all-black, boned foundation and heavy grosgrain petticoat.

From left to right:
Line drawing, front of dress
Line drawing, back of dress
Detail centre back of dress
Cocktail dress, pleated black chiffon. Christian Dior, winter 1947. *L'Art et la Mode*, October 1947.

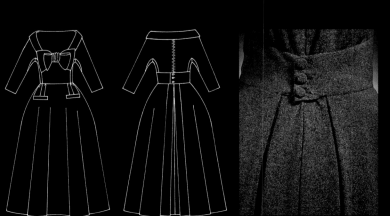
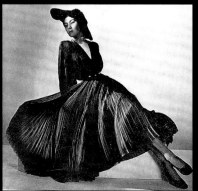

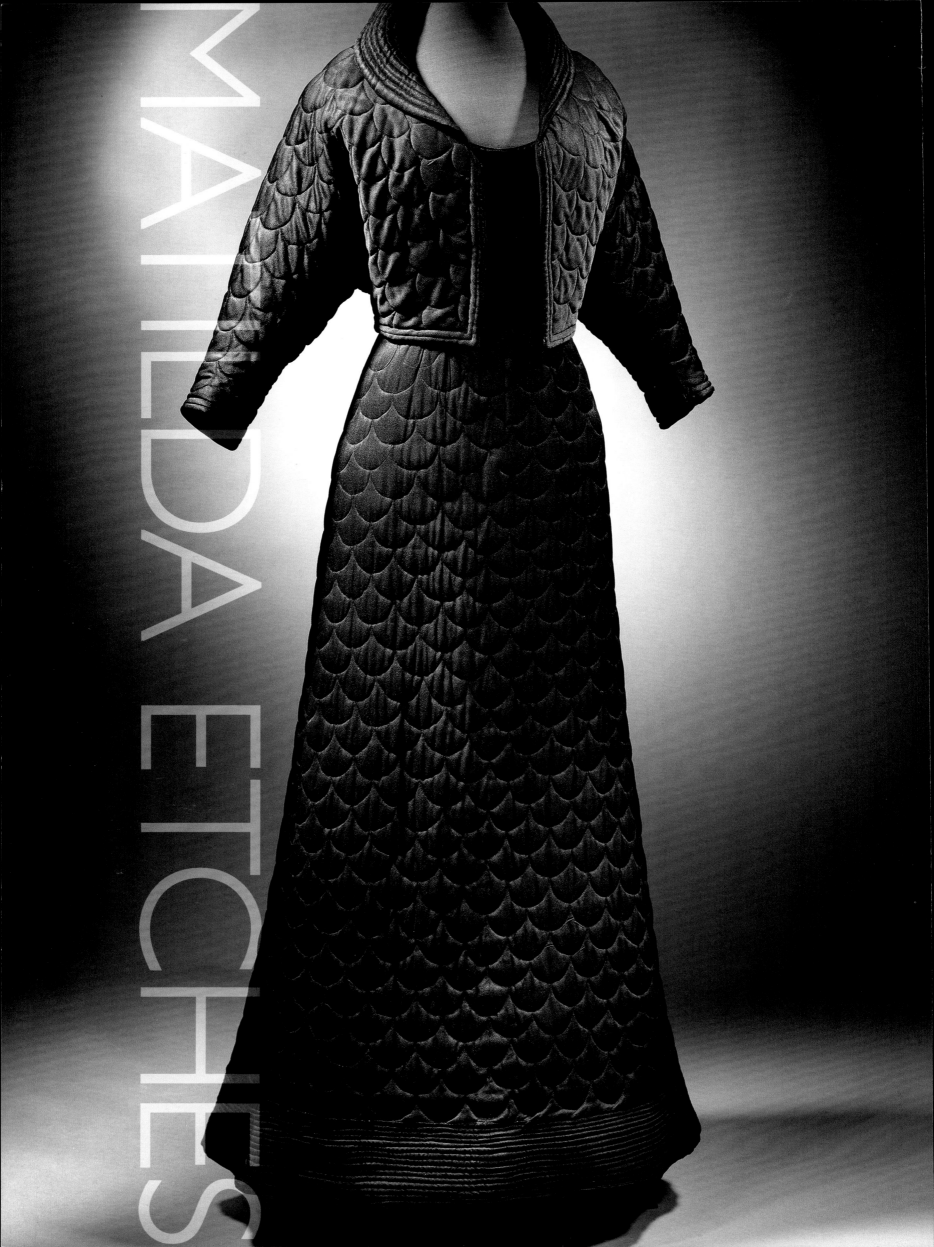

Evening ensemble, dress and jacket, Matilda Etches

London 1947

Given by Miss Hazel Armour

Quilted in a traditional manner, this cosy evening gown and jacket were specifically designed for winter evenings at a time when post-war coal shortages in Britain made the heating of public places spasmodic. *Country Life* described the ensemble as 'a sheath dress, ankle length, with a bolero to cover up the bare *décolletage*'. Matilda Etches (1898-1974) selected fine black crêpe to create an optical slimming effect and lined the jacket with an eye-catching vivid purple silk. Both garments are quilted in the popular shell pattern, which is skilfully adapted in the dress to fit closely to the figure and also create tiny winged sleeves. Finishing borders of tightly packed parallel lines of quilting give substance to the collar and hem.

Without formal training, Matilda Etches released her first fashion collection in 1935 at the Dorchester Hotel, London, displaying a number of designs in black, including a quilted crêpe paper cape and a chaste day dress inspired by a nun's habit. Within a couple of years she had abandoned mainline fashion to design and make costumes for film and theatre but returned to couture in 1947. Because she worked on an individual basis with her clients (including Vivien Leigh and Dame Ninette de Valois) she has never been accorded due recognition for her imaginative approach to fashion design. She invented a non-crushable, knife-pleated 'butterfly' evening cape that packed down to fit into an umbrella-size cover, while another fashion coup was to apply hundreds of heat curled strips of black organdie over a plain background to make a 'ravishing summer evening gown' (*Santa Barbara News-Press*, 4 July 1954). The quilted two-piece has a typical Etches twist – the jacket with just two seams (under the arms) can be worn either way up.

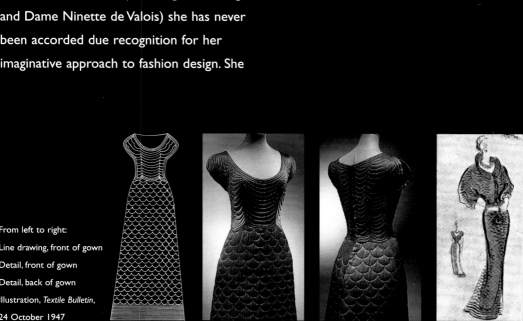

From left to right:
Line drawing, front of gown
Detail, front of gown
Detail, back of gown
Illustration, *Textile Bulletin*,
24 October 1947

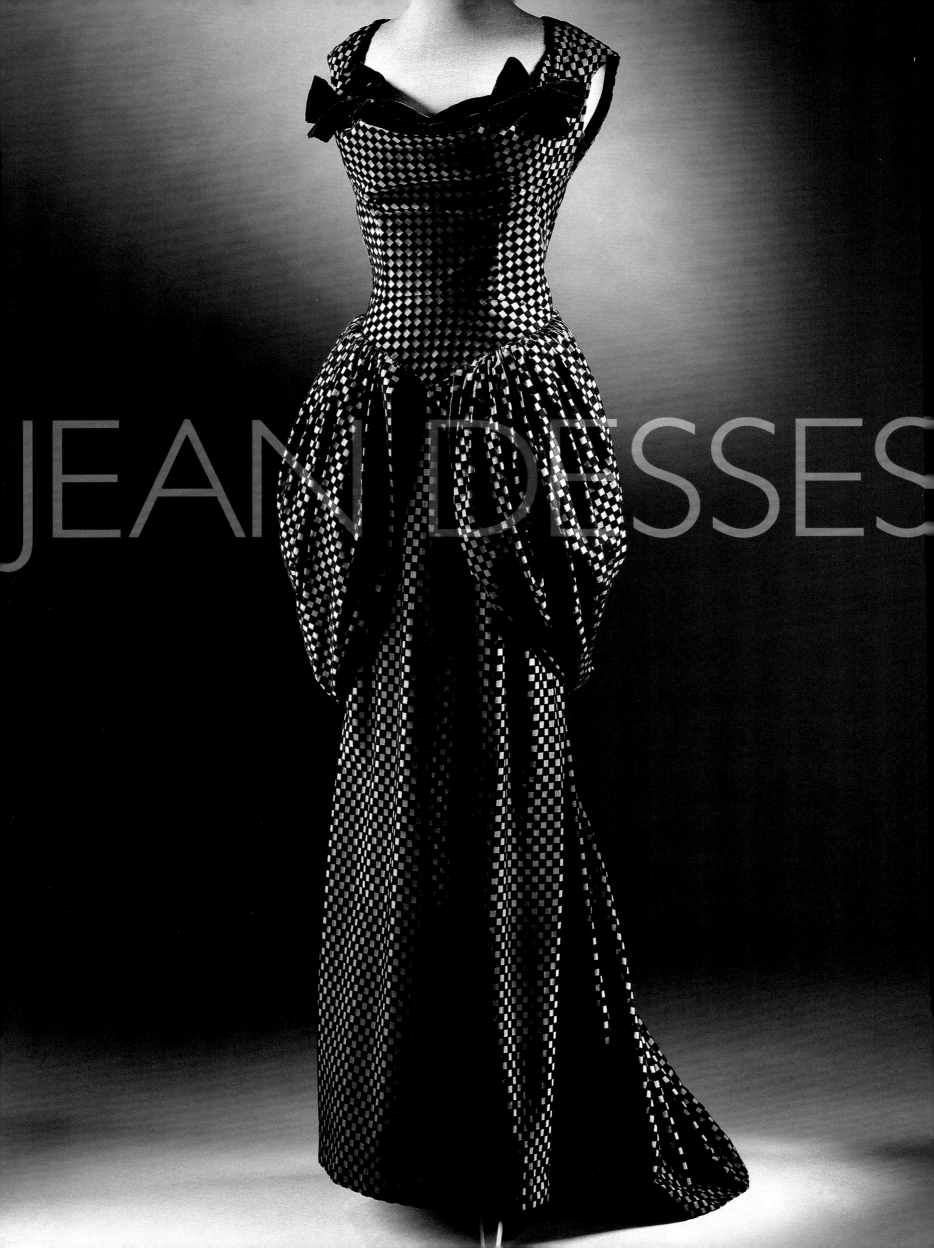

Evening gown, Jean Dessès

Paris 1948

Worn and given by the Hon. Mrs JJ Astor

Of Greek parentage but born in Egypt, Jean Dessès (1904-70) opened his Paris couture house in 1937. After World War II, along with forty other leading designers, he participated in the Chambre Syndicale's 'Le Thèâtre de la Mode', a travelling exhibition launched in 1945 of knee-high wire mannequins dressed in the latest styles, which announced to the world that Paris intended to regain its position at the epicentre of fashion. In the following years, with official support and freed from the extreme deprivations imposed by war, couturiers experimented, often in sophisticated black, with intricate ideas made up in lavish materials, such as this imposing evening gown. The formula of a

long, sheath dress teamed with fly-away panels, enormous bows or basques set at or about hip level became a couture favourite in the 1950s; unfortunately designers seemed to disregard the fact that, in order to succeed, this theme demanded extremely tall, willowy wearers. Fabric was stiffened, padded, weighted and underpinned to achieve impressive but often impractical garments. Dessès had a clientele of wealthy, elegant women who adored his imaginative but never shocking collections.

Bianchini-Ferier, the Lyon-based manufacturer of exclusive dress fabrics, wove this black chequerboard, voided velvet with the necessary stiffness to retain the sculptural forms devised by Dessès, who

was exploring the potential of bouffant shapes. The velvet created a powerful silhouette, giving the design instant drama. Intricately cut, the gown has a tightly fitted bodice with a low, stand-away neckline enclosing a bow-trimmed modesty in plain silk velvet. Over a long skirt with a fishtail train, side panels are gathered to form panniers (supported by net frills) which exaggerate the hips and then curve behind where they cross and ingeniously slot through each other. Known as 'La Ligne Corbeille', this was popular with Paris designers and, like Dessès, they often rendered it in black for maximum impact.

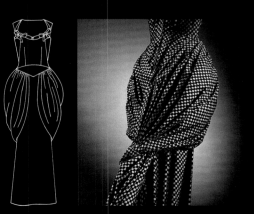 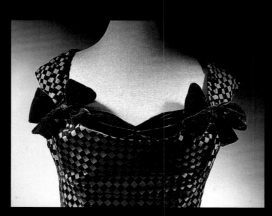 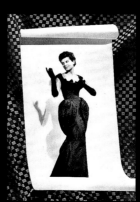

From left to right:
Line drawing, front of gown
Detail, back of skirt
Detail of bodice and neckline
Advert for Bianchini-Ferier
textiles, 1948

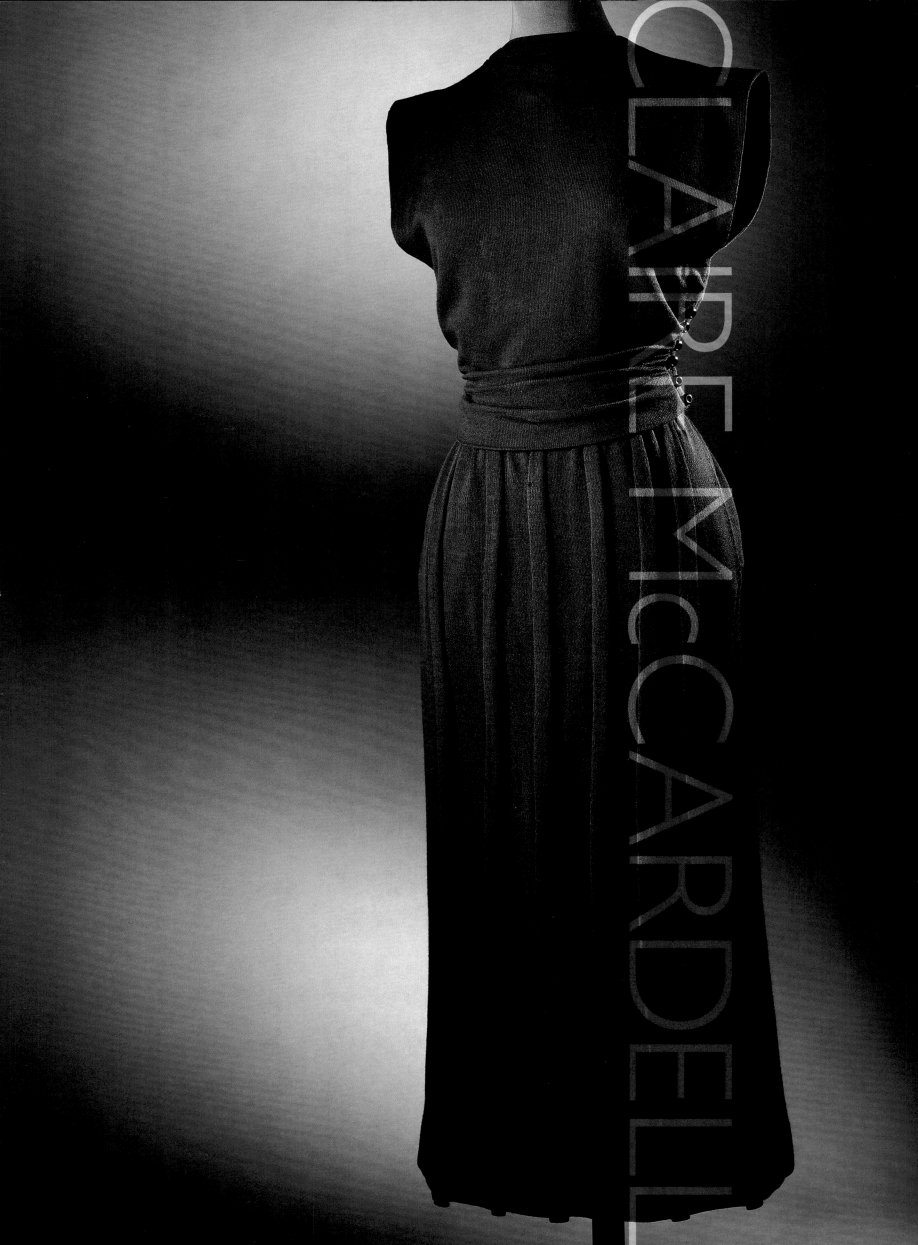

Day time ensemble – top and skirt, Claire McCardell for Townley Frocks

New York about 1950

Given by Mrs Adrian McCardell

Revered as the designer who created the 'American Look', Claire McCardell (1905-58) had an informal, relaxed attitude towards clothes. Her level-headed creed was that, above all else, garments had to be comfortable and functional. She studied fashion design at Parsons School, Manhattan, spending a year in Paris observing the workings of *haute couture*. In 1931 she joined Townley Frocks and provided them with designs for easy-to-wear styles in modest fabrics yet with a distinctive cut and details that made them exceptional. Black was not an overwhelmingly significant element in McCardell's repertoire but when appropriate she used it. Jersey, however, was her favourite material. She appreciated its no-nonsense flexibility and its resilience. In her amusing handbook *What Shall I Wear?* (1956) jersey was nominated one of her 'universal' fabrics redolent of elegance and good taste. She found that it was every bit as regal as velvet and asked: 'Isn't it wonderful to unpack wool jersey and thumb your nose at an iron?' Sally Kirkland (fashion editor of *Life*) recorded the fact that women who could easily afford higher prices often 'preferred the fluid lines, packability and versatility of Claire's jerseys'.

Typically in her beloved jersey, McCardell designed a supple top and skirt that could be worn all day in great comfort but was extremely chic. The skirt's slightly irregular, soft pleats are anchored so they would never go awry. With admirable economy, just one front and one back panel make the cap-sleeved top which loop-fastens at the left side and back neck with characteristic McCardell details – shining black buttons. Black resisted the ravages and grime of the nine-to-five grind and fulfilled McCardell's exhortation to 'choose clothes that won't look wilted after a day's wear'.

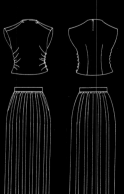
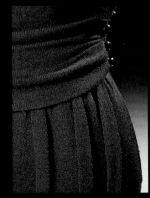

From left to right:

Line drawing, front of ensemble

Line drawing, back of ensemble

Detail, left side fastening of top

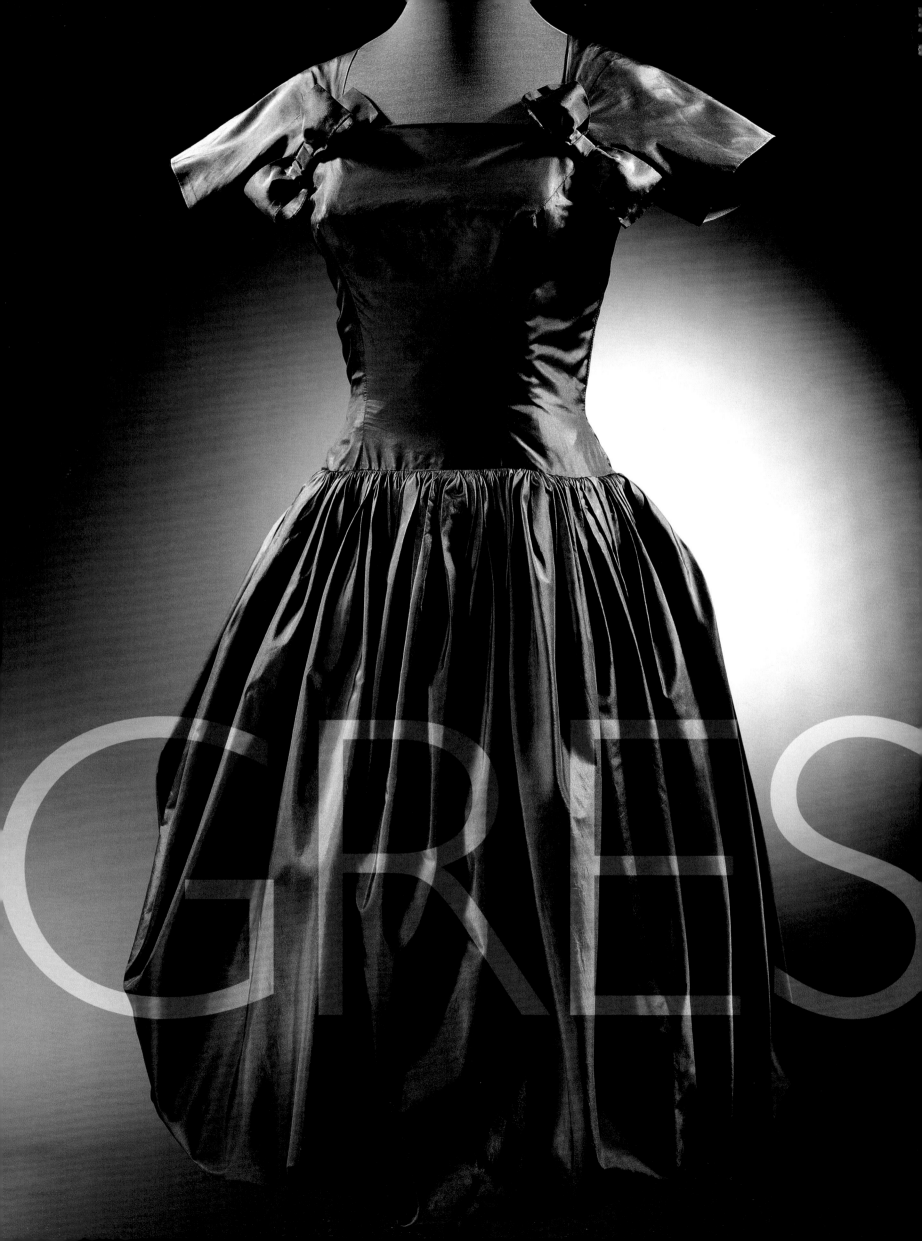

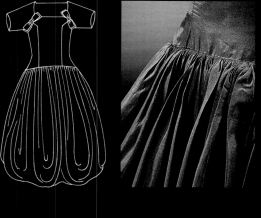
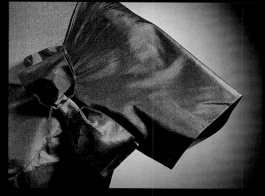
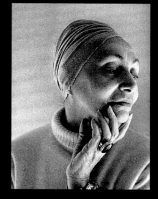

Cocktail dress, Grès
Paris about 1950

Madame Grès (1903-93) wanted to be a sculptress, but her desire was never realized. However, she became internationally famous for her creativity as a couturier and renowned for columnar, draped styles in supple silk jersey (frequently white). These classics remained in her repertoire for her entire career, being adapted slightly to suit the needs of each season. Not instantly recognizable as her work are up-to-the-minute designs that had a more fleeting fashion appeal, such as this resolutely black cocktail dress. Throughout the 1950s, in their search for new silhouettes, couturiers experimented with ballooned skirts, variously described by fashion editors as 'à la Zouave', 'pumpkin', 'tulip line', 'gonflé' or 'puffball'. These rounded shapes were difficult to achieve

and maintain – by sitting down a wearer risked deflating her skirt, though this danger was averted at cocktail parties where guests usually stood. Such early evening occasions with their mixed alcoholic drinks enjoyed a new lease of life in the 1950s, when fashion's agony aunts were united in their support of the appropriate attire – a little black cocktail dress.

Madame Grès composed this bouffant design by minutely gathering fine silk taffeta into a dropped waist and by attaching it at the hemline to a narrow, straight-line petticoat in matching taffeta. Contrasting with the skirt's gourd-like curves is a tightly fitted, long-line bodice with pert short sleeves. The top is boned and lined with silk organza which is extended into an inner roll beneath the gathers to shape and give

support. As was customary, the garment was superbly finished; even the zip head was fitted with a tiny silk pull to help the wearer (or her maid) fasten the dress. Gleaming black taffeta increased the drama of the design, and Madame Grès left the powerful, almost organic form uncluttered save for two discreetly tailored bows marking the corners of the low, square neckline.

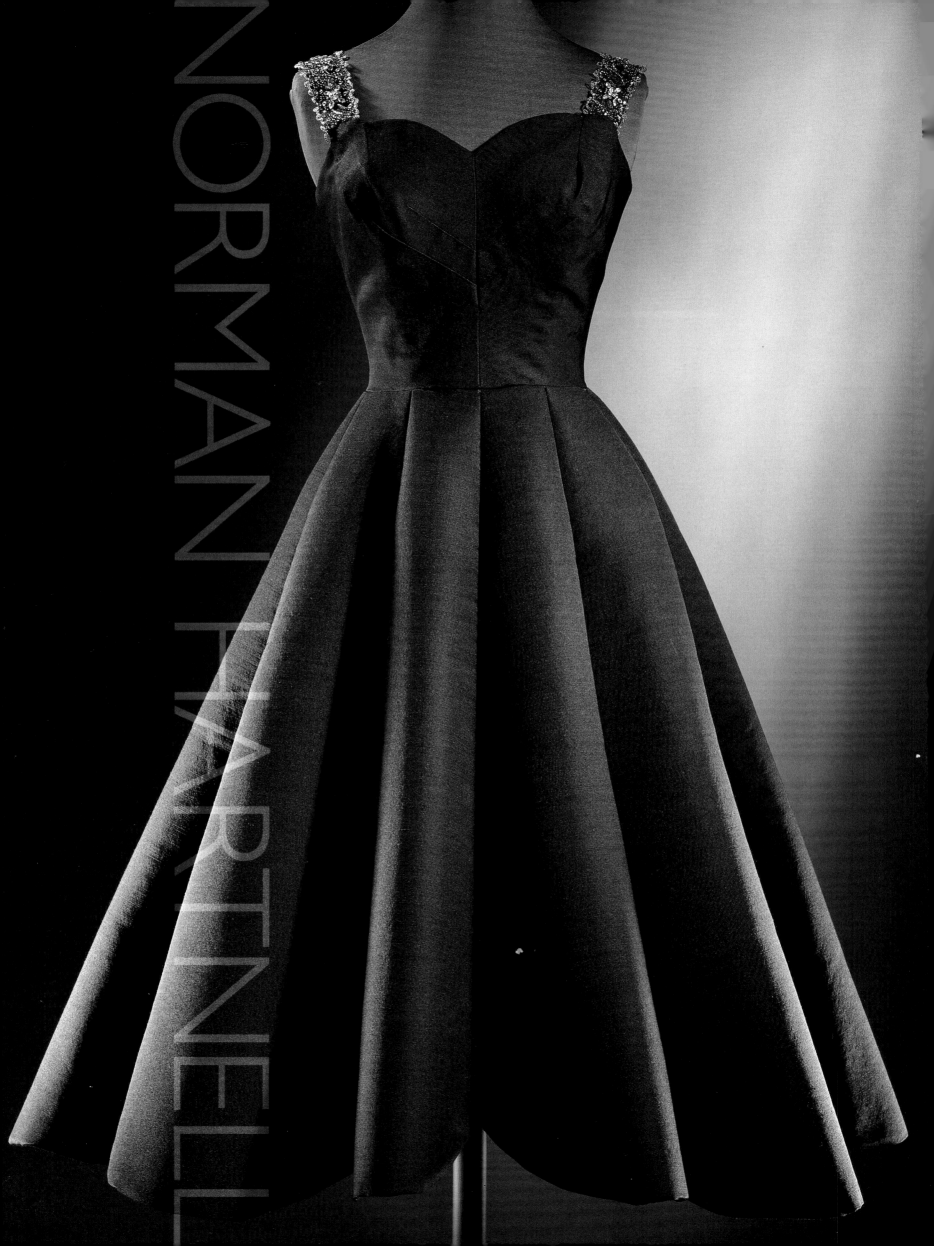

NORMAN HARTNELL

Evening gown,
Norman Hartnell

London early 1950s

Worn and given by

HRH Princess Margaret

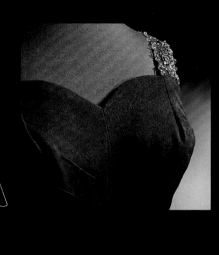

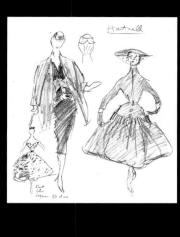

Norman Hartnell (1901-79) was best known as the couturier to the British royal family and in 1935 produced his first design for Princess Margaret (then five years old), who looked angelic in her pretty pale pink satin bridesmaid's dress at the wedding of the Duke of Gloucester and Lady Alice Montagu-Douglas-Scott. Unless in mourning or at solemn state occasions such as Remembrance Day ceremonies, it is unusual for royalty to appear in public wearing black. Indeed, on one notable occasion Hartnell was applauded for avoiding the inevitable black of bereavement. Queen Elizabeth's mother, the Countess of Strathmore, died a few weeks before the 1938 state visit to France and, although it was postponed, the revised schedule fell within the period of court mourning. Realizing that to plunge the Queen into deep black, purple or grey in high summer was neither sensible nor politic, Hartnell saved the day by composing a wardrobe in white – an alternative colour for mourning.

Throughout the late 1940s and 1950s, Hartnell was commissioned to design a wide range of clothes for Princess Margaret's official duties. Knowing her liking for Dior's 1947 New Look and to emphasize her tiny waist, he often designed dresses with tight bodices and spreading skirts.

In heavy black grosgrain, this evening gown indicates the Princess's taste for uncluttered simple lines with the minimum of decoration – in this case, just the shoulder straps are embroidered with silvered beads and *diamantés*. Interest is vested in the skirt, constructed in ten panels and finished with bold scallops at the hem. The substantial weight and density of the grosgrain maintains the skirt's flared profile and holds its umbrella-like undulations. Black was a perfect foil for Princess Margaret's translucent skin and blue-violet eyes.

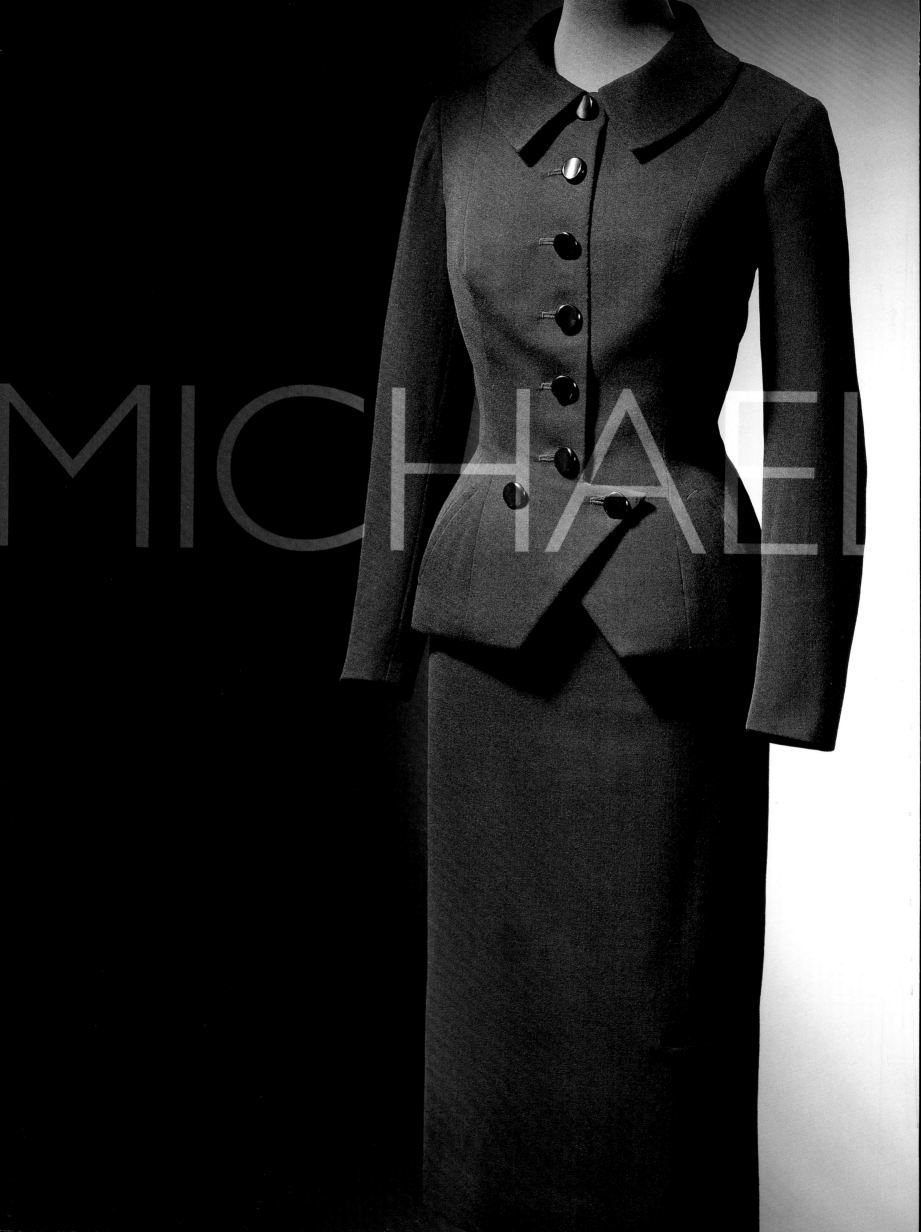

By the early 1950s little black suits had become indispensable to professional women at the office and were also ideal for shopping and taking lunch. Fashion magazines and etiquette manuals advised that a smartly tailored black suit was the perfect solution for town wear, being chic yet practical. *Vogue* led the way in 1950, praising the virtues of a black two-piece: 'For the woman-about-town or the girl-with-a-job this outfit (supported by a change of accessories) is the chic answer to those all-through-the-day engagements that end with a theatre or restaurant dinner' (British *Vogue*, October 1950). By assembling different accessories around the core of a fitted or semi-fitted jacket and skirt (slimline was preferred), looks ranging from boardroom severity to cocktail frivolity could be constructed. In the city it was modish to team such suits with pert hats, obligatory gloves, court shoes, bag and a long, slender umbrella.

Michael Donnellan (1915-85) joined Lachasse after the war to design tailored suits and subsequently (1953) opened his own house, Michael of Carlos Place. 'His understanding of the human body, superb tailoring and purity of line gave him a very high contemporary reputation, not least among his peers. He was often compared to his idol, Balenciaga…' (Elizabeth McCrum, *Fabric and Form: Irish Fashion Since 1950*, 1996). For this sharply cut worsted two-piece, he eschewed the usual V neck with revers and chose a high neck with a demure Peter Pan-like collar. The focal point is the line of bold, shining buttons fastening the jacket, and attention is drawn to the clever switch below the waist to a double breasted format with steeply cut-away fronts. Mathematically precise cut and construction ensure the perfect balance and success of this ensemble. The jacket has judicious padding and is carefully interlined and lined to mould the body and curve out gracefully over the hips. The skills of an experienced tailor achieved the exactly pointed panels and the meticulously bound buttonholes. Michael's collections regularly included these severe styles in black.

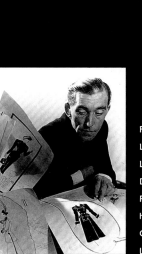

From left to right:
Line drawing, front of suit
Line drawing, back of suit
Detail, lower front of jacket
Portrait of Michael with
his sketches, late 1940s.
Courtesy of
Leonora Curry Barden

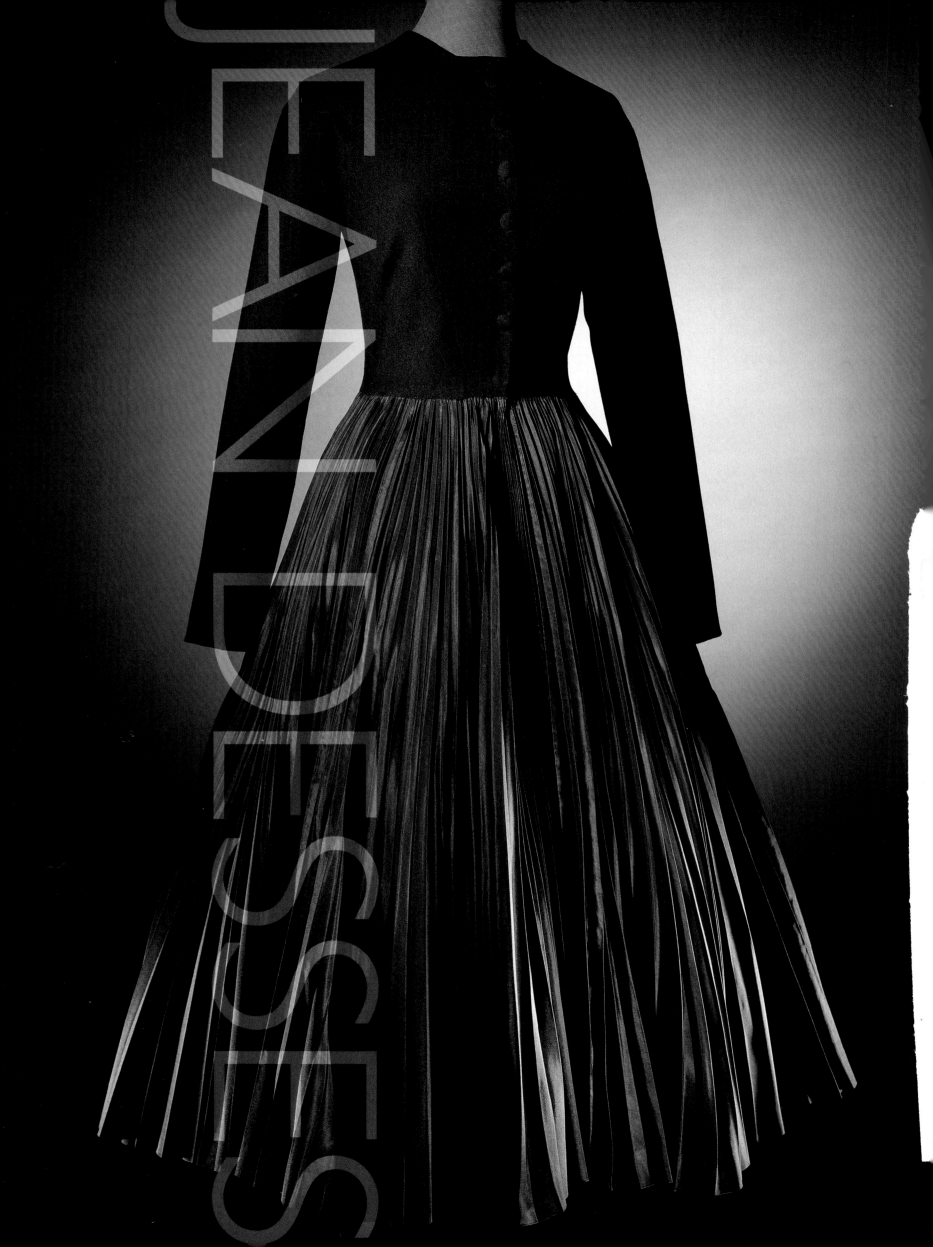

Day dress, Jean Dessès

Paris about 1955
Worn by Mrs Opal Holt and given by
Mrs DM Haynes and Mrs M Clark

Perhaps the most desirable little black dress was the model that could be worn in comfort during the working day and could go on into the evening, demanding nothing more than a change of accessories. It had to be smart but not too heavyweight and woolly for the glittering attachments and glamour of night-time. The idea of a fitted sweater in fine matt wool, attached to a pleated skirt with a sheen, caught on and, in the 1950s, became the standby of the professional woman.

Jean Dessès' version of this versatile dress has a modest, high-necked, long-sleeved bodice that front fastens with self-covered buttons. In non-reflective wool, it is cut and darted to fit the torso closely. From the narrow waist spreads a lustrous, calf-length, accordion-pleated silk taffeta skirt. In the post-war period textile scientists developed new permanent pleating techniques. In 1955 it was noted that 'mounting interest in pleating and pleated fabrics has no doubt been generated by the permanent pleatability of synthetic fabrics – a process which spread eastwards from the States, and has produced the biggest advance in pleating since its origins in the ancient world' (*Hard's Year Book for the Clothing Industry*, 1956). These advances generated a trend for finely pleated skirts; down-market versions were in the latest man-made fibres such as Terelyne, whereas only pure silk or wool met the needs of *haute couture*. For nine-to-five efficiency a black sweater-dress might be accompanied by a crisp white collar or cheerful scarf, matt leather belt, sensible shoes and a roomy handbag, and at the witching hour these could exchanged for evening pearls, patent belt, strappy shoes and a clutch bag. Fashion magazines of the 1950s were funds of such 'transformation' tips for the busy, well-dressed woman, and the basic black dress was a regular starting point.

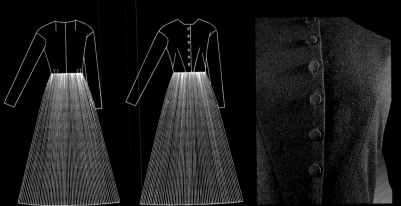

From left to right:
Line drawing, back of dress
Line drawing, front of dress
Detail of bodice front

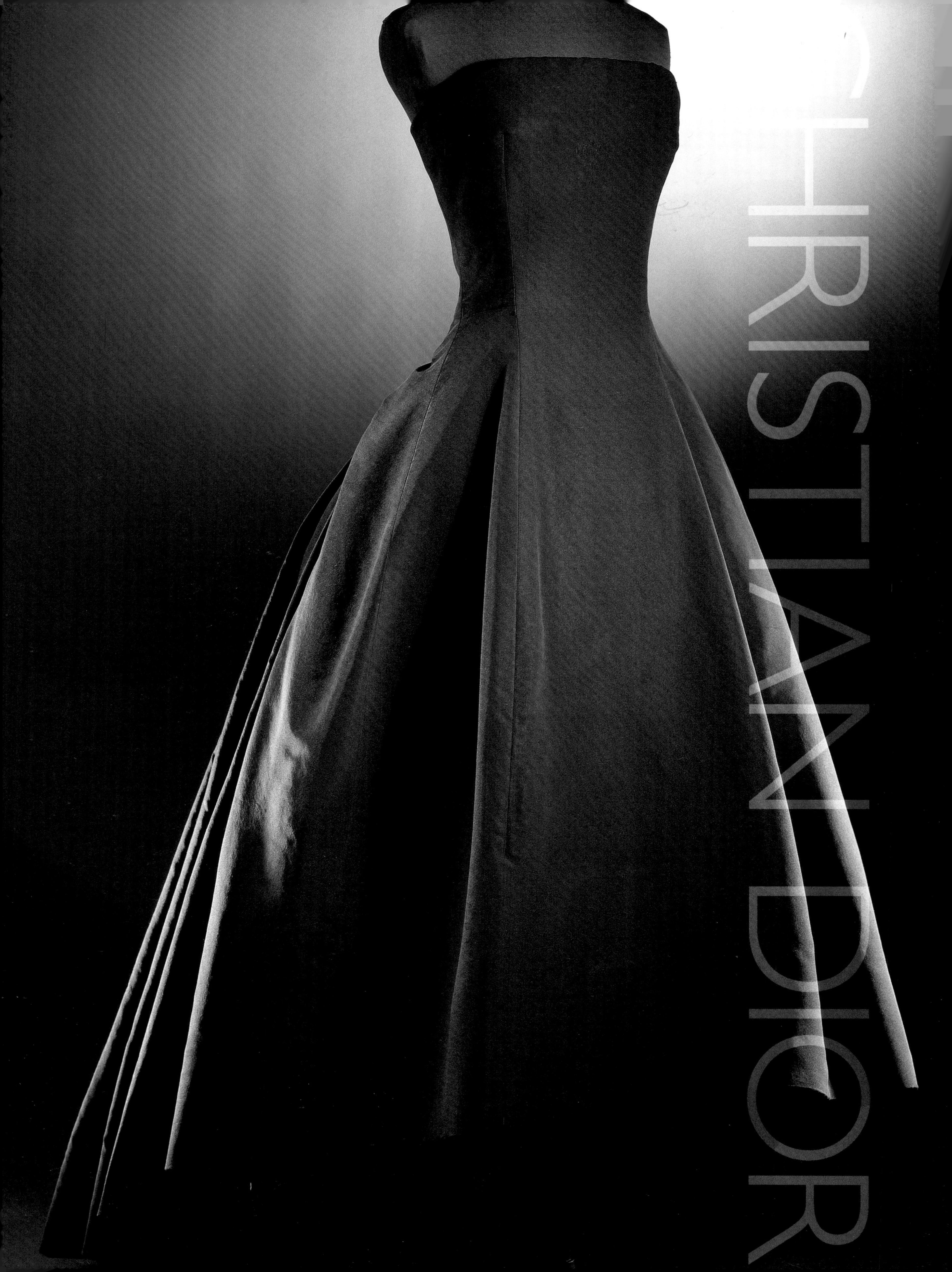
CHRISTIAN DIOR

Evening gown, 'Soirée de Décembre'
Christian Dior

Paris autumn-winter 1955
Worn and given by Dame Margot Fonteyn

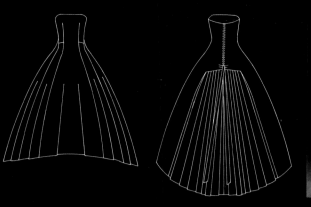

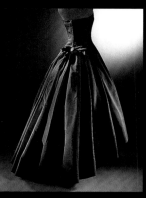

From left to right:
Line drawing, front of dress
Line drawing, back of dress
Gown back view

Black was of enormous significance to Christian Dior. He described it as 'The most popular and the most convenient and the most elegant of all colours. And I say colour on purpose, because black may be sometimes just as striking as a colour' (*Christian Dior's Little Dictionary of Fashion*, 1954). Black was rarely absent from his collections, and he frequently used it to create the defining statements for his famous lines. The habit of naming collections was not new when Dior opened his house, but his titles were catchy and had huge popular appeal. Particularly successful was his ploy of using letters from the alphabet to describe silhouettes of the mid-1950s: H line (autumn-winter 1954-55), A line (spring-summer 1955) and Y line (autumn-winter 1955-56).

Belonging to the Y-line period, Dame Margot Fonteyn's strapless, 'princess' style evening gown is a sculptural masterpiece (an inverted Y) in crisp silk faille, shaped by a boned foundation attached to a multi-layered tulle petticoat. The prima ballerina's slenderness, poise and streamlined elegance were perfect for the gown's strong lines. A favourite with *haute couture* was the trick of composing two dresses in one – the front skirt was short (here, lower calf level) but dipped to an imposing floor-sweeping train at the back. It offered the grandeur of a full-length evening dress but the mobility of a short style. In order to contain the dress within crisp borders, stiffening bands run within the neck and hem turnings. Remaining true to his belief that 'a simple black dress…triumphs by its very austerity' (*Dior by Dior*, 1957), Dior kept the gown's smooth lines uncluttered save for the restrained decorative note of streamers that tied at the back and trailed over the softly pleated centre panel.

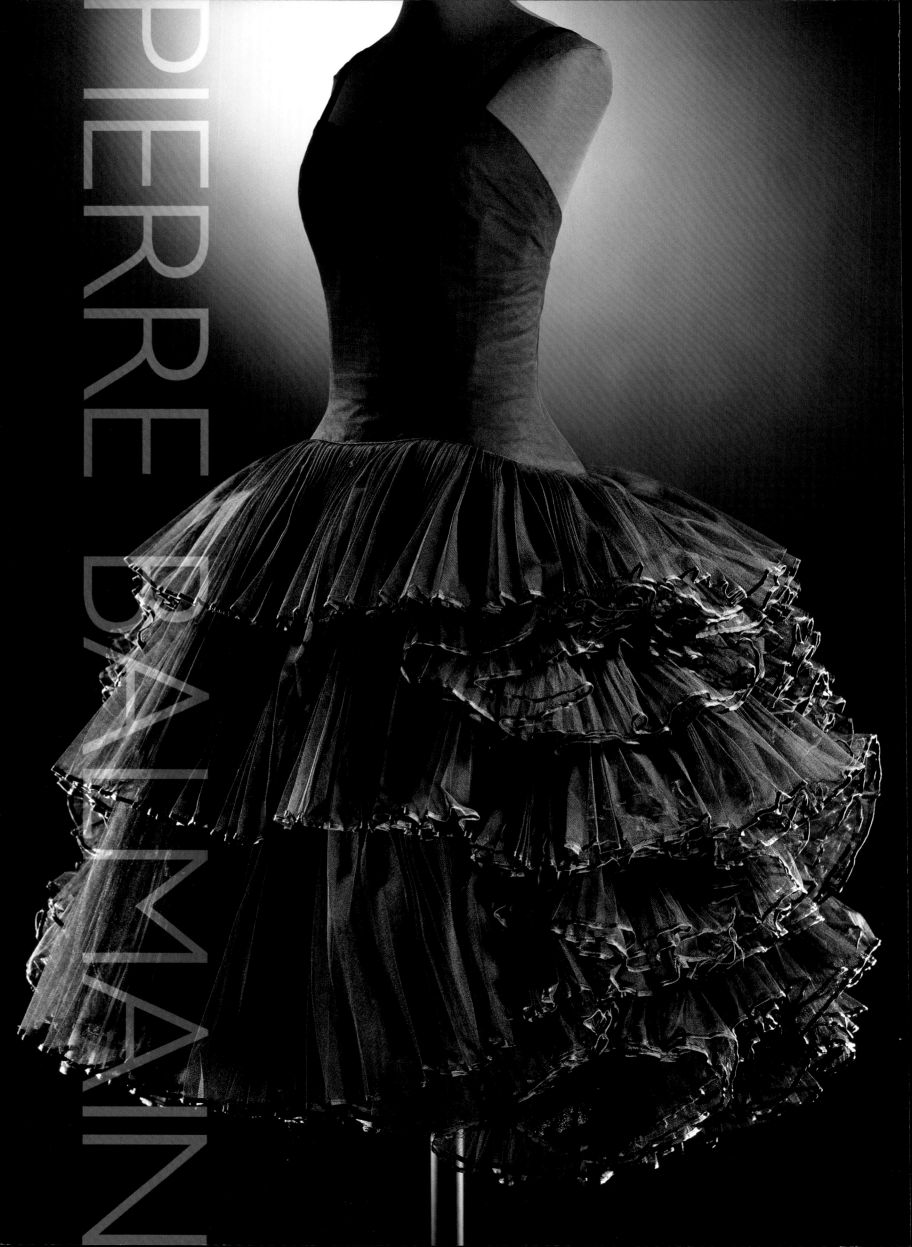

Evening dress, Pierre Balmain

Paris 1957

Worn and given by

Lady Elizabeth von Hofmannsthal

Between 1952 and 1959 Pierre Balmain (1914-82) gave his collections the generic name 'Jolie Madame', an ideal description for his overtly feminine and flattering designs. These qualities won the house a prestigious clientele known for its refined chic, a clientele that included Vivien Leigh and Queen Sirikit of Thailand. Balmain, according to Célia Bertin, was 'the last word in elegance, and encourages all kinds of extravagances as long as they are in good taste' (*Paris à la Mode*, 1956). His palette inclined towards pretty colours, but sophisticated black invaded for cocktails and grand occasions. Throughout the 1950s fashion decreed that skirts should be pencil slim or voluminous, and the most lavishly full styles usually graced evening events. Rumour had it that a certain *élégante*, in order not to crush her enormously bouffant skirt, was transported to a grand gala standing up in one of her horseboxes.

Taking inspiration from ballet costume, this evening dress has a severely plain top and a complex extravaganza of a skirt. Low necked and unadorned, the bodice drops to the hip level at the sides and is tightly fitted to the body by curved seams and long darts. It is of tulle stretched over taffeta and mounted on a firmly boned foundation. Springing from the lowered waist is a frou-frou skirt of accordion-pleated triple flounces in frail tulle edged with shining satin ribbon. At the sides additional fullness is achieved by tiers of enormous rosettes of pleated tulle interleaved with supporting ruches of nylon crin. To anchor this profusion and help take its weight, that regular feature of the innards of *haute couture* garments was provided, a grosgrain belt known as a waist-stay. The exuberant mass is held buoyant by two full and complicated petticoats of black nylon, stiffening and net frills.

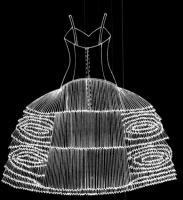
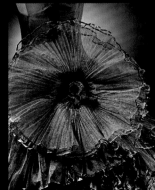

From left to right:

Line drawing, back of dress

Detail, construction of

side skirt

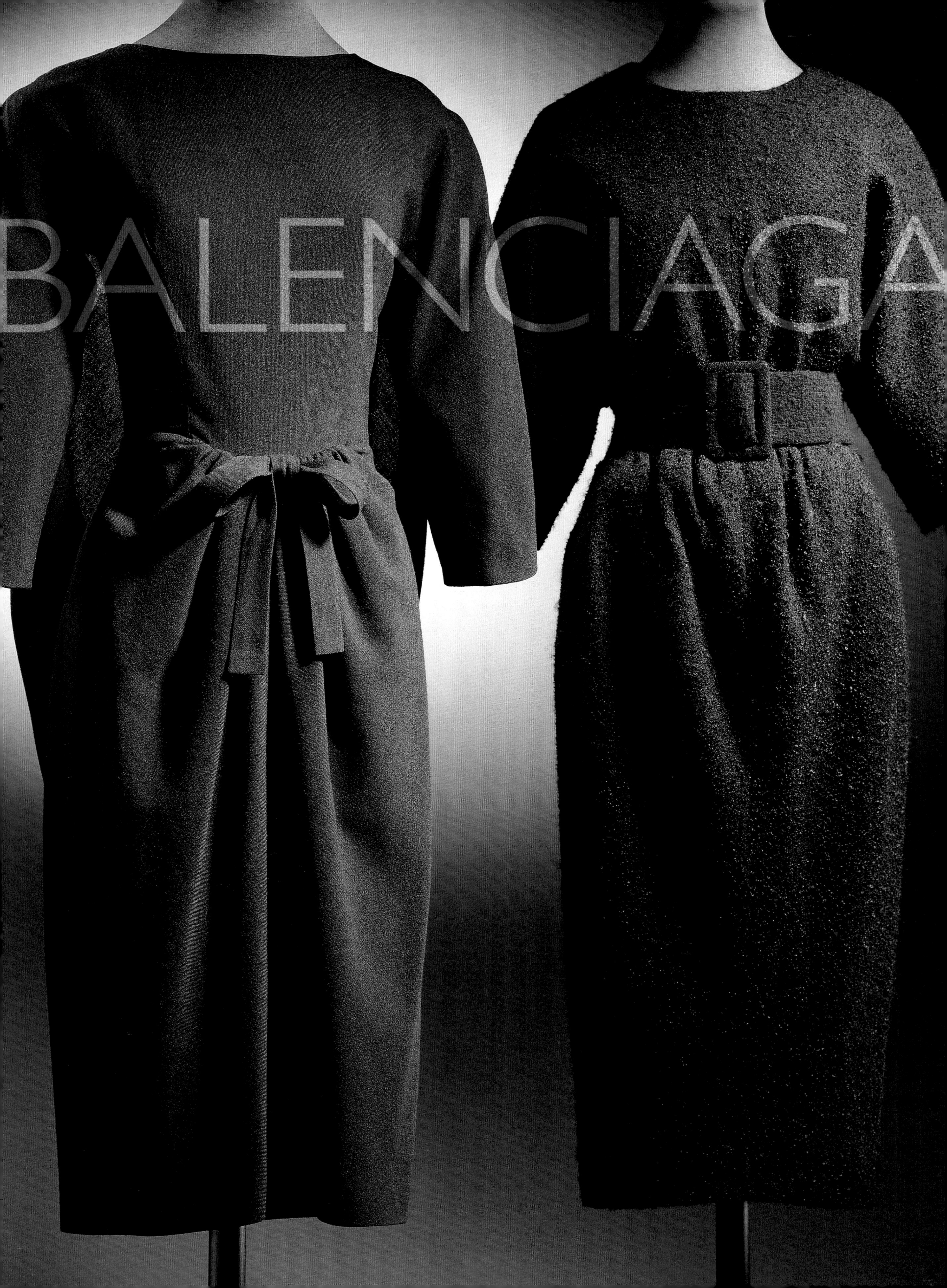
BALENCIAGA

Left, day dress, EISA (Balenciaga)

Spain autumn-winter 1957
Worn and given by Mrs S Hammond

Right, day dress, Balenciaga

Paris autumn-winter 1958
Worn by Martita Hunt,
given by Miss Catherine Hunt

Cecil Beaton (in *The Glass of Fashion*, 1954) declared that 'Balenciaga does not believe in the eternal novelty of the new, as so many fashion maniacs do'. Indeed, Balenciaga (1895-1972) saw no merit in change for change's sake. He worked methodically from season to season on specific ideas to refine and perfect them. He constantly revisited and reinterpreted elements of pared-down day wear in black and, as Jacqueline Demornex (Jouve and Demornex, *Balenciaga*, 1989) testified, 'every collection featured the discreet appearance of a little black dress made entirely by Balenciaga; he sewed it with his own hands. The dress was not simply a fetish. Its entrance marked that magical instant that gave the collection its own particular style and harmony.'

Throughout the 1950s he made advances in the lean line known popularly as the 'sack'. Two variations on this theme have a basic structure of a slender, semi-fitted outline with round neck, elbow-length sleeves and belt. However, different materials and details give the dresses identities of their own.

The dress (left) in plain weave wool has a cocoon-shaped, draped back and the EISA (his mother's name) label, identifying it as the product of one of Balenciaga's Spanish outlets, Barcelona, San Sebastian or Madrid. Clothes here were cheaper than their Paris equivalents, as they were made in less costly Spanish fabrics and business overheads were lower than in France. In a chunky woollen bouclé, the T-shaped dress (right) has a wide belt and a pair of pockets located on top of the hips. It makes a characteristically strong, simple and supremely elegant statement which caused fellow designers to hail Balenciaga as 'the Master'.

From left to right:
Line drawing, back of gown, 1957
Detail of centre front tie belt, 1957
Detail of centre front buckled belt, 1959
Croquis by Fernando Martinez, 1959.
Courtesy of Balenciaga, Paris

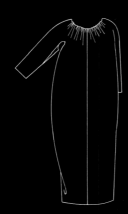
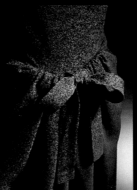
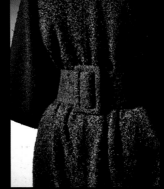
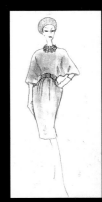

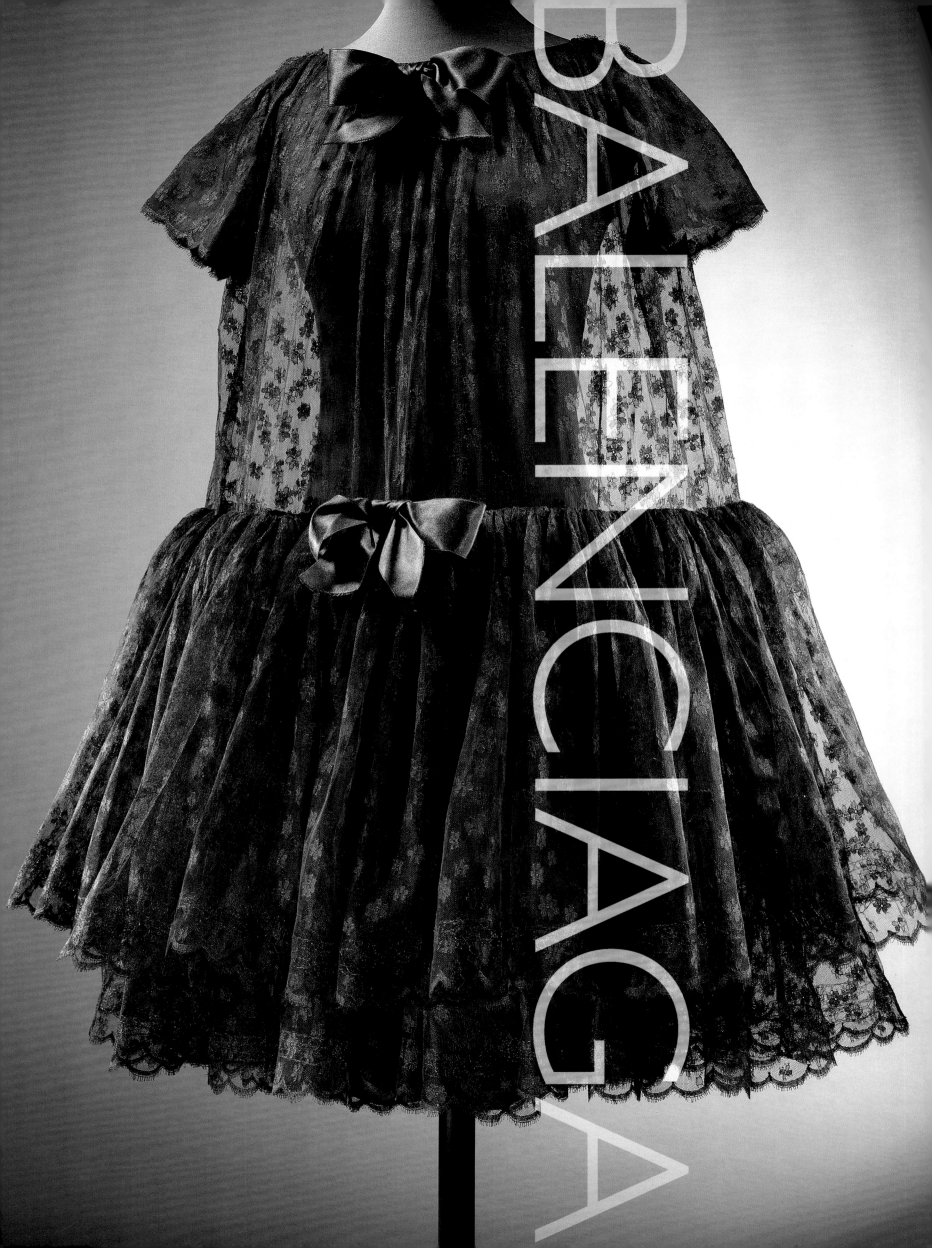

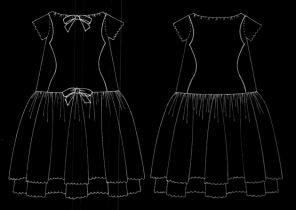 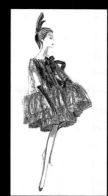

Evening dress, Balenciaga

Paris autumn-winter, 1958
Given by Sir Cecil Beaton

Balenciaga had a predilection for flounced black lace, a taste fuelled by his appreciation of traditional Spanish costume, including tiered flamenco dresses, mantillas and black lace fashions in portraits by Goya. Throughout his career he featured French lace in his collections, frequently using row upon row of black Chantilly to create spreading skirts, lavish evening capes or tight sheath dresses. To establish contrast and emphasize the texture and pattern of lace, he often set it over cream, baby blue or pink satin. In the same spirit he teamed the famous 'Le Mouton Noir', a voluminous evening coat of tightly packed layers of frilled black lace, with narrow, tapered, cream satin trousers. Balanciaga was known for his purist ideals, which culminated in timeless classics, and he tended to remain aloof from short-lived fashion trends, apart from the occasional indulgence.

Released in 1956, the film *Baby Doll* portrayed an adolescent as a sex object dressed in girlish clothes which inspired a plethora of short, flared styles. It is not recorded if Balenciaga was directly influenced by this phenomenon or indeed by the almost contemporaneous publication in Paris of Nabokov's *Lolita*, but the description 'Baby Doll' was applied to a group of flounced lace dresses he produced in 1957 and 1958.

A dichotomy is created in the V&A's 'Baby Doll' by a suggestively tight black crêpe de Chine underdress – clearly visible through the semi-transparent, extremely wide, flared black lace overdress. The latter has short sleeves and a dropped waist into which is gathered a flounced skirt. Two giant black satin bows mark the centre neck and centre waist, adding to the child-like theme.

An almost identical version in white at the Balenciaga Archive in Paris has an aura of youthful innocence, whereas black lace gives the design a knowing, almost wicked, adult gloss.

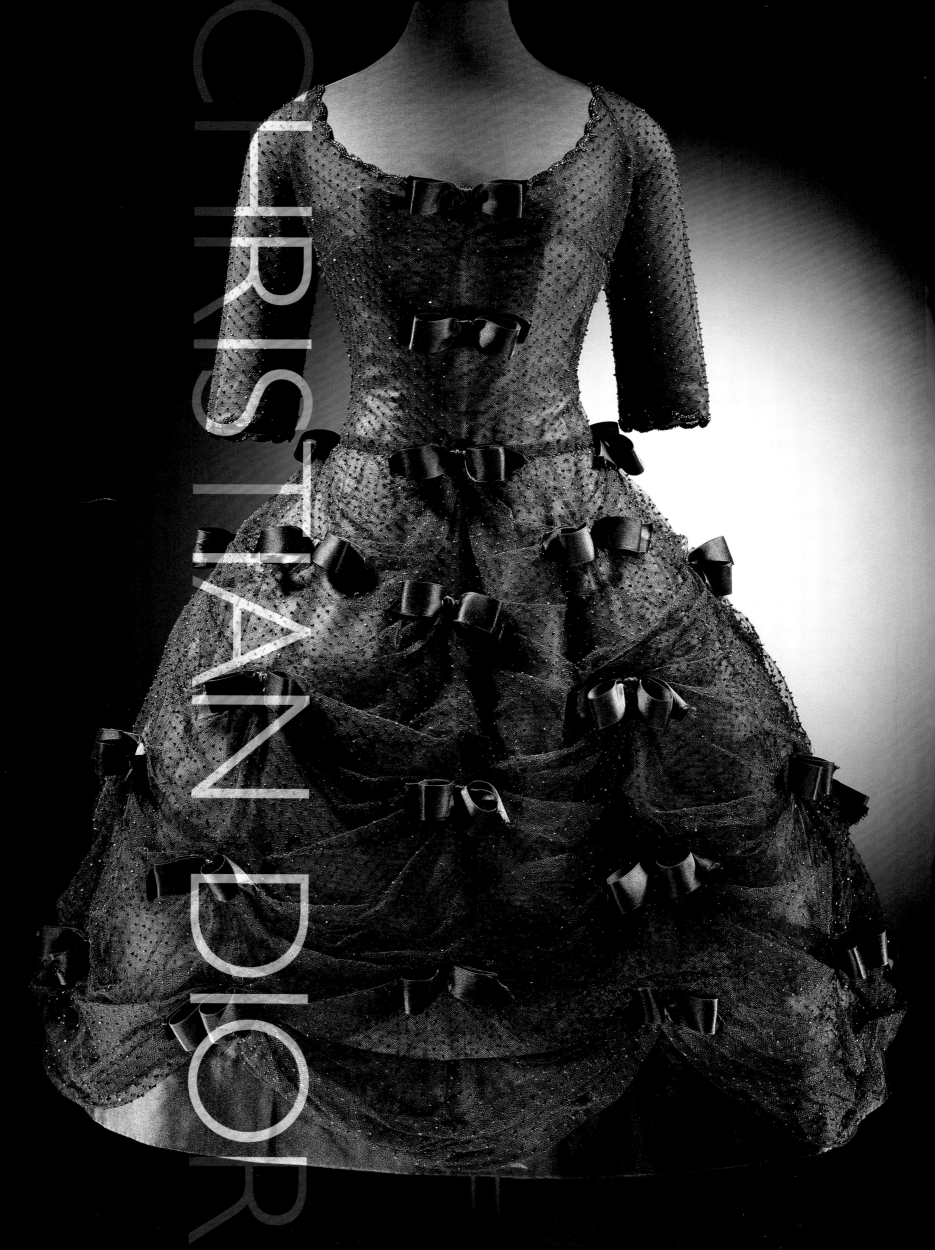

Evening dress, 'Bal Masqué', Yves Saint Laurent for Christian Dior

Paris spring-summer 1958
Worn and given by
the Duchess of Windsor

Throughout her life the Duchess of Windsor (1896-1986) dressed in an elegant manner, patronizing top Paris designers (Dior was a particular favourite). She was often photographed in pride of place, front row at the collections, and was sixty-two years old when she selected this froth of a black evening gown from Yves Saint Laurent's spring-summer collection for the house of Dior. Always impeccably groomed, with a youthful appearance and an angular slenderness maintained by careful dieting, she made sure that she always had the very latest mode. In *The Windsor Style* (1987), Suzy Menkes gathered evidence of Wallis Simpson's affinity for black, pin-pointing such comments as: 'You have to wear black, ageing or not, because when the little black dress is right, there is nothing else to wear in its place'. When sketching Mrs Simpson for American *Vogue* (February 1937), Cecil Beaton wrote: 'My sitter is at her best in a nondescript black dress that she makes smart by wearing'.

Indicating how slim the Duchess was, this dress has a tiny bodice tapering to a waist measuring 23 inches (30.5 cm). Stylistically, the dress makes reference to 1860s bell-skirted fashions, and there are even some constructional parallels in its cream silk strapless foundation of a tightly fitted, boned corset and domed skirt supported by a layered petticoat. Like many late nineteenth and early twentieth-century evening fashions, the frivolous outer shell of swathed tulle, bows and beads has a fragility that belies the firm, highly structured underpinnings. A symphony in black, the lightweight overdress is a double layer of spotted black tulle, studded with sparkling black bugle beads and arranged in festoons caught at intervals by forty-two bows of satin ribbon.

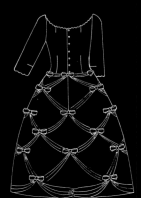
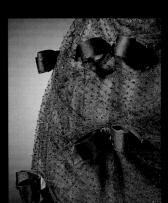
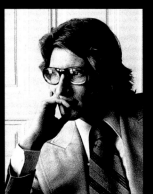

From left to right:
Line drawing, back of dress
Detail of skirt
Portrait of Yves Saint Laurent
by Cecil Beaton, 1971

GALANOS

Evening dress, Galanos

American autumn 1959

Worn and given by Miss Eleanor Lambert

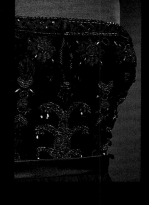
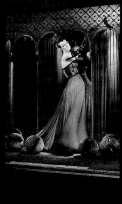
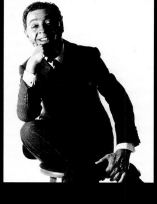

From left to right:
Detail of bodice front
Gown on display, 1959
Portrait of James
Galanos. Courtesy
of the designer

James Galanos (b. 1924) launched his own label in 1951, deciding to create his ultra-sophisticated high fashion collections in Los Angeles, a city better known for the manufacture of outdoor leisure and activity wear. The cosmopolitan elegance of black has always assumed an important place in Galanos's work, and Melinda Watt (Martin, *Contemporary Fashion*, 1995) revealed that after forty years in business 'he still relishes the challenge of creating the perfect black dress'. From his experience as a designer in New York and Paris (with Robert Piguet), he brought a thorough knowledge and appreciation of the skills that make custom-made clothes so special, and as an independent continued to operate at the

very top of the market. His label is noted for meticulous hand finishing and splendid embroidery. Galanos was particularly fond of chiffon and by the mid-1950s was renowned for slender-line evening dresses with supple skirts composed of layers of this sensual fabric, every inch of the many metres of hemline being rolled and stitched by hand or finely picot edged.

Galanos made regular trips to Europe to select fabrics and trimmings from specialist manufacturers; this chiffon came from the Lyon silk weavers Bianchini-Ferier. In 1959, using that successful formula of pairing black with one colour, he chose to offset a triple-layered black chiffon skirt with a strapless bodice in dark crimson

velvet sumptuously embroidered with fleurs-de-lis and rosettes in black bugle beads, chenille and soutache. The combination is eminently successful – the fitted, slightly high-waisted bodice has an almost ecclesiastical effect and is separated by a simple satin ribbon waistband from the ethereal black chiffon skirt. The donor, Eleanor Lambert, American fashion's most powerful press agent, was described by Marilyn Bender as 'a tireless matchmaker between fashion and art' (*The Beautiful People*, 1967). Miss Lambert was instrumental in the foundation of the Council of Fashion Designers of America (1962) and in the same year persuaded Congress that it should recognize fashion as an art form,

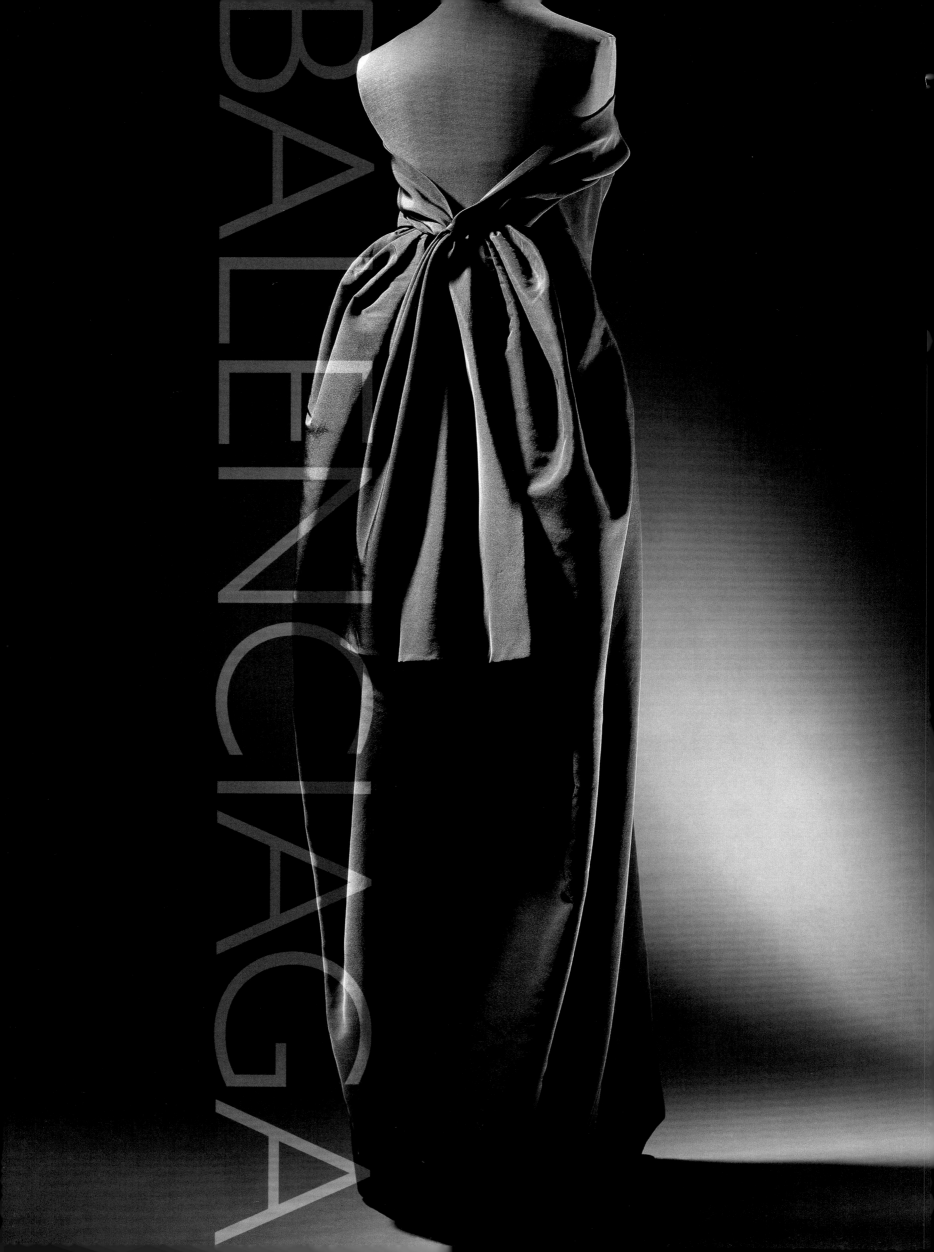

The 'Amphora' line, evening gown, Cristobal Balenciaga

Paris 1960
Worn and given by Mrs Loel Guinness

Balenciaga had a natural affinity for black – his native Spain provided abundant inspiration in the black of peasant garb, of traditional mourning, of religious orders and of courtly attire as depicted by such artists as Velazquez and Zurbaran. In 1938, a year after he opened his Paris house, *Harper's Bazaar* described 'the striking impact created by the new Balenciaga salon with its high collared black dresses. This is the black of Spain, so deep in tone that all other blacks seem grey beside it ...' Balenciaga used black in an uncompromising manner to create powerful fashion statements that attracted clients with a taste for drama. He composed evening gowns that were adventurous in their explorations of volume but never strayed into the realm of the outlandish. He used silks with a weight and substance necessary to achieve and retain unusual silhouettes: taffeta, *cloqué*, Gazar (by Abraham) and ribbed fabrics – poult, faille and grosgrain.

By 1960 fashion was moving away from the high-waisted line known as Empire or Josephine but, as usual, Balenciaga followed an independent route and kept faith with this style (one of his favourites), a decision that resulted in a number of outstanding designs, including the 'Amphora'. Balenciaga had an expert knowledge of fabrics and was always true to their nature, never imposing complicated underpinnings to bring about artificial shapes. Thus the cocoon-like back was achieved by clever cutting and by using a silk with the crispness necessary to hold the convex form. With a typical stroke of bravura, Balenciaga finished the back with an enormous knotted sash. From the front the gown is a lean sheath with a strapless neckline, slightly padded to stand away from the body.

Mrs Loel Guinness was one of Balenciaga's favourite customers. Bettina Ballard described her as a slim, dark Mexican who was 'apt to wear the same black jersey dress over and over, with two strings of priceless pearls and a black mink Balenciaga coat – all to Balenciaga's complete approval because this is the way she looks best' (*In My Fashion*, 1960).

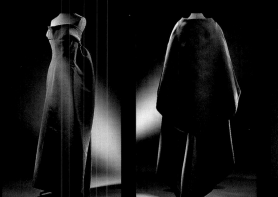
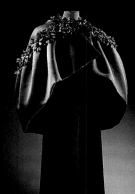

From left to right:
Gown, front view
Back of cape and dress,
Balenciaga, 1967.
Worn and given by
Mrs Loel Guinness
Front of cape and dress,
Balenciaga 1965.
Worn and given by
Ava Gardner

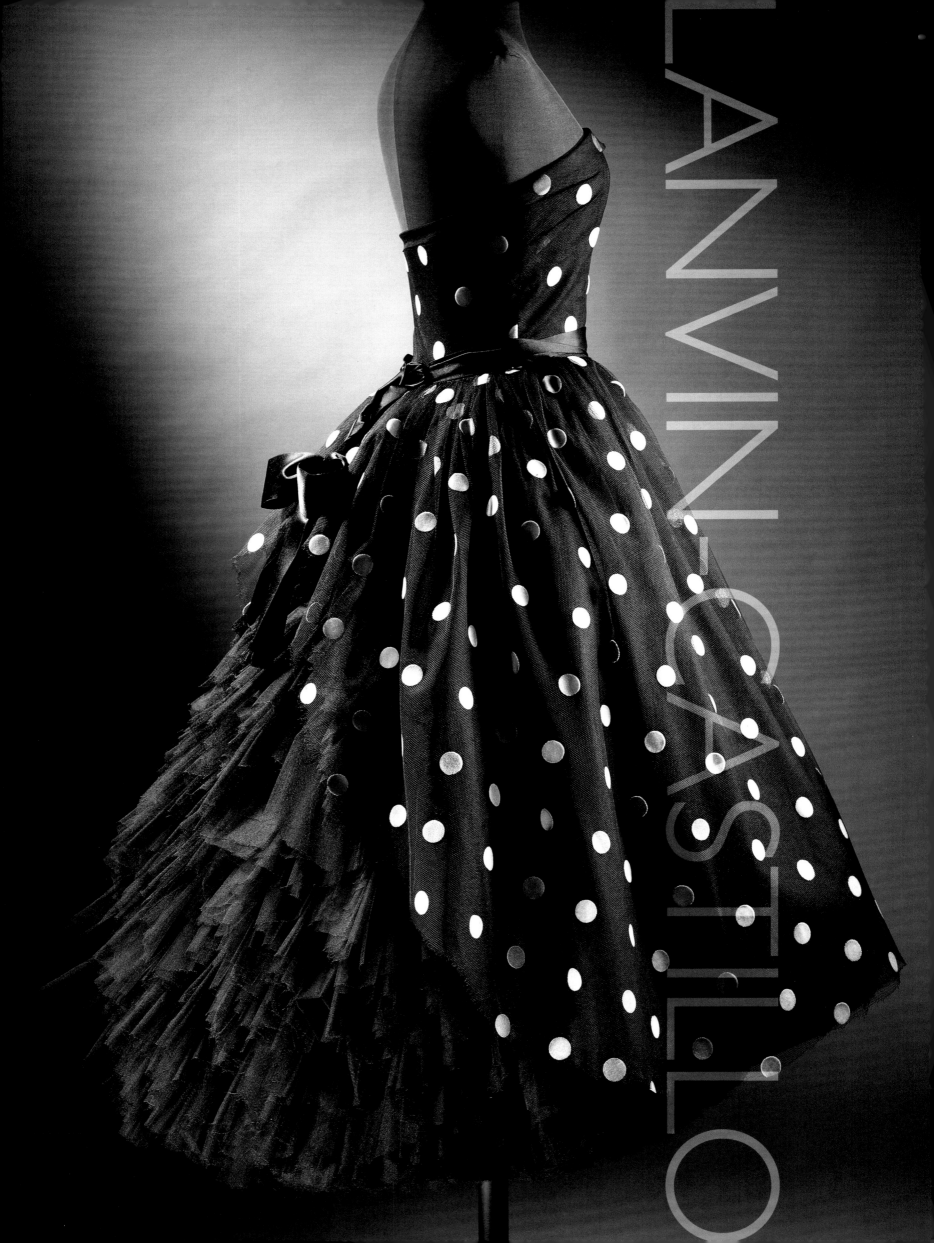

Evening gown, Lanvin-Castillo

Paris about 1960

Worn and given by Stella, Lady Ednam

The Spanish-born designer Antonio del Castillo (1908-84) joined the long-established house of Lanvin in 1950, bringing a new spirit to the collections and introducing the joint label Lanvin-Castillo. Like his countryman Balenciaga, he had a penchant for bright colours as well as Hispanic black. Bettina Ballard revealed the secret of his post-war success: 'Lanvin-Castillo is the only house that designs with certain smart women in mind and who adapts dresses to the individual tastes and purses' (*In My Fashion*, 1960). Using inky tulle, he created lavish evening gowns with such extravagantly full skirts that they could not fail to make an impact. Tightly fitted bodices, either strapless or provided with insubstantial spaghetti straps, were perched above the spreading skirts. A shape-forming and supporting substructure was all important and, for a black dress, was customarily made in matching black.

The formula consisted of an outer shell sitting over a corset-like, boned foundation (with or without suspenders) attached to a voluminous petticoat of layer upon layer of net stiffened with deep bands of nylon crin. An innermost, straight-line crêpe de Chine underskirt prevented the scratchy net from tearing stockings to shreds. This type of skirt could be exceedingly heavy, so to help take the weight and anchor the entire construction it was attached to a waist-stay of sturdy grosgrain that fastened with substantial hooks and eyes at the centre back. Illustrating the fact that black with white is a successful and eye-catching ploy, Castillo glued oversize white felt dots over the bodice and overskirt. The latter is apron-like and in a saucy gesture is divided and cut away at the back, permitting the petticoat's frou-frou to cascade out in a bustle-like manner. In a final audacious touch, a black satin ribbon belt circles the waist to the centre back, where it is knotted into a pigtail finished with a bow that sits perkily over the posterior.

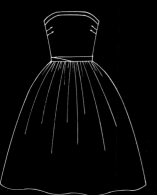 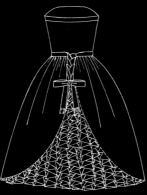 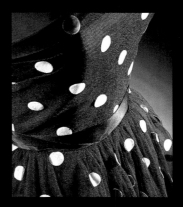

From left to right:
Line drawing,
front of dress
Line drawing,
back of dress
Detail of felt spots
on bodice and skirt

81

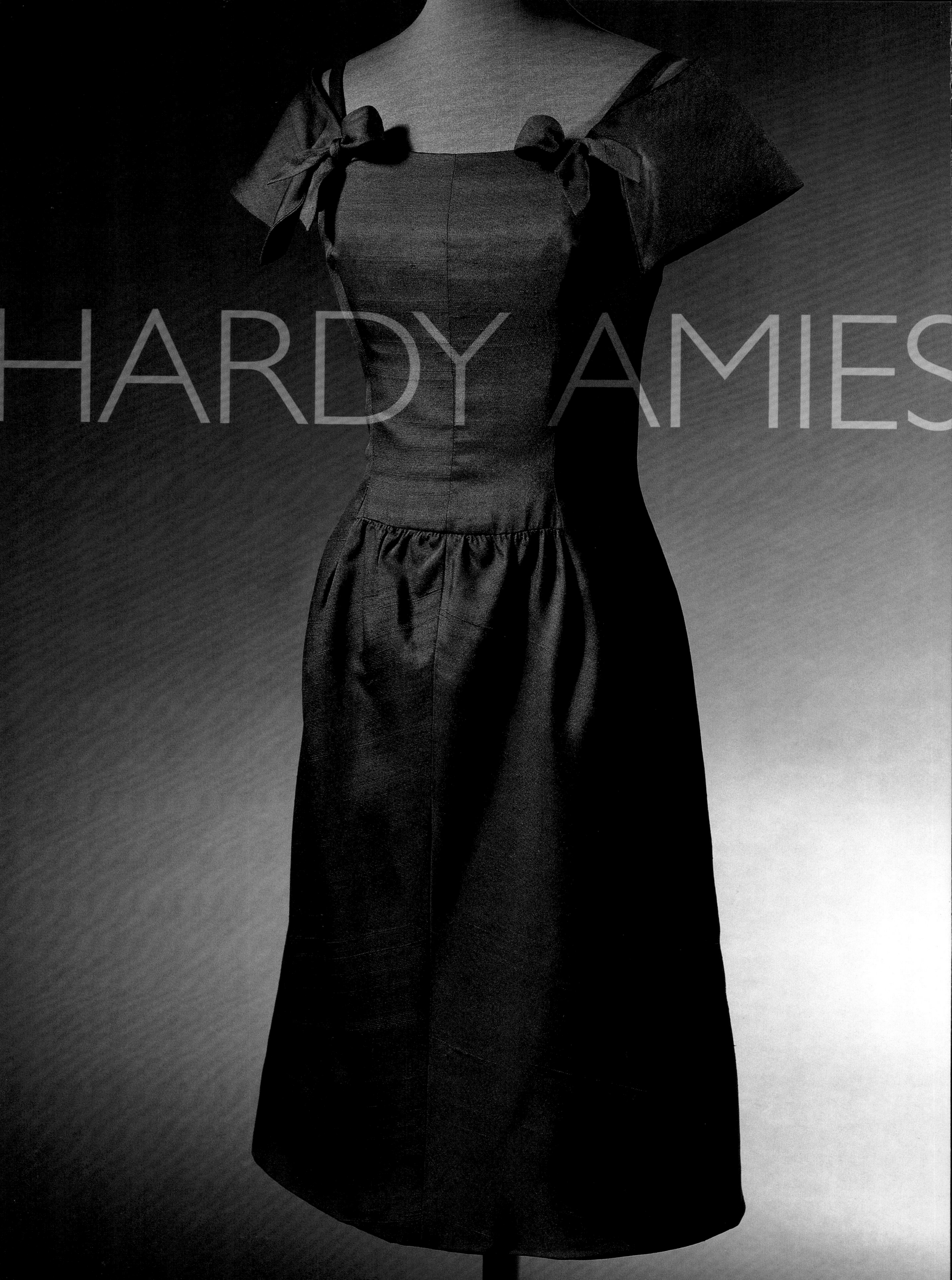
HARDY AMIES

Cocktail dress, 'Epigram',
Hardy Amies

London 1960

Given by Mrs RJ Rickett

For over fifty years Sir Hardy Amies (b. 1909) has provided a discerning clientele with elegant clothes that make a virtue of the understatement. He has always avoided outlandish gestures in favour of designs with the quiet good taste that has proved perfect for his private couture customers. They relied on Hardy Amies to supply them with durable, well-tailored suits and coats as well as evening gowns with romantic appeal. With his very English talent for modesty, the debonair couturier admits to a conservative approach, advocating evolution rather than revolution in fashion.

Since 1950 the house has supplied a wide range of designs for the public appearances of Queen Elizabeth II. Though black is usually confined to mourning in the royal household, Amies described the care lavished on a particular 'almost' black dress of 1980. Intended for Her Majesty's audience with Pope John Paul II, Amies was delighted with the black Chantilly lace over layers of white and grey tulle. However, he was disappointed when the Queen did not appear in this gown, concluding that 'our dress was not conventionally black enough for a church occasion but it would be perfect for wearing at private dinners whenever the Palace was in mourning' (*Still Here*, 1984).

Catering for the decorously dressed English lady in the post World War II period meant attending to her every need, including providing appropriate attire for the taking of cocktails. The 1950s witnessed a boom in cocktail parties, for which a little black dress became *de rigueur*. Hovering between a day dress and a fully-fledged evening gown, the cocktail dress usually featured diminutive sleeves and a short skirt. In this model in slubbed black silk, attention centres on pretty shoulders adorned with straps, bows and cape sleeves. In keeping with Sir Hardy's belief that a lowered waistline is flattering, the dress has an elongated bib front and, teamed with slimming black, it creates desirable lean lines.

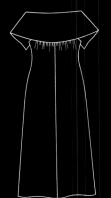
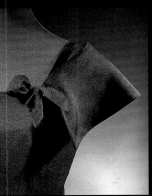
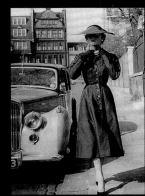

From left to right:
Line drawing, back of dress
Detail of left 'sleeve'
Afternoon dress in black
silk (by Ascher),
Hardy Amies, 1954

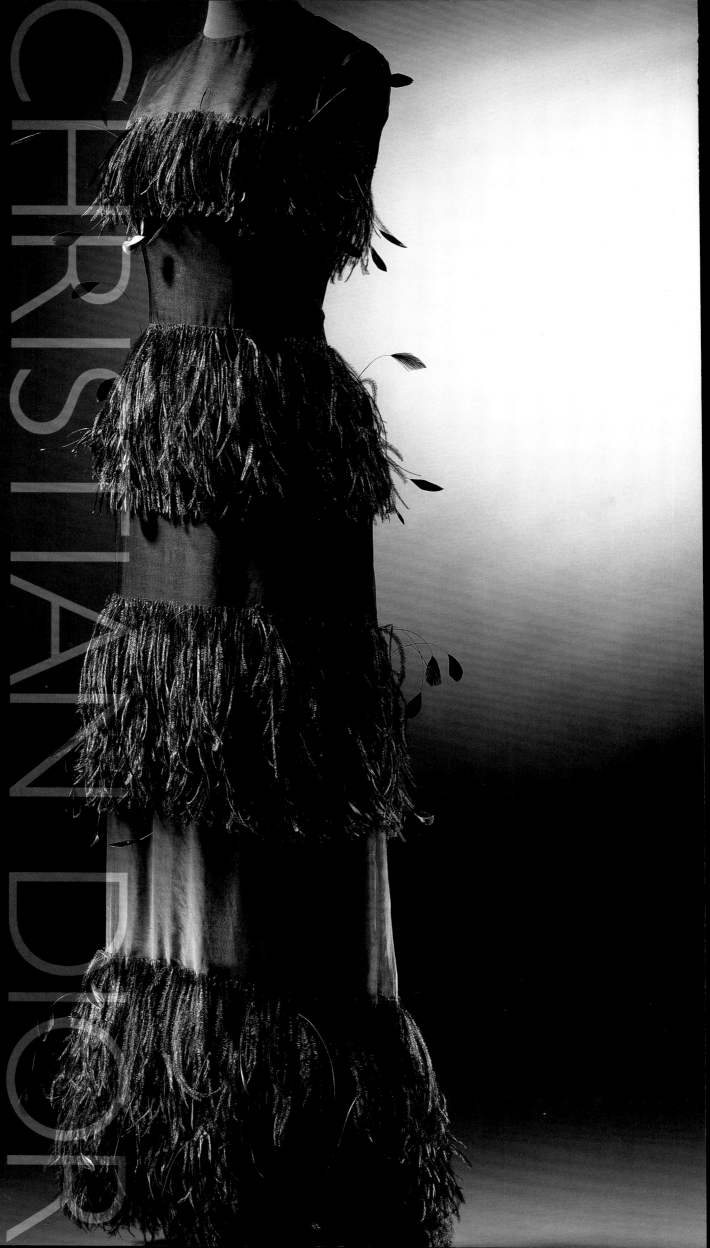

Evening gown, Marc Bohan for Christian Dior

Paris spring-summer 1967

Worn and given by Mrs Walther Moreira Salles

In August 1986 Marc Bohan (b. 1926) gave *L'Officiel* a graphic account of his apprenticeship with the couturier Robert Piguet. For each collection, this formidable teacher insisted that his young designers made two or three ensembles from scratch, unaided by the workrooms. Aged nineteen, Bohan first created two black dresses, for which he made twenty-five attempts before they were absolutely perfect – he has commented, somewhat ruefully, that he could make them today with his eyes shut. After Piguet he joined Molyneux and then Patou. In 1960 he moved from Christian Dior-London to take the helm in Paris at the prestigious avenue Montaigne headquarters, here, in Brigid Keenan's words, for nearly thirty years 'never failing to produce beautiful, feminine clothes' (*Dior in Vogue*, 1981). Bohan's skill and deft touch kept the house in the limelight and satisfied the demands of its elite clientele. His long experience in Paris couture enabled him to maintain the traditions of refined design that he combined with a contemporary appeal. Black had always been a regular and successful component of the Dior look, and

Bohan maintained the custom. He ensured that a little black dress with the Christian Dior label was impeccably made and the height of chic. For day wear Bohan preferred clean, uncluttered lines with minimal decorative effects, but for evening he created notable extravaganzas.

Here Bohan constructed a simple, sleeveless shift of lightweight organza, form a frail background for horizontal bands of feathers dyed a glistening black. In order n to distort the delicate silk, ostrich plumes were painstakingly divided up and rows of tiny individual strands glued into position. Adding a further exotic dimension, *coq* feathers shaved into diamond shapes arc a random out from the ostrich quills. The insubstantial organza floated over the bod and the slightest gesture caused the plume to tremble and nod. Black feathers have always occupied an important place in fashion, their gleam, texture and movement having special night-time allure.

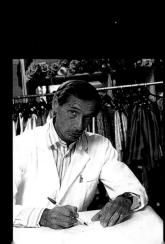

From left to right:
Detail of feather bands
Portrait of Marc Bohan.
Courtesy of the
Dior Archive

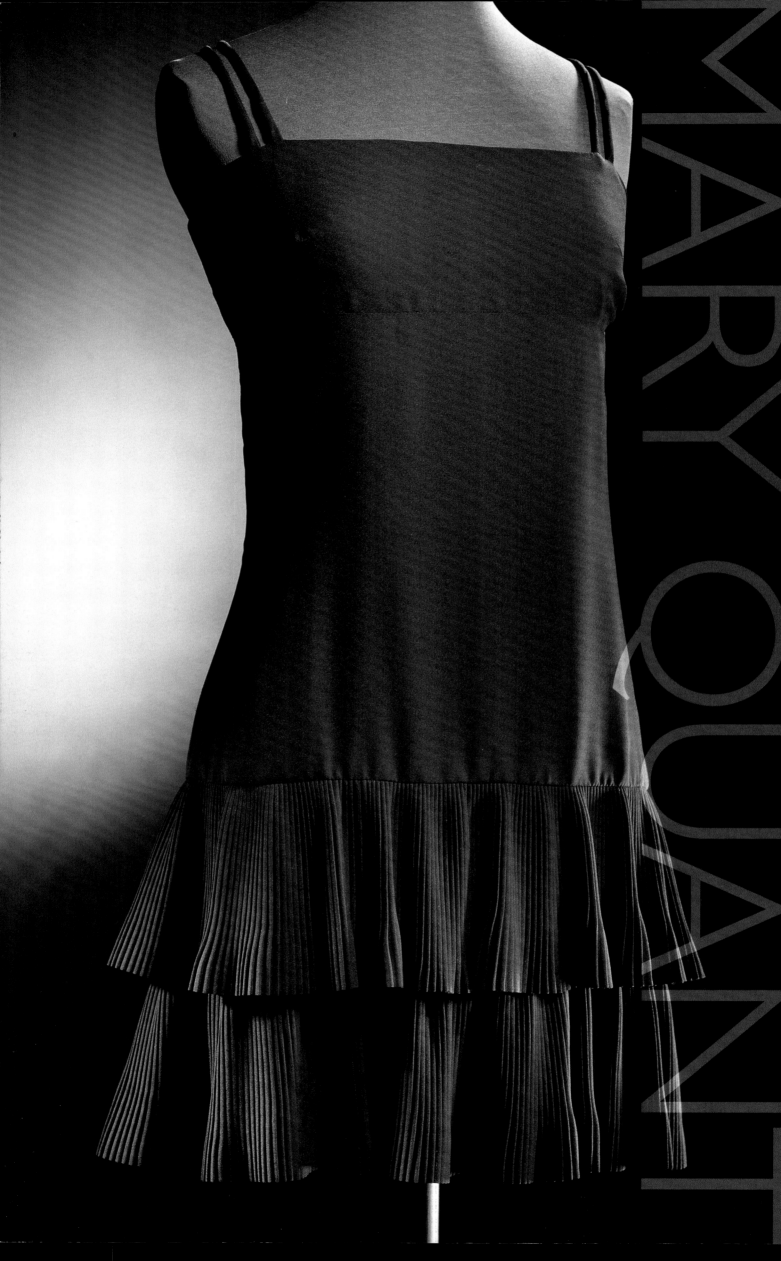

From left to right:

Line drawing, front of dress

Detail of pleated frills

Mini dress by Mary Quant

Portrait of Mary Quant.

Courtesy of the designer

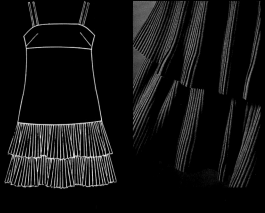
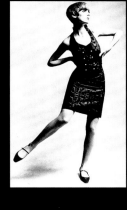
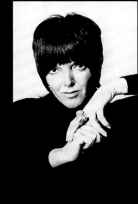

Mini dress, Mary Quant

Ginger Group, London 1967-68

Given by Mrs A Walford

Black in fashion had a struggle in the 1960s when it was modish to signal one's youth by flaunting either bright primary colours or baby blues and pinks. Mary Quant (b. 1934) spearheaded the 1960s revolution in fashion that put 'Swinging London' in the international limelight. Customers flocked to Quant's King's Road shop, Bazaar; in its zany window displays she deliberately experimented with the psychology of colour to attract buyers. Soon, however, her name became associated with the predominantly black Chelsea look with its beatnik overtones – 'high black leather boots, black stockings and black leather coats' (*Quant by Quant*, 1966). She was responsible for a series of fast-moving 'must have' styles for young women who were thrilled to be offered exciting alternatives to the diluted versions of staid, matronly garments then masquerading as teenage clothes. Black peppered her early collections and, in 1963, when she launched the innovative 'wet look' collection in PVC,

World famous for championing the mini skirt, Quant's Ginger Group collections launched in 1963 often featured black minis. A 1967 group of diminutive dresses in medium-weight jersey knit caught the spirit of the time, especially a day-time mini in black with a high neck and front zip christened 'Banana Split'. Black for evening survived and one of the perkiest black dresses in the V&A's collection is this resolutely modern Quant mini that makes reference to 1920s tubular shifts as well as 1950s cocktail dresses. In moss crêpe, with spaghetti straps, it is seamed under the bust then glides over the body to finish in a double tier of permanently pleated frills.

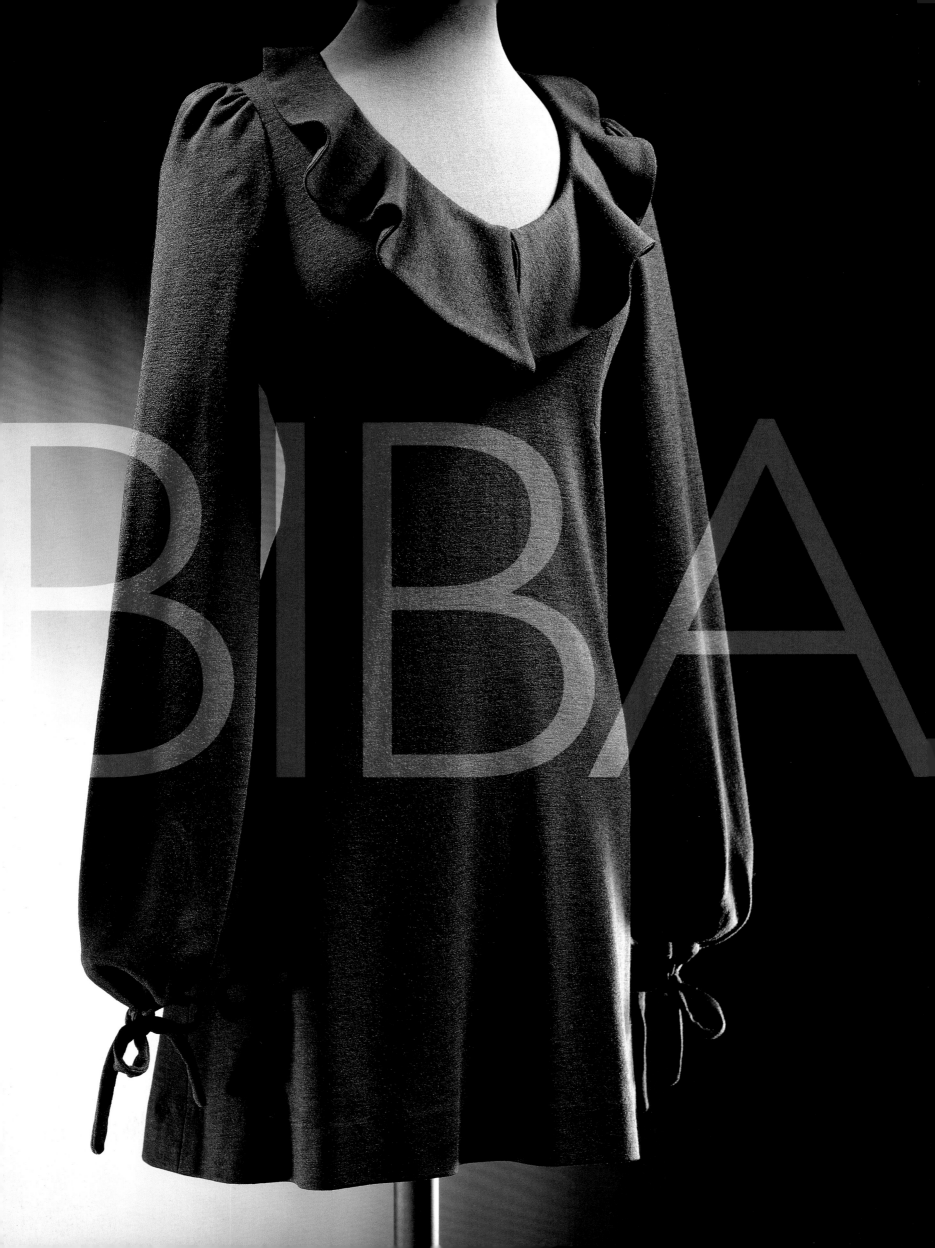

From modest beginnings as a home-based mail order concern in 1964, Barbara Hulanicki (b. 1936) and her husband developed Biba into London's liveliest boutique of the 1960s and early 1970s. It became the mecca for the young and trendy, who delighted in the moody, pastiche art nouveau and art deco interiors featuring low lighting, velvety banquettes and bentwood coat stands on which the merchandise was hung with considered negligence. Decadence was an important part of the Biba image and was vested in the sludgy purples, maroons and pinks that became its hallmark colours, though black always punctuated the collections. As a young fashion illustrator, Hulanicki was thrilled to find a new shop in the Kings Road with a 'simple black dress with no nasty buttons or detail…I immediately went in and bought the black dress, which was 20 guineas – a fortune in those days' (*From A to Biba*, 1983).

This late 1960s body-skimming mini dress in cotton jersey knit typifies the Biba look, being audaciously short with a scoop neck and droopy bias-cut collar. The bishop-style sleeves were also characteristically Biba, with the tightest possible, circulation-hindering armholes, from which they flare out to voluminous sleeve ends gathered into long rouleau ties. The latter could prove hazardous when eating, especially when soup was on the menu. This mini was worn with pale, opaque tights and bar shoes (preferably from Anello and Davide) with button fastenings and clumpy heels.

Cotton jersey proved a best seller, as it was comfortable to wear and easily maintained. The fashion T-shirt was Biba's big breakthrough. In addition to skimpily short dresses, Biba offered maxi-length versions with similar flowing sleeves – they were so popular that young women queued to wrench them from the stands. After the birth of her son, Hulanicki was appalled at prissy pink and blue baby clothes so, declaring that 'My baby was going to wear purple and black…', she launched a worldly-wise collection for children.

From left to right:
Line drawing, front of dress
Detail of lower sleeve
T-shirt dress, scarf and hat in
jersey. Photograph Hans Feurer.
Biba mail order catalogue, 1968.

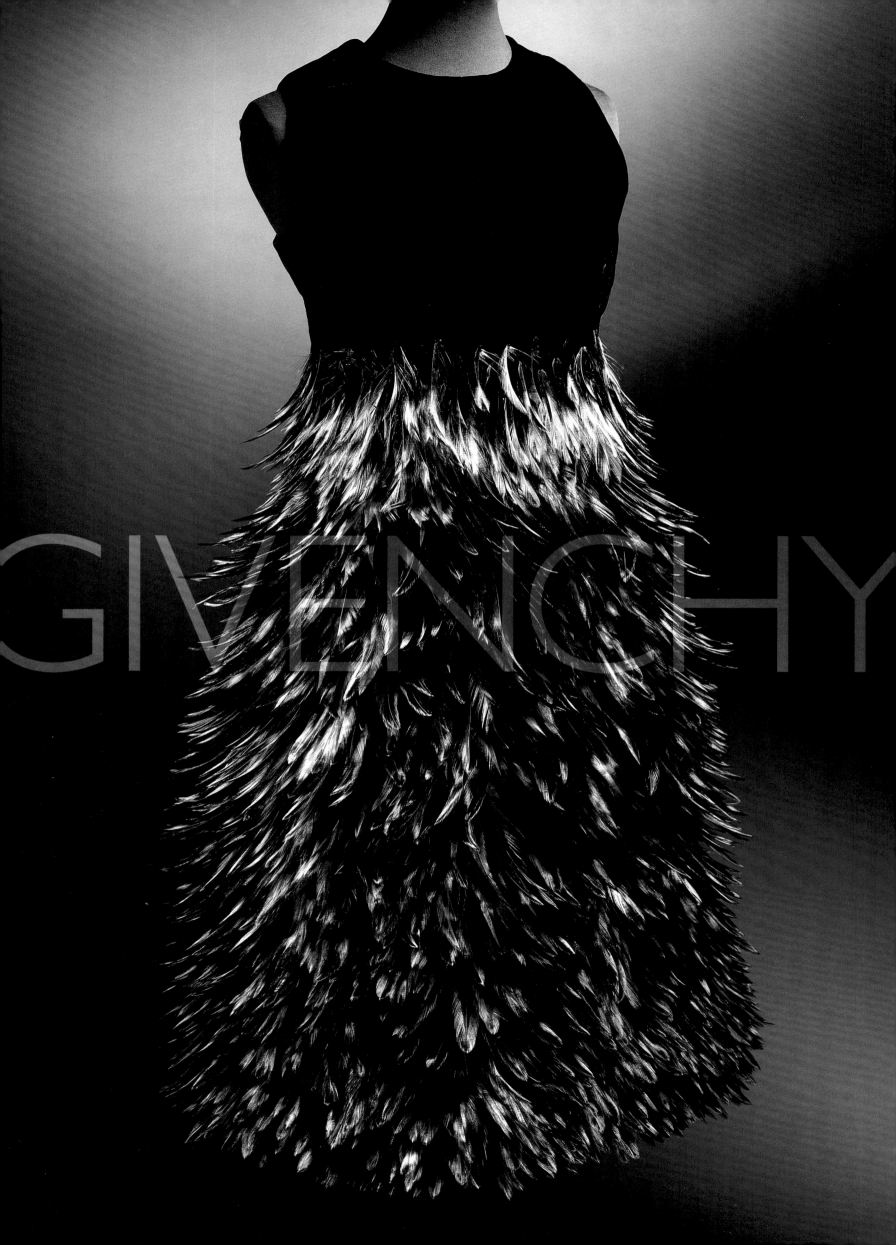

At his première in 1952, Hubert de Givenchy (b. 1927) revealed his understanding of the classic nature and power of the neutrals when he presented a collection featuring interchangeable separates that were predominantly black, white and grey. Instantly successful, the clothes (many in cotton) were heralded as young, feminine and easy to wear, enduring characteristics of Givenchy's work. He adored creating with a wide range of colours, but only rarely in the next forty years were black dresses absent from his collections. Givenchy met his muse, Audrey Hepburn, in 1953 when she was in Paris filming *Sabrina Fair* and from then until her death in 1993 she inspired some of his most outstanding designs. Together with Edith Head and Pauline Trigère, he was responsible for Audrey Hepburn's wardrobe as Holly Golightly in *Breakfast at Tiffany's* (1961), when she wore a simple, sleeveless sheath dress that became the most famous little black dress in the history of the cinema.

Givenchy met his mentor, Balenciaga, in 1953, beginning a friendship that lasted until Balenciaga's death in 1972. Devoted to their *métier*, they met regularly to discuss their collections and couture techniques. In 1991 Givenchy avowed that 'Balenciaga was a revelation to me…In one of his ensembles, with just a single seam in the middle of the back, the line was so pure, so clear that it conveyed simplicity in its very perfection'

(Catherine Join-Diéterle *Givenchy: 40 Years of Creation*, 1991). When Balenciaga closed his house in 1968 he recommended that his clients should go to Givenchy – as his natural successor.

Like Balenciaga, Givenchy had a sure hand when composing with black. In this lively mini dress, a sleeveless bolero in velvet, edged with rows of gleaming exotic feathers dyed black, sits over a bodice attached to a Gazar skirt covered entirely in matching black feathers. The jaunty, outward curling quills reflected the lights of night-time festivities and in motion imparted an attractive tremble and sway to the ensemble.

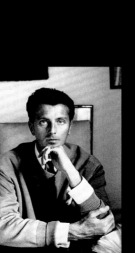

From left to right:
Detail of feathers on skirt
House photograph, design
number 201, 6 August 1968
Portrait of
Hubert de Givenchy by
Cecil Beaton, 1958

VALENTINO

Evening dress, Valentino

New York 1969
Worn and given by
Princess Stanislaus Radziwill

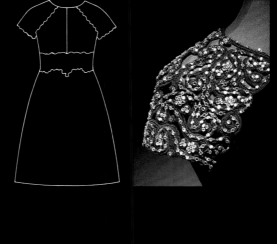

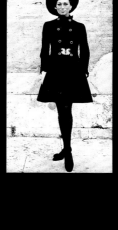

For over thirty years, from headquarters near the Spanish Steps in Rome, Valentino (b. 1932) has created ultra-sophisticated collections to delight his wealthy and glamorous clientele. Seen as one of the peers of couture, he was dubbed 'the Rolls Royce of fashion' by the *International Herald Tribune* in November 1967 and 'The Roman Emperor of Fashion' by *W* in 1987. A versatile and adventurous colourist, he particularly enjoys making dramatic statements in his signature Valentino red – a vibrant crimson. However, black and white, alone or combined in optically powerful designs, are rarely excluded from his collections. Fashion editors and customers alike heaped praise on his

all-white (from head to toe) collection of 1968, and Valentino 'the Chic' has been consistent in his employment of that cornerstone of couture – sleek black. The Valentino retrospective exhibition in Rome (1991) was remarkable in its exciting presentation and meticulous attention to detail. Mannequins were specially made, and each ensemble, including the numerous black dresses, was provided with exactly correct accessories.

The best-dressed sisters Jacqueline Kennedy and Princess Stanislaus Radziwill were confirmed Valentino supporters – Mrs Kennedy wore Valentino for her marriage to Aristotle Onassis in 1968. The younger Lee Radziwill had a professional knowledge

of fashion, having been an assistant to Diana Vreeland when Vreeland was fashion editor of *Harper's Bazaar*, and then she modelled for *Vogue* after Vreeland became its editor-in-chief. With a natural flair for clothes and an up-to-the-minute style, she shopped with discrimination at top designers as well as at boutiques. She chose this trendy yet refined little black velvet dress, featuring late-1960s nude-look peepholes at the midriff and shoulders from Valentino, New York. Infills of black soutache, glistening with *diamantés* arranged in a filigree pattern, permitted glimpses of the body (or body stocking) beneath.

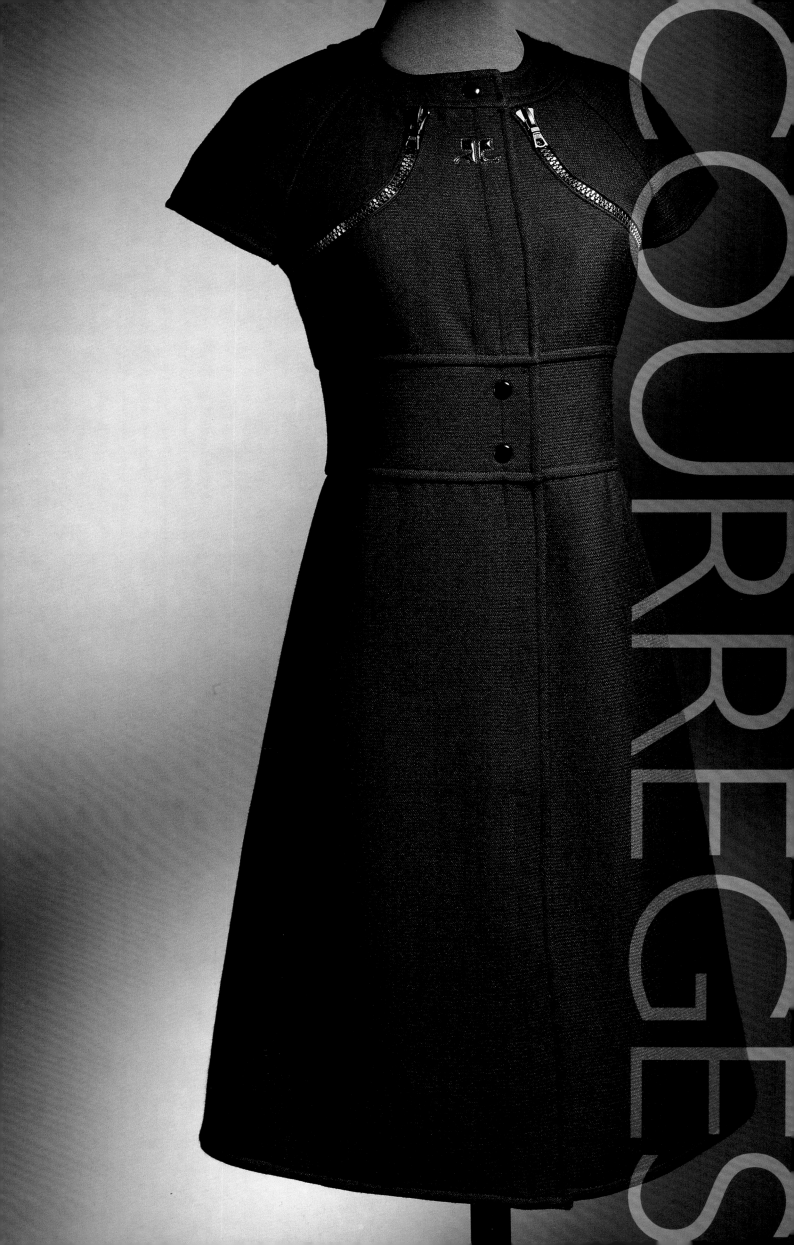

Day dress, Courrèges

Paris 1972

Worn and given by
Mrs Christine Dupont-Nangle

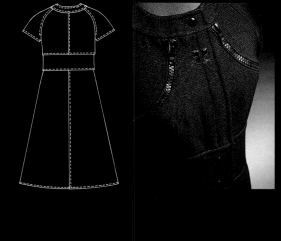

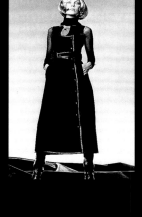

André Courrèges (b. 1923) is best known for championing pure, bright colours as well as his favourite space-age white, which he equated with 'sun and laughter'. Black was not a primary feature of his work, as Ann Ryan commented in 1972: 'There were no "little black" cocktail dresses in Courrèges' collections...' (Ruth Lynam, *Paris Fashion*, 1972).

Courrèges astounded an audience of buyers and journalists assembled in 1964 to see his spring collection with ultra-short, resolutely modern clothes worn by athletic young models radiating fitness and good health. Describing his ideal customer, he stated: 'She is active, moves fast, works, is usually young and modern enough to wear modern intelligent clothes' (*Paris Fashion*, 1972). Admiring his modernism

to couture in 1967. Ignoring short-lived trends and retro movements, he remained faithful to his original vision centred upon pure lines and gently flared shapes, usually made in smooth-faced gabardine. His spectrum came to encompass black which, like white, suited his strictly disciplined, minimalist designs.

From his *couture future* line, this severe day dress in figured black worsted has perfectly executed welt seams that emphasize each constructional section, and the only concessions to decoration are a pair of bold, black plastic zips and the 'ac' monogram.

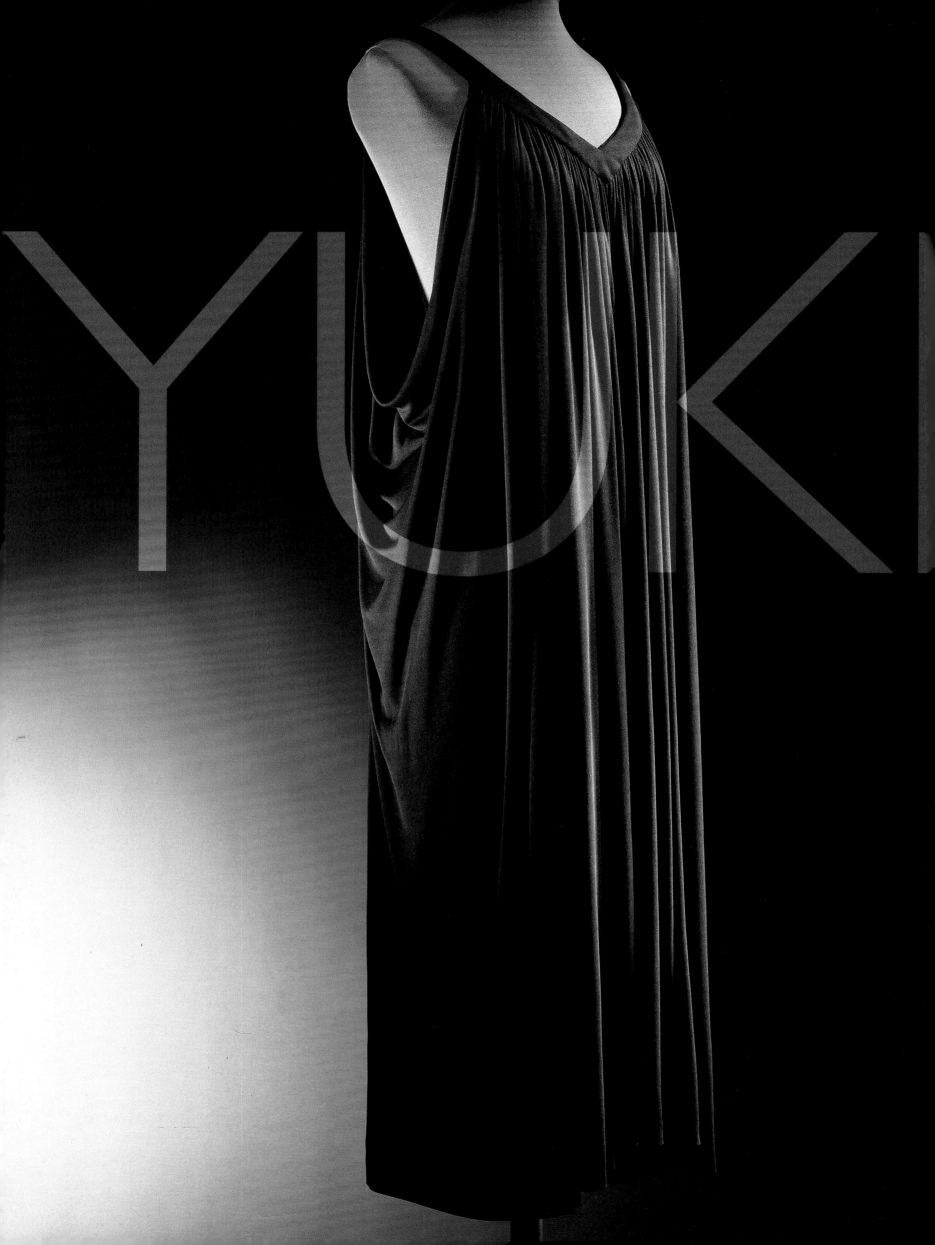

Evening dress, Gnyuki Torimaru (Yuki)

London about 1975

Worn and given by Gayle Hunnicutt

With extraordinary skill and infinite patience, Gnyuki Torimaru (b. 1937) has achieved draped garments that are remarkable for their balance and flow. In the early 1970s he found that supple polyester jersey was an ideal fabric for these fluid and timeless innovations. In stark white, deep red or severe black they make particularly strong statements suggestive of the pleated, draped and wrapped costumes of ancient Greece and Rome. Suzy Menkes explained in her foreword: 'Yuki creates a noble architecture, sculpting soft fabrics so they follow the body, yet take on a shape of their own' (Etherington-Smith, *Yuki*, 1998).

Designing in a modern idiom, Yuki draws upon a rich background – his Japanese roots, his training as a textile engineer, architectural studies and a time in Paris couture in Pierre Cardin's studio. Rather than cut and shape cloth using conventional Western tailoring methods, he prefers to compose in a less wasteful manner, with basic geometric shapes, especially square panels of fabric. His drapery is accomplished by controlling myriads of soft pleats and folds from starting points at the neck or shoulder; in this evening dress they cascade from a band forming a low V neck.

A perfectionist, Yuki works on a dressmaker's mannequin, meticulously pinning and adjusting each minute fold until he is completely satisfied with the drape. Polyester jersey is not the easiest fabric to handle, and though the technique is demanding the result is paramount, an ideal that is captured by Yuki's own description: 'the fabric falls free and is entirely detached from the body. So when people move, the fabric ripples like a wave on the water. Then, when they are still, the drapes fall back to exactly where they were.' Unadorned black suited Yuki's purist ideals and was an excellent foil for the chestnut-haired beauty of the Texan-born film star Gayle Hunnicutt.

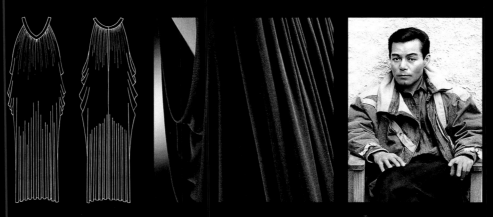

From left to right:
Line drawing, front of dress
Line drawing, back of dress
Detail, side of dress
Portrait of Gnyuki Torimaru.
Courtesy of the designer

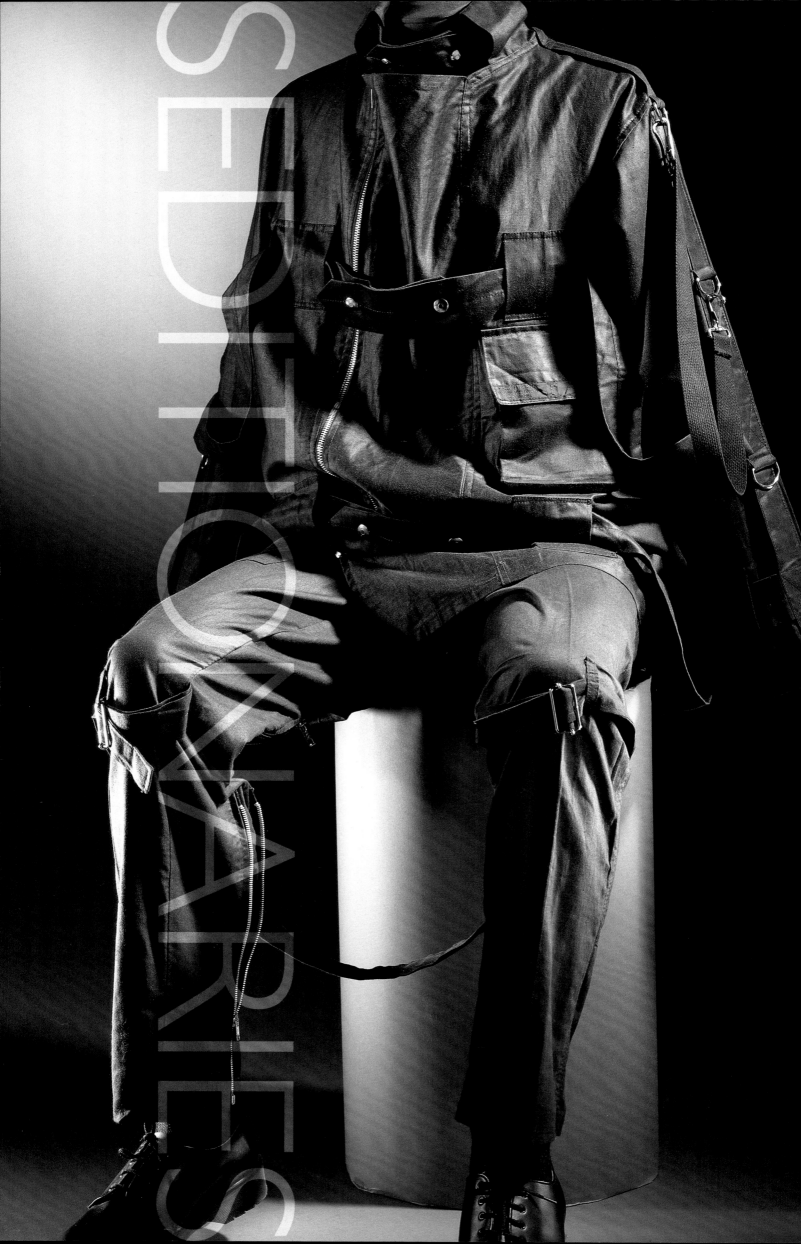

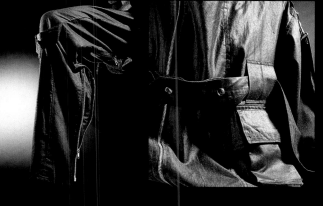

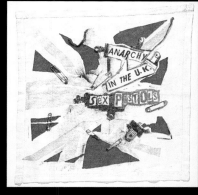

From left to right:
Detail of right trouser leg
Detail, front of jacket
Printed handkerchief,
Anarchy in the UK,
Jamie Reid, 1976

Bondage suit,
Vivienne Westwood and Malcolm McLaren

London 1976

Given by Vivienne Westwood
and Malcolm McLaren

As a symbol of rebellion and dissension, black is an indelible part of subcultural dress. In the second half of the twentieth century this embraced the existentialist black of Paris Left Bank intellectuals; the black of bikers' leathers; the subversive black of punks; and the fantasy black of goths. For each group, black clothing, however fashioned, was a powerful means of uniting the members in a shocking and defiant separateness, of setting them apart from what they perceived to be normal and mainstream. In the mid-1970s Vivienne Westwood (b. 1941) and Malcolm McLaren (b. 1946) became style monarchs for punks. From their Kings Road shop, SEX, and its successor, Seditionaries, they devised the look for the infamous punk rock band the Sex Pistols. Music and fashion were fused to create a barrage of sound and style that mocked and threatened. In 1976 Johnny Rotten was photographed in their archetypal punk outfit – a black sateen bondage suit.

Borrowing elements from army combat pockets and non-functional straps provided with snap fasteners, D-rings and spring links. The trousers were rendered remarkable by a zippered seam under the crotch, a detachable, black towelling bum flap (emulating a primitive loincloth) and 'hobble' straps (borrowed from fetish wear), which fettered the legs between the knees and inhibited movement. Jane Mulvagh told an amusing story about their mobility: 'Once, when Vivienne was accompanying a punk to hospital, the nurses wondered how she could move freely in her funny trousers. In answer she cartwheeled the length of the corridor into Casualty, to the amazement of the staff, patients and even the drunks' (*Vivienne Westwood*, 1998). It was easy for those who could not afford designer punk to customize the menacing look with black drainpipe jeans, striped mohair sweaters, black bin liners, ball-and-link chains and safety pins.

ZANDRA RHODES

Evening dress, Zandra Rhodes

London 1977

Given by Miss Zandra Rhodes

Zandra Rhodes (b. 1940) is famed for romantic dresses in floating silks decorated with her inimitable lyrical and colourful prints though occasionally, as in this evening dress, she strikes blacker, down-beat notes. This radical departure was the highlight of her 1977 'Conceptual Chic' collection, which was inspired by the predominantly black clothes worn by London punks as well as by historical fashion in the V&A, including a Schiaparelli dress of 1938 with a powerful *trompe l'oeil* print of torn fabric and seventeenth-century costume with slashed decoration. In *The Art of Zandra Rhodes* (1984) she describes the thrill of 'punk in the raw', vibrant but threatening clothes seen at the Roxy club – black plastic garbage bags secured by safety pins, torn black rubber T-shirts and laddered black stockings. These oppressive elements of punk dress fed into her menace-free designs for up-market evening wear.

Rayon jersey forms the clinging, sophisticated sheath with a slashed, asymmetrical hemline and neck embellished with ball-link chains, beaded safety pins and glinting *diamantés*. Sewn in bright blue thread, the seams are on the outside of the garment and, in an unpunk-like manner, top stitching around the slashes prevents fraying. Emphasizing its divorce from a streetstyle fashion, the 'Conceptual Chic' collection was shown in editorials paraded by glamorous mannequins (including super-model Jerry Hall) with tall, slender bodies, manes of glossy hair and wearing Manolo Blahnik's strappy, high gold sandals. This high fashion concept, which Zandra Rhodes feels was a major landmark in her work, was the forerunner of a genre of ripped black clothing with expensive designer labels. No longer were hole-ridden and worn (the fashionable term being 'distressed') garments confined to the poor and underprivileged, and with their carefully conceived holes, high fashion designs ranged from sexy, skin-tight evening dresses to big-look winter sweaters.

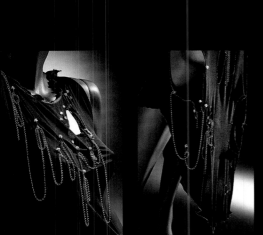

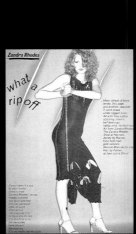

From left to right:

Detail, top of dress (front)

Detail of lower dress (front)

Photograph by Lothar Schmid, *Vogue*, September 15 1977. Courtesy of Condé Nast Publications

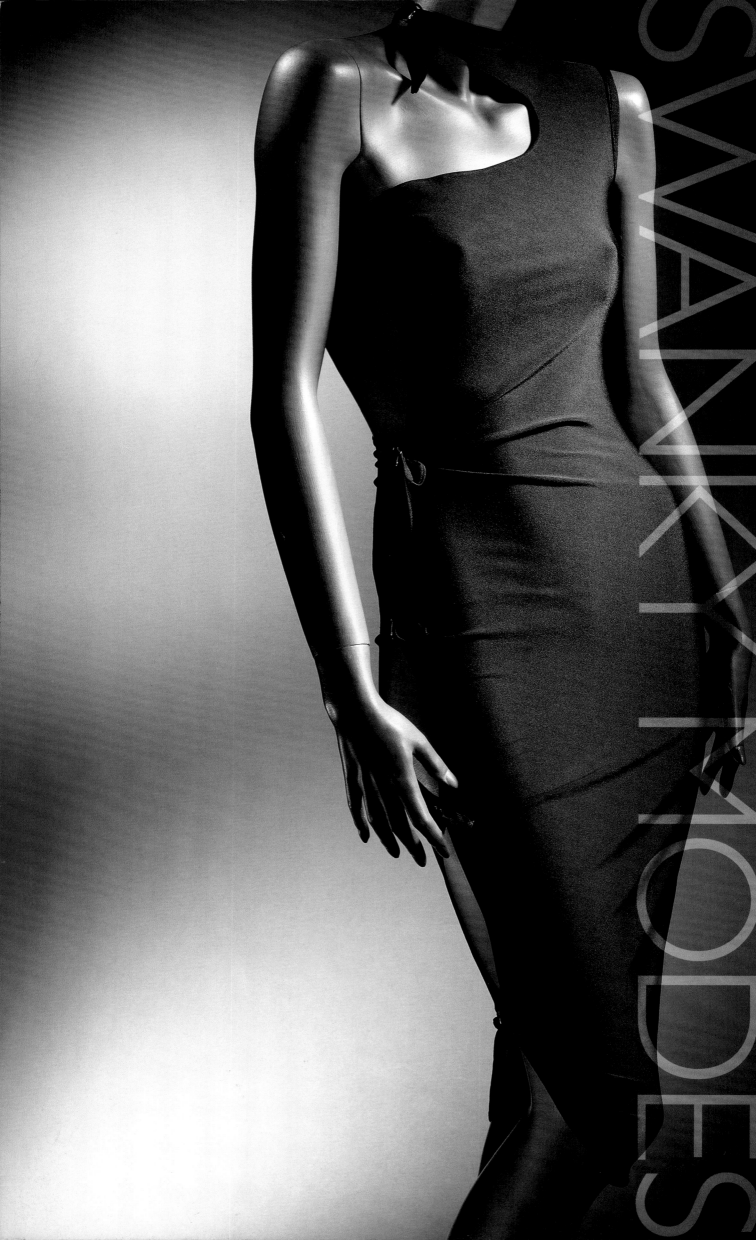

Disco dress, Swanky Modes

London 1978

Given by Swanky Modes

Founded in 1972, Swanky Modes, based in London's Camden Town, was a team of four youthful, inventive designers, Judy Dewsbury, Melanie Herberfield, Willie Walters and Esme Young. Located on a traffic-laden route, their shop window displayed extraordinary designs, often in fluorescent colours punctuated by black, which never failed to catch the attention of passing drivers and pedestrians. Their extrovert ideas for the young and intrepid were part of the vibrant London fashion scene led by emerging talents (many trained in Britain's unique art schools) who, as Brenda Polan observed, had an understanding of the semiology of dress, an inborn sense of style and extraordinarily few inhibitions about expressing both' (The Fashion Year, 1983).

The disco-dancing craze of the 1970s ran in parallel with the keep fit mania that spread from the USA to Europe. Though special clothes were designed for these respective activities, a degree of stylistic cross-fertilization took place, with the consequence that exercise gear and disco wear became almost interchangeable. Sleek-look, mix-and-match leotards, leggings and little wrap-around skirts were at home on the disco floor as well as in the gym. The remarkable stretch-and-recover fibre Lycra was instrumental in bringing about this revolution in 'second skin' clothing. Dubbed 'the fitness fibre', it was introduced in 1959 but took time to move from corsetry to sportswear and body-fitting fashion. In 1977 John Travolta in the film Saturday Night Fever set the seal on the popularity of disco dancing.

At the height of the boom, Swanky Modes used a swimwear fabric for their best-selling disco dress that opens out flat and is fastened tight around the body by side straps pulled through steel D-rings. The nylon and Lycra mix took dye well, resulting in a dense black that washed and dried quickly. Its clinging nature and daring cut-outs dictated a minimum of underwear but for a serious dancer, with a well-toned physique, it was ideal, being cool, flexible, streamlined and sensuously black.

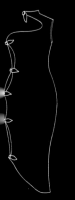 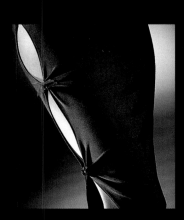 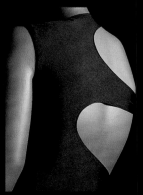

From left to right:
Line drawing,
front of dress
Detail, lower right
side of dress
Detail, back of dress (top)

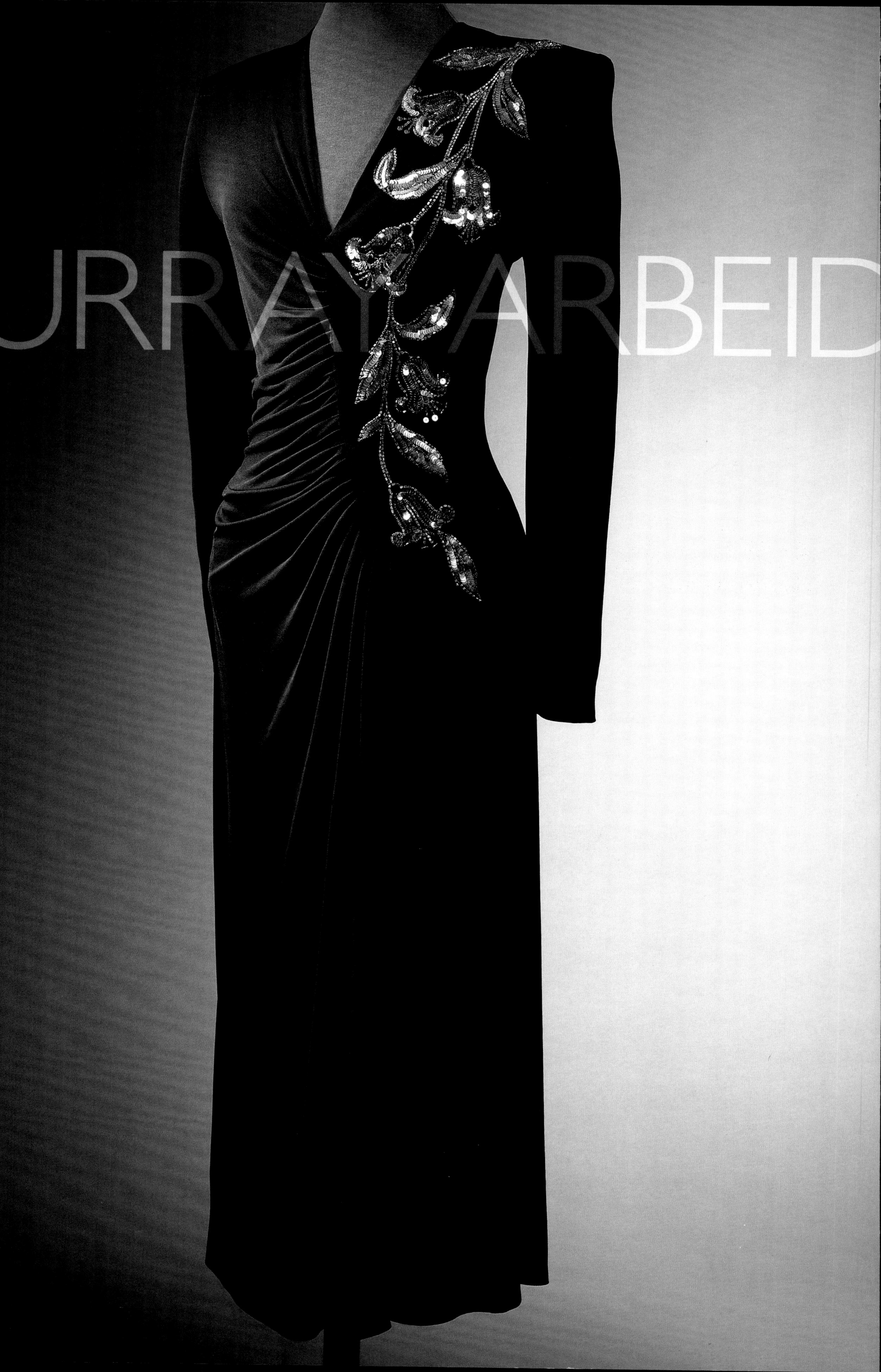
URRAY ARBEID

Evening dress, Murray Arbeid

London 1978

Given by Murray Arbeid

Making sure that women were well dressed has always been the aim of Murray Arbeid (b.1935). Knowing that he wished to be a fashion designer, he left school at the age of fifteen to train in pattern-cutting at the Paris Academy in London. The following four years were divided between mass production and the rarefied atmosphere of Michael Sherard's couture atelier. The latter he described as 'glamorous, exciting, sophisticated' – he often designed stage clothes for celebrities, including Marlene Dietrich. This wide-ranging experience proved invaluable when he opened his own establishment. In the mid-1970s, he moved to share premises with the royal milliner Frederick Fox in Bond Street, where they frequently collaborated (and still do) to achieve top-to-toe ensembles.

Murray Arbeid chose supple black jersey for his reinterpretation of the curvaceous styles of early 1940s dresses (Hollywood movies had the most seductive) in soft synthetics with drapery and an asymmetrical construction. Big shoulder pads (forerunners of the 1980s 'power' shoulders) emulated the wide, sharp-cornered 1940s profile, providing a hard, mannish line in contrast to the gentle arcs, shirring and floral embroidery below. Panels on the right drape seductively over the body into a seam that sweeps from a deep, V-shaped *décolletage* over the left hip. Meandering down the left torso, a spray of lilies is worked in gold and silver sequins and bugle beads in homage to 1940s large-scale embroideries. In keeping with the spirit, Frederick Fox created a black jersey turban trimmed with a high curving aigrette.

Young women in the 1970s were thrilled with 'retro chic' and adored forties revivalism, whereas older women who had worn wartime fashions were not entirely captivated. Announcing Murray Arbeid's

appointment to design c
Hilary Alexander (*The D
1988) remarked upon h
'deliciously irreverent at
recognition of the signif
fashion, he had decided
would open with a little
'L B D Mark 1' and clos
wedding dress named 'C

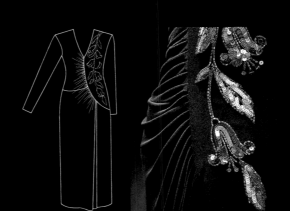

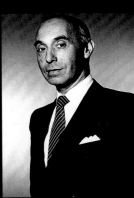

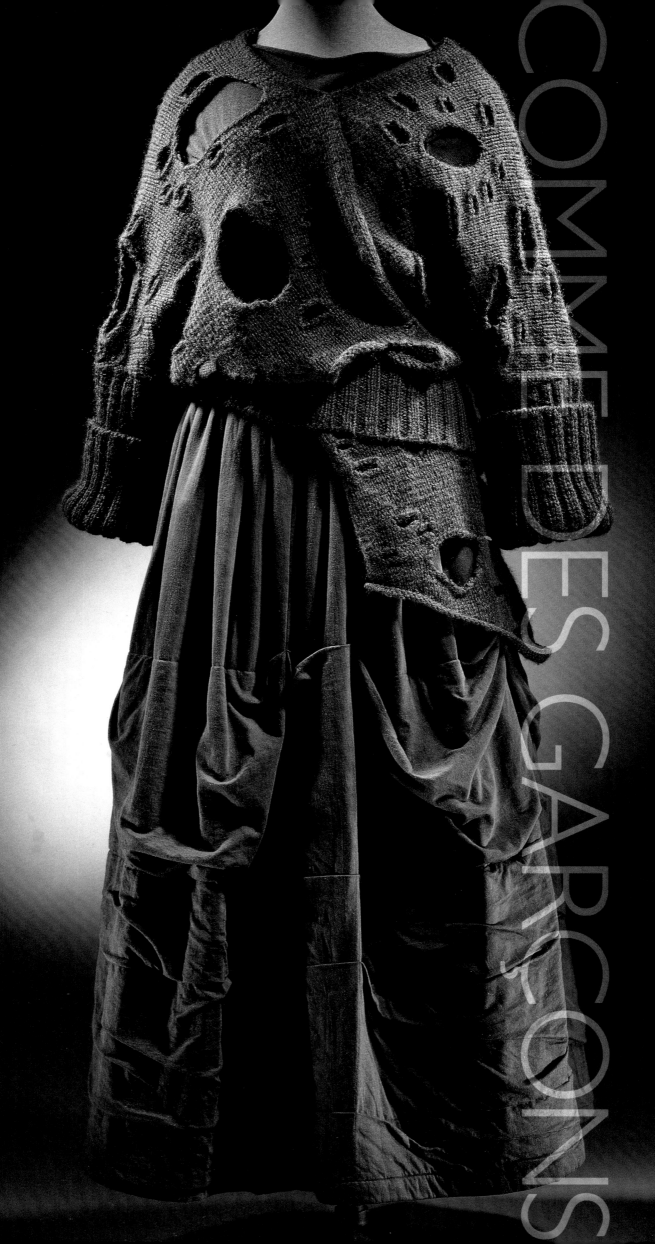

Though she now explores a wide and exciting spectrum of colour in her work, Rei Kawakubo (b.1942) and her company Comme des Garçons are indissolubly linked with black. This is based on her emphatically black collections of the 1980s, a bias that prevailed until March 1988 when she proclaimed (to the astonishment of some) that 'red is black'. Deyan Sudjic wrote of her deep involvement with the achromatic, explaining that it was a draining experience that demanded the investment of 'so much emotional energy' (*Rei Kawakubo and Comme des Garçons*, 1990).

Rei Kawakubo had been designing in Japan for some ten years before astounding an audience in Paris (1981) with an extraordinary collection of capacious, wrapped clothes. This marked the start of the company's expansion in the West and the opening of Comme des Garçons stores, which illuminated the validity and versatility of black and neutrally dyed garments, offering the 'complete experience' of revolutionary clothes in avant-garde interiors. A few fashion commentators had problems comprehending her unorthodox techniques, extensive palette of blacks and the giant volume of her designs, but others, smitten by the strength and austerity of her vision, outnumbered them.

The black hand-knitted 'lace' sweater caused consternation and ill-considered references to bag lady clothes and radical feminism. In fact it is an immaculately hand-knitted piece that utilizes the decorative potential of post-punk random holes. Made in chunky but extremely light wool, the asymmetrical pattern is ingenious, incorporating a deep welt that sits on the hips and gives form to the sweater. Rei Kawakubo established an interplay of textures and blacks – of the fine woollen undersweater; the big 'lace' sweater; and the sturdy, asymmetrically quilted cotton jersey skirt with its deliberate washed-out grey-black. She told Leonard Koren that her affinity for black was based upon the fact that she felt comfortable with it, and she commented: 'I don't know why but my feeling for black is stronger than ever these last ten years' (*New Fashion Japan*, 1984).

From left to right:
Line drawing, back of sweater and skirt
Detail, centre front of sweater and skirt
Detail of left shoulder
Photograph of 'lace' sweater by Peter Lindbergh.
Courtesy of Comme des Garçons

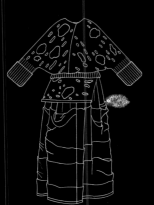
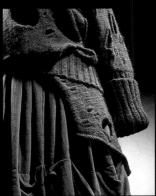
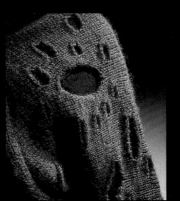
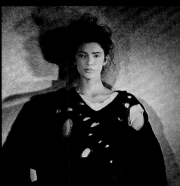

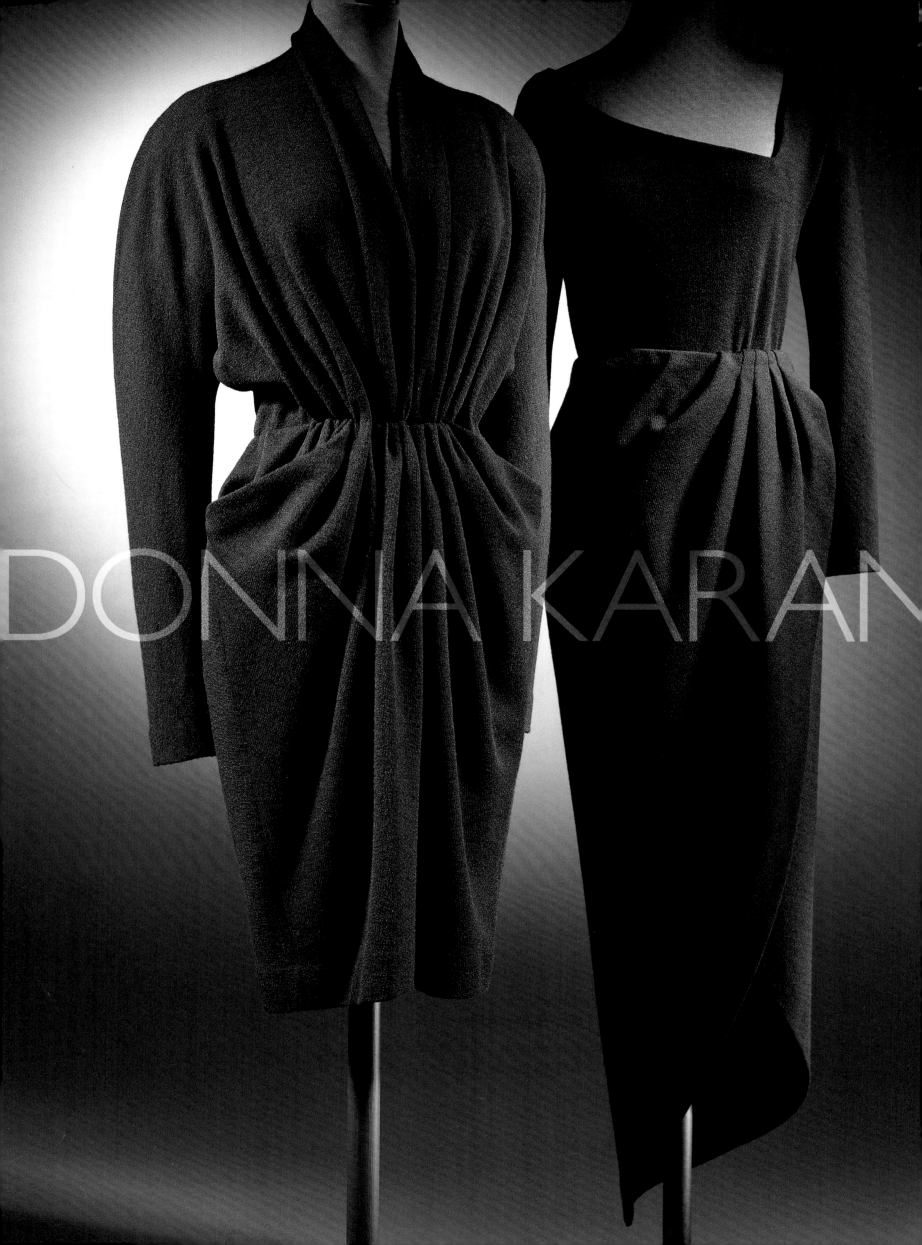

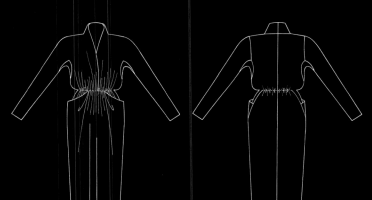
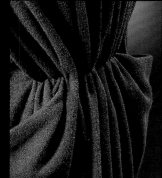

Day dresses, Donna Karan

New York 1985-86

Worn by the Baroness Birk of

Regent's Park and given by her family

Women's Wear Daily in 1985 had nothing but praise for the first own-label collections of Donna Karan (b. 1948), pin-pointing the fact that 'Black is the pivotal colour', and indeed black has remained a significant component in her work. As a hard-grafting professional designer and mother, she has an intimate knowledge of the needs of the cosmopolitan working woman. Her special insight into the demands of the hectic pace of New York life led to the creation of clothes with a powerful chic and a comfortable fit – a perfect partnership for the workplace. She regularly returns to black fabrics, often employing luxuriously soft woollen jerseys that will accommodate her body-conscious approach. Her practical attitude and special solutions won her an avid following and international commercial success. To avoid the annoying way that separates ride up and bunch, she used bodysuits as a basis for her designs, ensuring that torsos always had clean, unbroken lines. Interviewed by *Women's Wear Daily* in the late 1980s, she outlined her fashion philosophy: 'This is a time marked by speed and energy. Clothes have to be relaxed with an element of drama. My whole collection is based on options and flexibility.'

Two sophisticated, big city black dresses in textured wool jersey indicate the strength of her concepts. The stark simplicity of a long-sleeved body with an eye-catching asymmetrical neckline is offset by the soft drapes of a lean, wrap-around and tuck-in skirt (right). A sister day dress (left) was given assertive broad shoulders but an ultra-feminine curvaceous shape and capacious pockets over the hips to counterbalance the padded shoulderline. Asked by Barbaralee Diamonstein to advise about a basic wardrobe in 1985, Donna Karan counselled: 'I would start with black; I always prefer black as the base' (*Fashion: The Inside Story*, 1985).

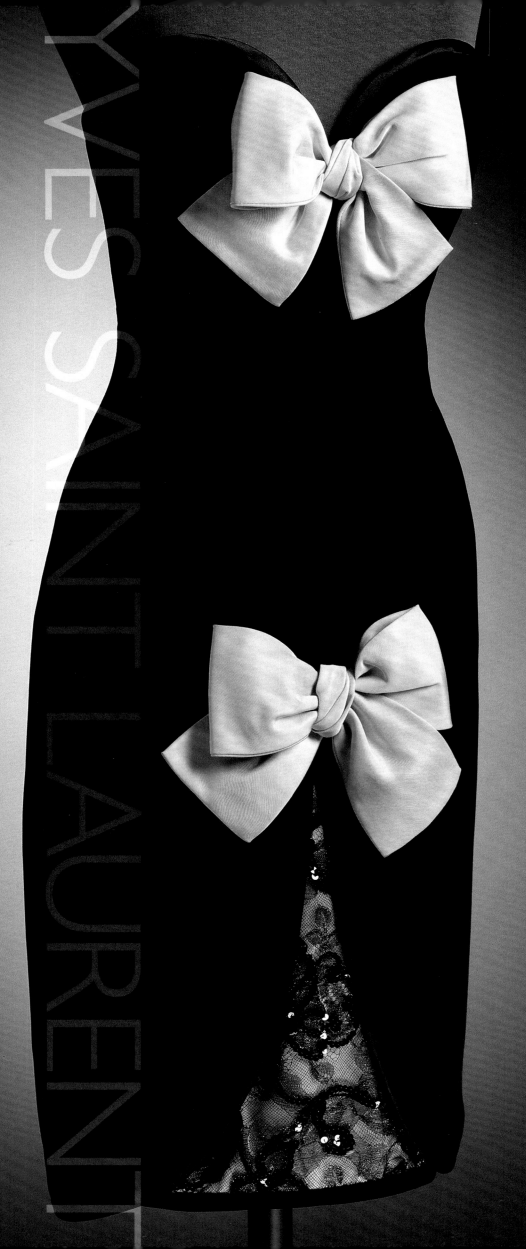

Evening dress, Yves Saint Laurent

Paris about 1985

Given anonymously

At the age of eighteen, Yves Saint Laurent (b.1936) was already aware of the power of black in fashion – he won first prize in the International Wool Secretariat's second competition (1954) with his design for a black cocktail dress. Judged by Balmain, Fath and Givenchy, the short dress with a draped asymmetrical neckline and narrow skirt was made up in Givenchy's atelier. Recognizing his evident talent, Christian Dior employed Yves Saint Laurent in 1955 and, after Dior's sudden death (1957), the twenty-one-year-old Yves Saint Laurent took over as head designer. With triumphant first seasons, he was heralded as the saviour of Paris couture, though his autumn-winter 1960 'young look' collection was 'nearly fatal'. An outcry in the press followed this so-called 'beat' collection (inspired by the black clothes of bikers and Left Bank beatniks). The ideas, summarized by *Vogue* as 'pale zombie faces; leather suits and coats, knitted caps and high turtleneck collars, black endlessly' (British *Vogue*, early September 1960), were simply too avant-garde for Dior's conservative clientele.

After the break with Dior and opening his own house in 1962, Saint Laurent was free to design for a more adventurous market. The very first dress by the newly independent designer (exhibited twenty-one years later in his retrospective at the Metropolitan Museum, New York, in 1983) was in black crêpe georgette with a bodice embroidered with jet. A sensational colourist working with a vibrant palette, he excelled at exotic, clashing combinations using bright pinks, reds, oranges and purples. Balancing this exuberance, he perfected restrained little black dresses and tailored designs executed in severe black; especially famous are trousers suits based on 'le smoking' and the city suit.

Throughout his career, Saint Laurent has made evening wear exploring the potential of black, particularly narrow, body-fitting designs (long or short) often enlivened with bold details in a single colour – 'that give the "little black one" wit and sex appeal' (*Yves Saint Laurent*, 1988). Svelte and strapless in glistening black silk velvet, this evening gown has a curved *décolletage* echoed by the cut-away hem, and the entire garment is immaculately edged in black satin. The focal points – two huge pastel green, grosgrain bows – gain authority against the pure lines and stark simplicity of black velvet.

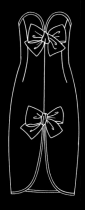

Line drawing, front of dress

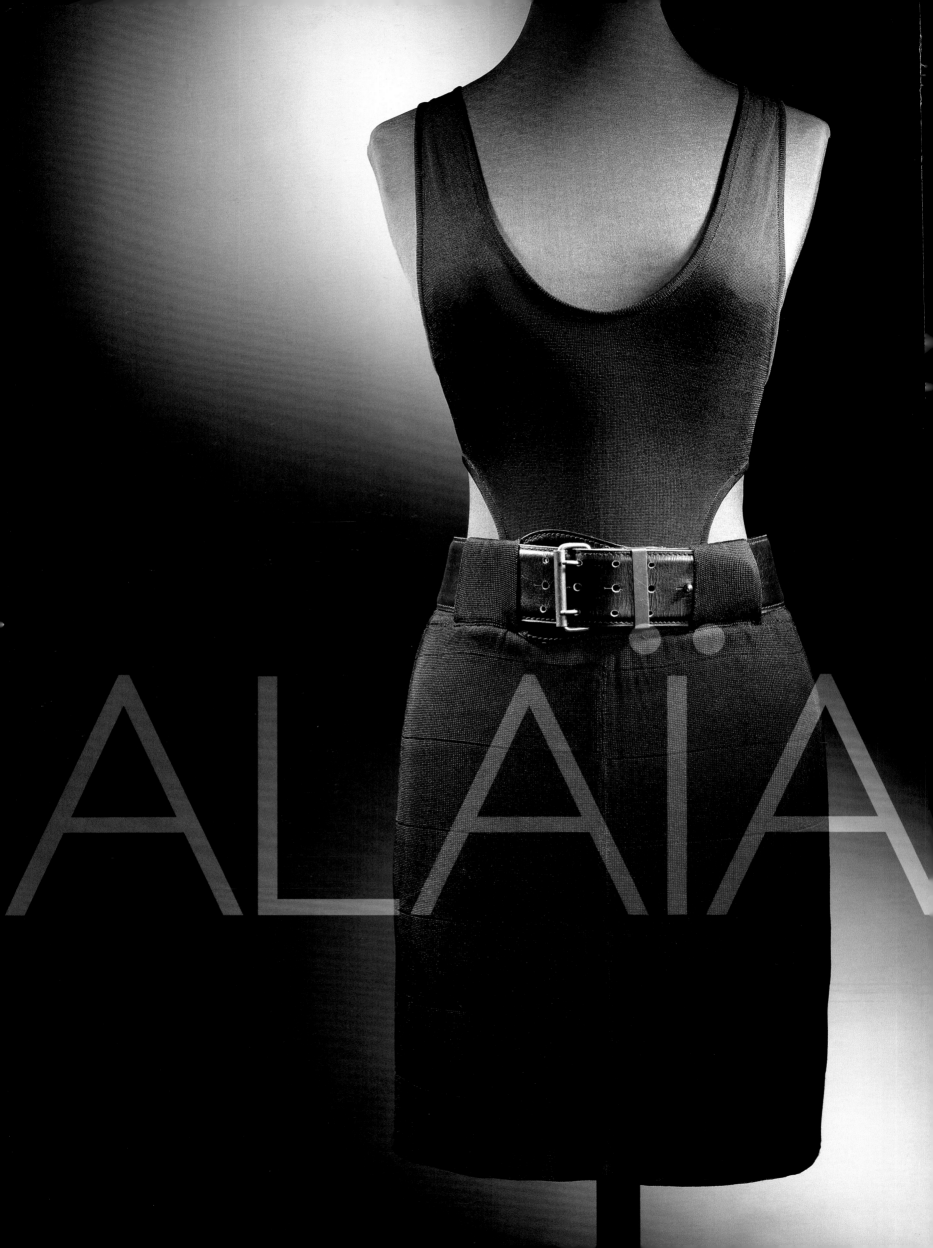

Summer ensemble, Alaïa

Paris 1985

Given by Azzedine Alaïa

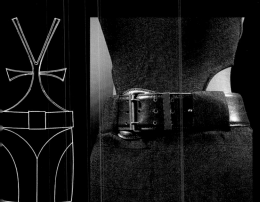
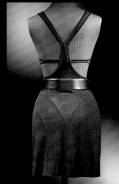

From left to right:
Line drawing, back of dress
Detail of centre front
Back view of dress

The flowing lines and perfect body-fitting designs of Tunisian-born Azzedine Alaïa (who declared 'I am as old as the pharaohs') make them among the most sensuous in recent couture. For many years he worked for private clients in Paris before introducing a ready-to-wear collection in 1980. Supple jersey knits in silk, acetate or fine wool and luxurious glove leathers dyed black are his favourite materials. With these he creates second-skin clothes that demand

lean, well-toned physiques and attract an international array of celebrity clients accustomed to the limelight – from super-models to pop stars. Georgina Howell named him 'The Titan of Tight'. Tina Turner told her: 'he gives you the very best line you can get out of your body… Take any garment he has made. You can't drop the hem, you can't let it out or take it in. It's a piece of sculpture' (USA *Vogue*, March 1990).

Gleaming black acetate was machine knitted to shape this bare-look, mini-skirted, pinafore dress and, in sharp contrast to the pliant jersey, a hard, wide leather belt sits defiantly at hipster level. The revealing scoop-necked, vest-like top is reduced to pairs of slender straps at the back and is so scanty that it precludes any underwear. A technical *tour de force*, the skirt back has structural lines meticulously arranged in a V-shaped band, which suggestively follows

the curves of the posterior. Alaïa told Marina Sturdza: 'I stress the body and I have to try my things on a living body because the clothes I make must respect the body' (Brenda Polan, *The Fashion Year*, 1983). For moments when confidence was at a low ebb, or to provide warmth when the sun went in, Alaïa gave the body-defining pinafore a matching, big-look, T-shaped top. A pair of Rayban sunglasses was the finishing, up-to-the-minute touch for this triumph of 1980s minimalist fashion.

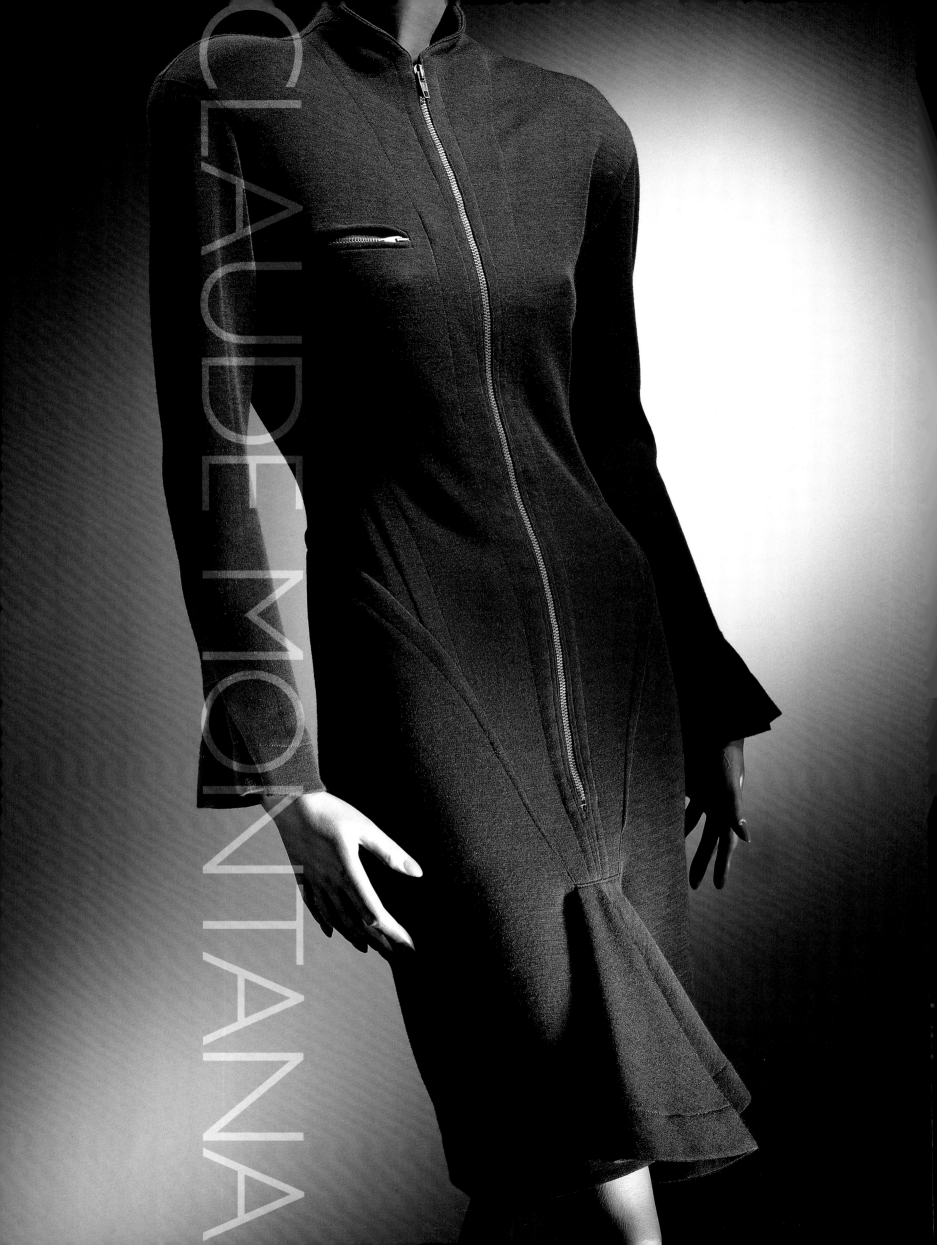

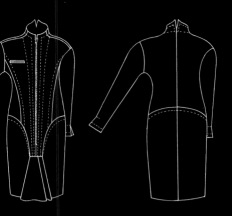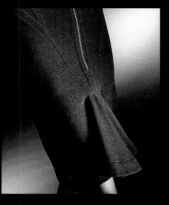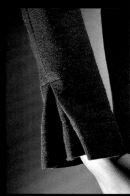

Day dress, Claude Montana
Paris about 1985

The big-shouldered look was the perfect guise for the tough, go-getting, professional woman of the 1980s; in the boardroom it gave her a dominance and physical presence to rival any male colleague. In black it resembled the city suit of the banker and businessman. The most intimidating shoulders were available from Claude Montana (b. 1949), famed for his aggressive and futuristic designs, which were sometimes cartoon-like in their exaggerated forms. Richard Martin observed: 'What became the power look in women's clothing in the mid-1980s is derived from Montana's aesthetic, so persuasive was it as an option for assertive presence without sacrifice of the female form' (*Contemporary Fashion*, 1995).

Throughout the late 1970s and 1980s he devised powerful silhouettes that gained even more impact when executed in black. Early on in his career he began to work with leather and developed skills which enabled him to handle it like a pliable textile rather than as an intractable skin. Favouring soft black glove leather, he translated hefty-shouldered biking gear and military uniforms into adventurous high fashion looks, only to be castigated for his outlandish vision of women. He took risks with visual quotes from the underworld of sex and martial violence, expressing them in threatening black. Undeterred by the critics,

Montana perfected a curvaceous top-heavy style featuring hugely padded shoulders below which fabric was cut to fit sensuously close to the body. This won him a following of confident, strong-minded clients who wished to assert their authority yet retain their femininity.

In addition to leather, Montana found wool jersey to his liking; it has the elasticity to cling to the body's contours and can be moulded to a streamlined finish. The front of this overtly sexy day time dress is a fluent linear composition featuring a bold, central zip and pairs of welt seams that accentuate voluptuous hips. The constructional lines meet above a flirtatious, flared kick pleat.

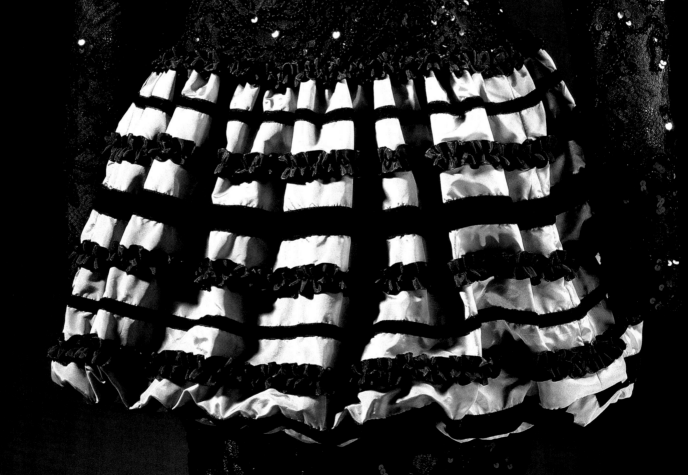

Evening dress, Givenchy

Paris 1987

Given anonymously

Givenchy updated the puff-ball silhouette (a favourite of the 1950s) and combined it with a sheath dress to achieve a witty and perfectly balanced evening dress for 1987. Carefully calculated proportions ensured the success of the perennial fashion strategy of black with one colour. Having spent time at Lelong, Piguet, Fath and Schiaparelli before opening his own house, Givenchy had a complete understanding of the complexities of *haute couture* (though modestly he claimed that he knew nothing before meeting Balenciaga). He was dedicated to the art and craft of high fashion. Together with a small and ever decreasing number of top couturiers, he maintained the practice and upheld the exacting standards of Paris couture through difficult years from the 1960s onwards. The tradition of made-to-order was threatened (and still is) by the commercial megalith of ready-to-wear and a studied negligence advocated by the influential youth lobby. In this maelstrom, Givenchy astutely launched his own ready-to-wear line, Givenchy Nouvelle Boutique, but continued his collections of refined, exquisitely made *haute couture* clothes. Marie-José Lepicard described them as bubbles to keep women 'safe from the outside world; they are dresses that suggest a certain remoteness, "protection against evil", says Audrey Hepburn' (Catherine Join-Diéterle, *Givenchy: 40 Years of Creation*, 1991).

Illustrating his skill with luxurious fabrics, Givenchy selected a sequinned lace (by Marescot) to form a twinkling, slender central pillar of black, adding a counterpoint of a gathered, bouffant, eau-de-Nil silk faille overskirt embellished with horizontal rows of black velvet bands and ruched silk ribbon (by Jacob Schlaepfer). Jane Mulvagh recorded the labour-intensive nature of couture and the fact that 'Givenchy's deceptively simple black velvet and taffeta sheaths' took a minimum of forty hours to make (*Vogue History of 20th Century Fashion*, 1988).

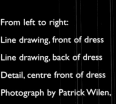

From left to right:

Line drawing, front of dress

Line drawing, back of dress

Detail, centre front of dress

Photograph by Patrick Wilen,

L'Officiel September 1987

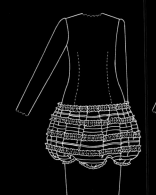
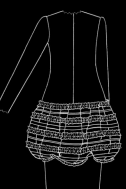
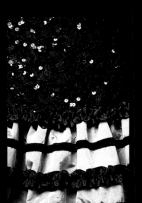
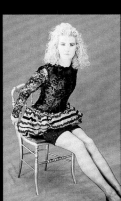

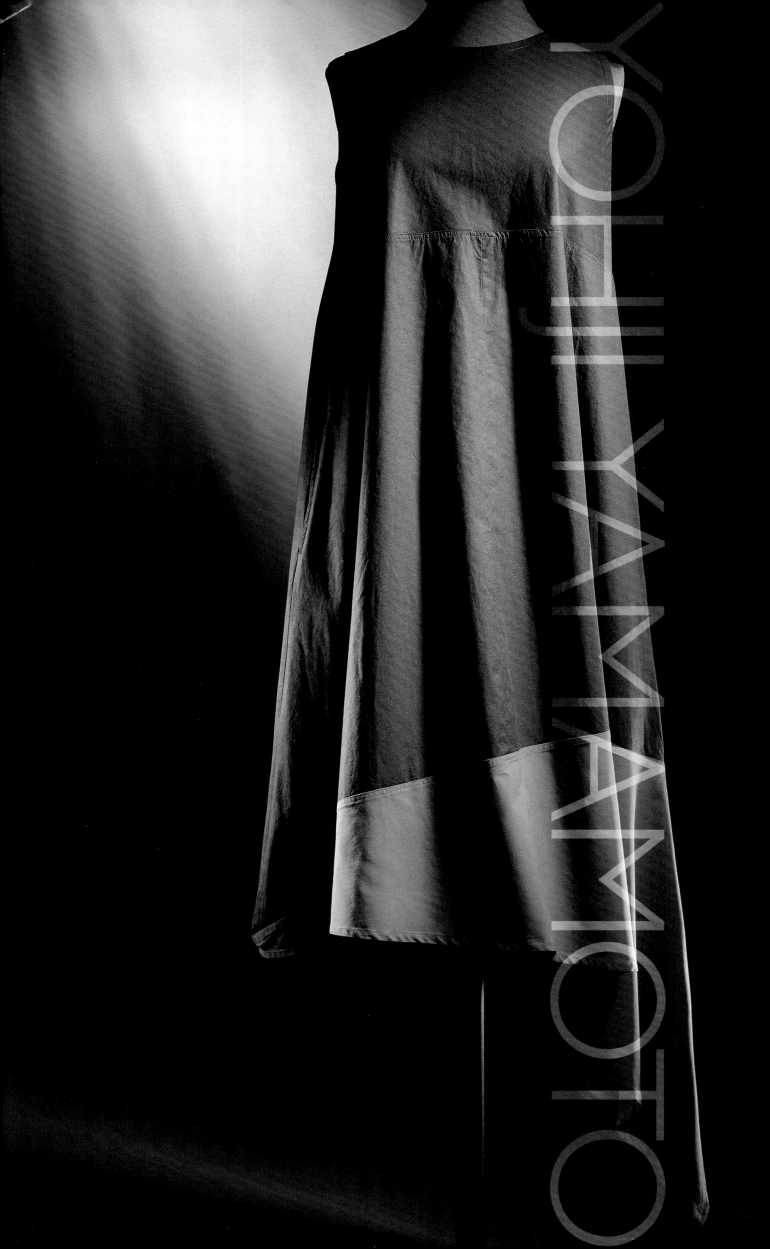

From left to right:

Line drawing, front of dress

Line drawing, back of dress

Detail, left side view

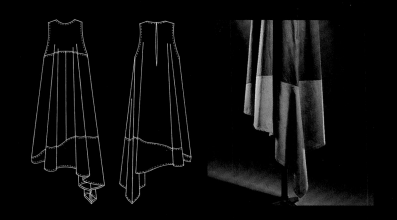

Summer dress, Yohji Yamamoto

Tokyo 1988-89

Given anonymously

Interviewed in 1989, Yohji Yamamoto (b. 1943) revealed his reliance on a sombre palette: 'I always wear black or navy, my only concession to colour being a white shirt or T-shirt' (*The Sunday Times Magazine*, 26 February 1989). In tandem with a radical rethink of cut and construction, 'anti-fashion' black was the most important component of the early 1980s revolution spearheaded by a trio of avant-garde Japanese designers, Issey Miyake, Rei Kawakubo and Yohji Yamamoto. After training in Japan and Paris, Yohji Yamamoto presented his first collections in Tokyo in the mid-1970s and by the early 1980s had astounded the international fashion press and customers alike with his new wave concepts. While preferring plain fabrics and eschewing conventional forms of decoration, such as embroidery and printed pattern, he advocated asymmetry and added fascinating if perplexing points of interest to black in the form of cut-outs, non-functional flaps, irregular hems and uneven collars. He took to placing labels that read 'There is nothing so boring as a neat and tidy look' in the ready-to-wear range that he produced for the young.

Very occasionally, as in this utterly simple yet distinctive sleeveless summer shift, he relieved the dominance of black with a slice of colour – here a triangle of burnt orange. Volume is all important; the panels of crisp, tightly woven cotton poplin are cut generously so that the garment would never restrict or impede movement. This is a perfect garment for oppressively hot days: the armholes are elongated slits; the centre back seam is caught at the neck but is open to the lower spine; while the floating conical shape permits the maximum air flow to cool the body. In keeping with his explorations of asymmetry, the orange hem dips almost to the floor on the left and has an unusual cupped finish on the shorter right side.

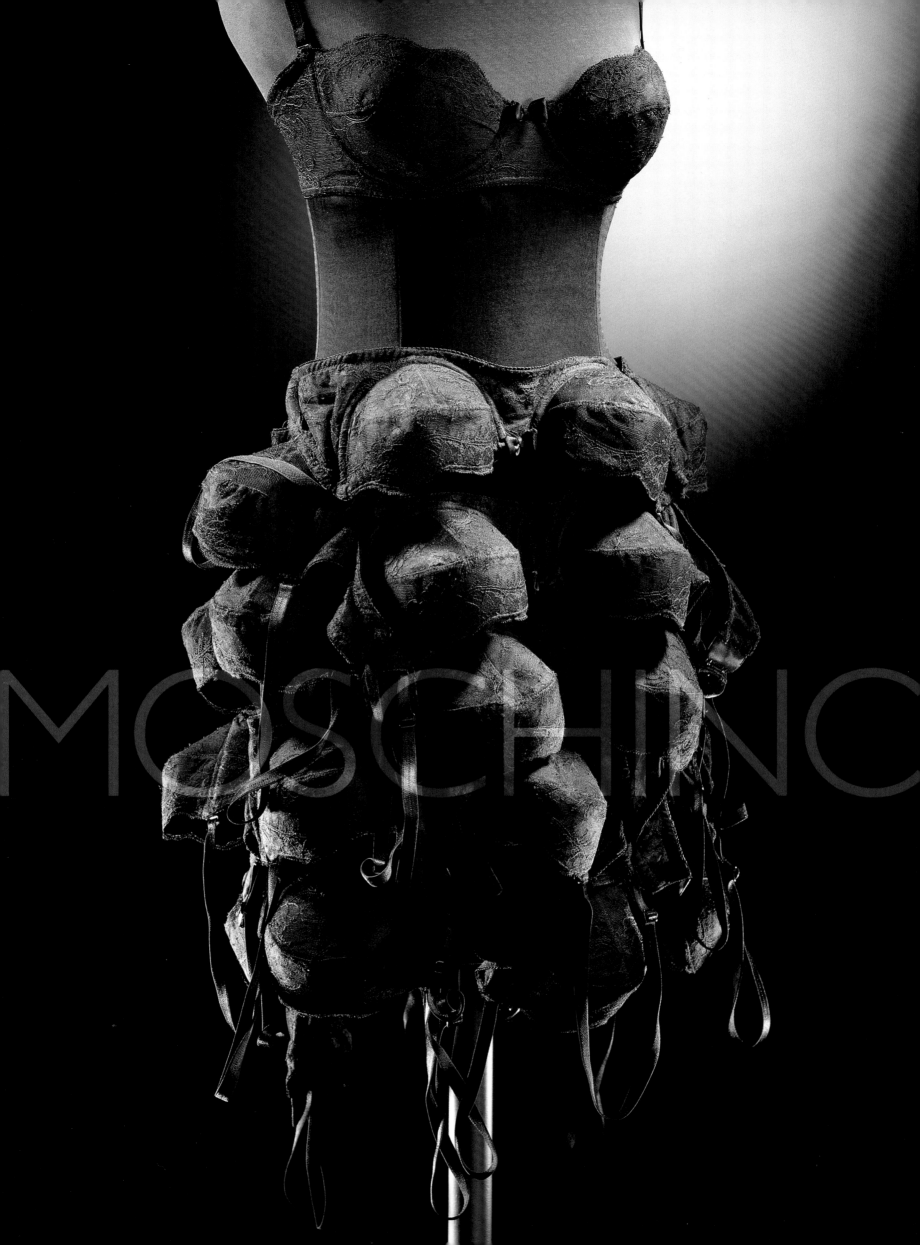

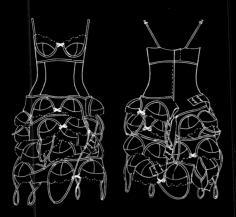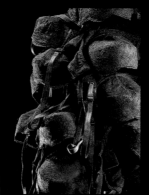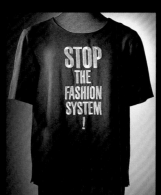

From left to right:
Line drawing,
front of dress
Line drawing,
back of dress
Detail, side of skirt
Embroidered silk
T-shirt, Moschino, 1988

Evening dress, Moschino

Milan 1988

Given by Franco Moschino

Franco Moschino (1950-94) revelled in the role he invented for himself – that of the 'bad boy' of international couture. Inspired by the art of the Dadaists and Surrealists, whose work he admired for questioning and threatening tradition and the status quo, he produced lively, amusing clothes that parodied the mores of the fashion industry and its customers. He studied art and worked for Gianni Versace, followed by Cadette, before establishing his own label in 1983.

Black was rarely absent from Moschino's collections. He used it for entire outfits and also as effective T-shirt backgrounds for his now famous slogans challenging the more fatuous elements of the fashion round. He was adept at producing immaculately tailored black suits with neat jackets and short skirts and rang the changes by decorating them with visual jokes and puns,

such as incongruous gilt knives, forks and spoons, vivid red hearts and bill board sized embroidered messages like 'Expensive Jacket'. Slogans for shirts included 'For Fashion Victims Only', 'Signed Garment' and 'Money Doesn't Make The World Go Around'. The monograph *X Anni de Kaos! 1983-1993* (1993) charts the commercial success of Moschino's iconoclastic designs and publishes his jibes at the fashion world, including a set of rhyming couplets, 'This is Why', beginning 'As we told you once before/Fashion shows are now a bore: /All the fuss and all the mess/Fail distinctly to impress…'

A perfect example of Moschino's desire to shock is this little black dress – from a distance it has the appearance of a non-controversial, slightly bell-skirted evening dress, and only as the viewer gets closer do the petticoat top and the twenty

fulsome bras composing the skirt come into focus. In the footsteps of unorthodox designers Vivienne Westwood and Jean Paul Gaultier, who audaciously employed brassieres and corsets as outerwear, Moschino takes the concept a stage further and makes an entire outergarment from saucy black underwear.

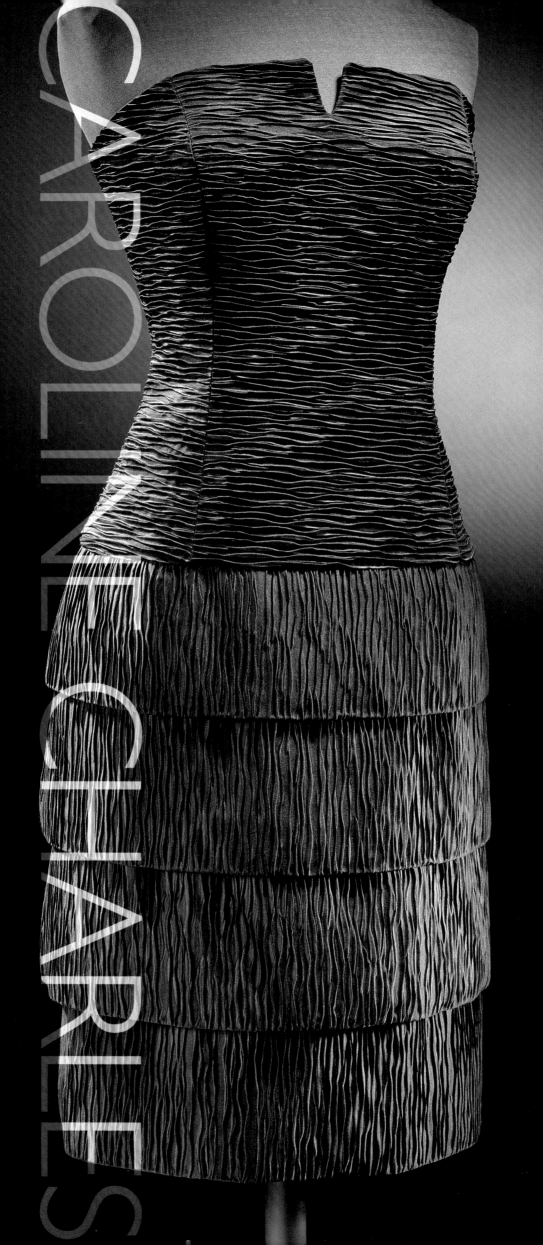

Evening dress, Caroline Charles

London 1989

Given by Caroline Charles

Caroline Charles (b. 1942) usually wears plain dark hues or black. In a studio surrounded by colour and pattern, she explained: 'You are forever holding fabric against yourself and you don't want what you're wearing to be a distraction' (The Telegraph Magazine). A disciplined and practical designer, each season she compiles a little uniform of two or three things' for herself as an instant and efficient solution to the quandary of 'what to wear today?'

After training with couturier Michael Sherard and a spell with Mary Quant, she went independent in 1963 and opened her first shop in 1975 in London's exclusive Beauchamp Place. Architectural Digest (September 1989) stated that she was 'one of the most English of designers. Her suits are of very good English tweed or paisley; her silk dresses are perfect for Ascot or Glyndebourne; embroidered jackets and long velvet skirts fend off drafts in chilly stately homes. She has a sense of occasion and knows exactly the English way to dress for an English event.' Adept at designing with jewel-like colours for evening and with camouflage browns or startlingly bright tartans for country day wear, she has given advice as colour consultant for the benefit of many multinational corporations. Every detail counts, and a skylight at Beauchamp

Place allows customers to try colours in natural light away from the distortions of electric illumination. Sophisticated black is rarely unrepresented in her collections, though in 1989 she declared that 'Ivory and gray are my ideals – I'm trying to resist black altogether' (Architectural Digest, September 1989).

Fortunately, a black tree bark polyester, by the Italian company Bogliani & Dossi, proved irresistible, resulting in the 'crinkle' dress. Charles created a simple evening statement that was the perfect vehicle for such a bold, highly textured fabric. In the strapless, long-line bodice, with a notched neckline, the deep striations circle the torso horizontally, while the tiered short skirt has the tree bark lines running in a slimming vertical direction.

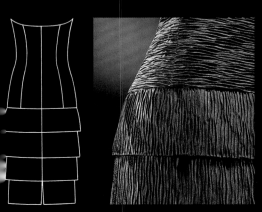
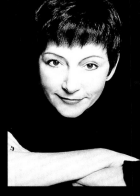

From left to right:
Line drawing, back of dress
Detail, top of skirt
Portrait of Caroline Charles.
Courtesy of the designer

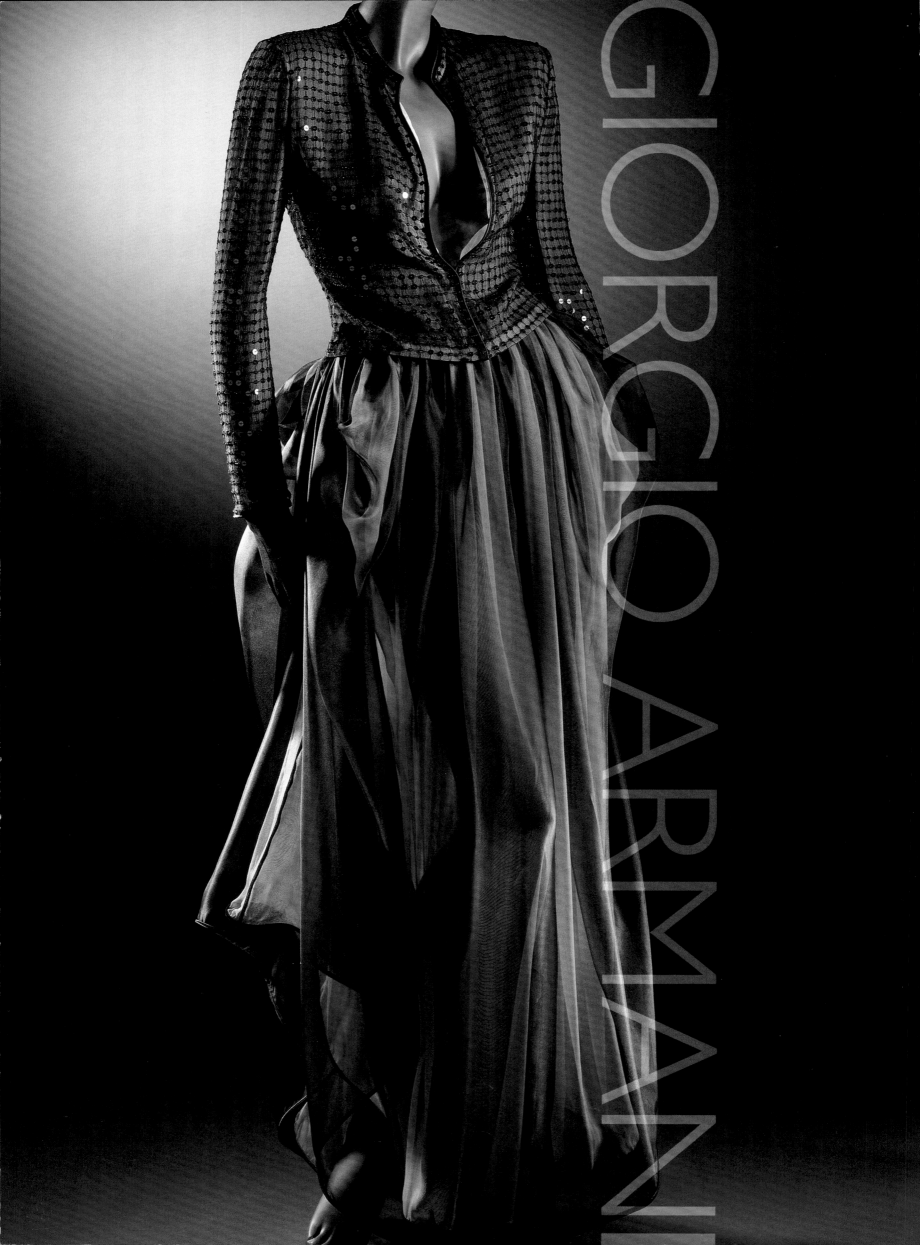

GIORGIO ARMANI

Evening ensemble, jacket and culottes, Giorgio Armani

Milan 1990

Given by Giorgio Armani

The master of cool beige, taupe and grey, Giorgio Armani (b. 1934) asserted: 'Evening used to be all black gowns. I eliminated black in my collection for night' (Lois Perschetz (ed.), *W The Designing Life* (1987), and a few months later in *La Stampa* fashion journalist Lucia Sollazzo agreed that 'Armani is impervious to the tyranny of black'. However, black did not desert his work completely. Although subdued colours dominated, the autumn-winter collection of 1986-87 opened with a long, austere black velvet dress, and throughout the late 1980s and 90s softly tailored clothes in a favourite inky blue-black made compelling, young-look window displays in his Emporio Armani outlets.

In the mid-1970s Armani revolutionized menswear with oversized suits devoid of rigid padding and interlinings. He then introduced feminized versions of this look in his influential collections for women. The suit remained a mainstay of Armani's work, including evening clothes. His brand of modern chic combines practical 'put them on and forget them' shapes with *de luxe* fabrics. Such is Armani's skill with jackets that he has been called the 'jacket wizard' and, long or short, fitted or straight, they always have the Armani hallmark – clean cut, unfussy lines. Relaxed styling informs all his designing activities, and it is his choice of fabrics that distinguishes day from evening wear.

To avoid the solidity and harshness of all black, and to add subtle tones, white chiffon lines the black chiffon and organza of this ethereal ensemble of jacket and culottes. The long-sleeved cropped jacket with its neat mandarin collar is fitted but not uncomfortably tight and would be demure but for its daring *décolletage* and embroidered trellis design with glittering black sequins. Appealing to women 'with subdued sensuality', the culottes glide over the body, their fullness gathered, pannier-like, over the hips.

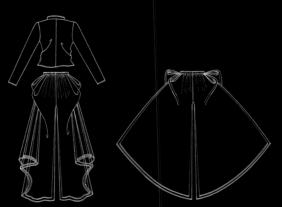 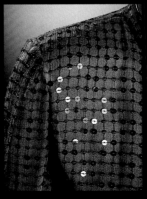

From left to right:
Line drawing, back of jacket and culottes
Line drawing, culottes spread out flat
Detail, right shoulder

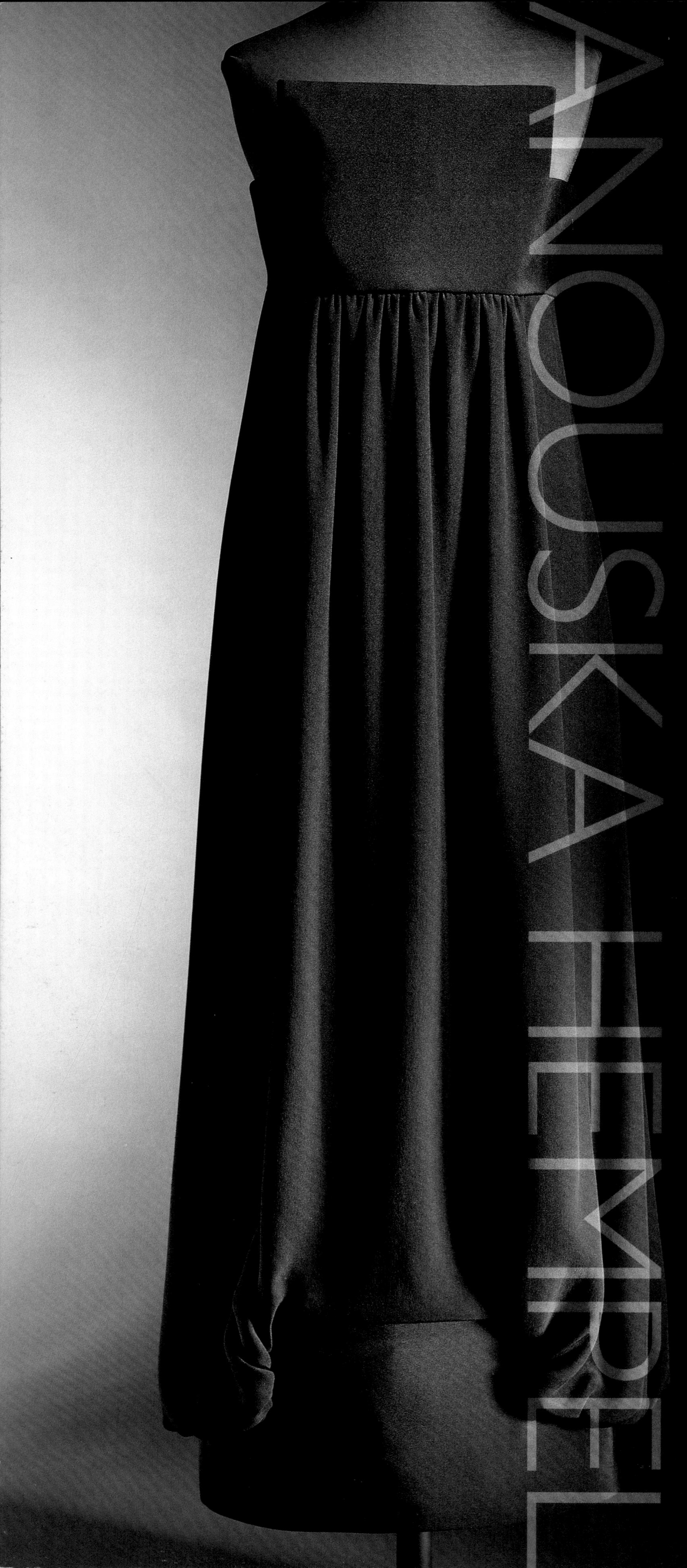
ANOUSKA HEMPEL

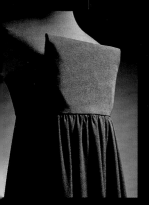
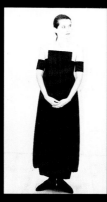
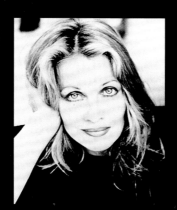

Evening gown, 'Marta',
Anouska Hempel

London 1991

Given by Lady Weinberg (Anouska Hempel)

Anouska Hempel opened her couture house in London's Pond Place in 1988. Almost immediately she achieved her intention of providing made-to-order 'after five' clothes and simple day wear for an elegant and wealthy coterie of women. A self-confessed perfectionist (and workaholic), she deliberately targeted this small and exclusive market; as she told Avril Groom, 'I'm not interested in having a large factory and bigger production problems' (*The Scotsman*, 23 January 1991). She did not have a formal training, but her energy, determination and innate sense of style brought about success. Petite and blonde, she herself wears black or deep anthracite grey as an ideal foil for her porcelain-like complexion.

Black as a background for opulent deep colours and luxurious fabrics became the mainstay of her sumptuous interiors and fashion collections in the late 1980s and early 1990s. The Pond Place shop with its black floor (marble), ceiling and walls was described as 'a doge's palace of draped

midnight blue and black silk. Swagged and swathed silk columns frame doorways, Venetian mirrors rise ceiling high, antique lanterns swing from taffeta ropes and attar of roses hangs in the air' (*City and Country Home*, September 1991). Anouska Hempel has always been concerned with quality rather than quantity, believing that her customers must have the best and that a garment should be as immaculate inside as it is outside. Interviewed by Liz Tobey for *Vogue* (July 1987), she revealed her conviction that women were increasingly happy to be dressed by women and her desire to 'make a person feel good'. A team she trusts translates her ideas into finished garments.

In weighty black silk with a low lustre, this high-waisted, pillar-like gown emanates power. The soft gathers of the tulip-like skirt are contained within the two flat, square-cut planes of bodice and bandeau hem. It is characteristic of her use of black for assertive yet feminine clothes to be worn by women with confidence.

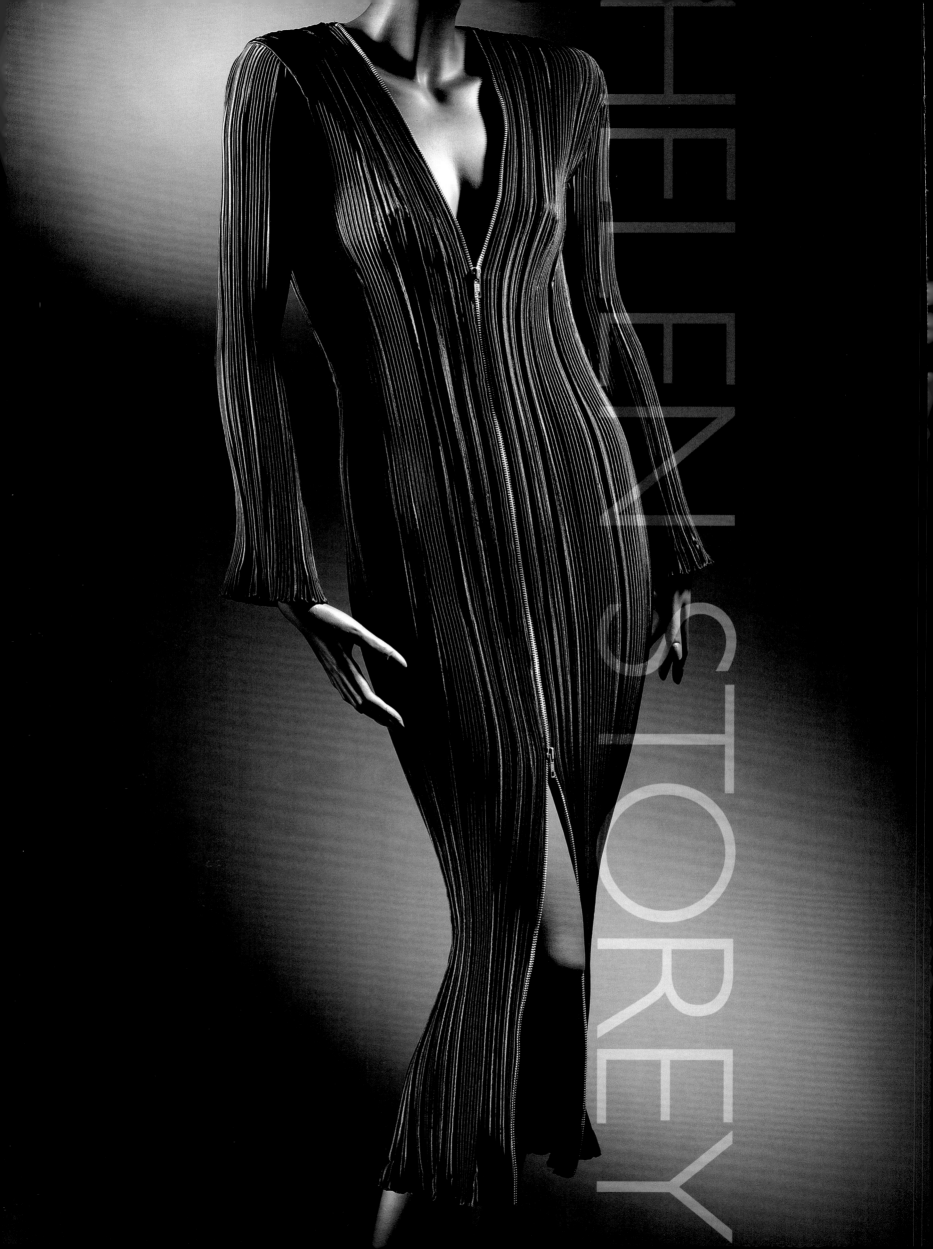

HELEN STOREY

Sheath dress for clubwear,
Helen Storey

London 1993

Given by Helen Storey

Throughout the 1980s and 1990s, vibrant young London fashion was in the hands of a group of talented designers in their twenties and thirties, including Helen Storey (b. 1959). Under the Amalgamated Talent label in 1984 it was apparent that she was completely in tune with, and frequently part of, the multiplicity of creative yet at times bewildering strands of UK streetstyle. Her compelling autobiography *Fighting Fashion* (1996) tracks her career; her husband's life-threatening illness; the collapse of her business; as well as her determined exploration of new routes for fashion. In 1997 this included collaboration with her sister, Dr Kate Storey, to produce the exhibition 'Primitive Streak, A Fashion Collection' at the Institute of Contemporary Arts in London which chronicled human embryonic development.

By the end of the 1980s she had gained an enthusiastic following for her glamorous nightclub clothes, attracting the likes of Madonna, Prince and Sandra Bernhard. Inevitably black played a key part in her clubwear designs as she manipulated the night-time power of black that comes out to play and seduce. Storey has made her preference for strong and theatrical statements (often in black) abundantly clear. In *The Guardian* (14 June 1995) Sally Brampton recorded the designer's violent reaction to conventional images of femininity: 'To me, a Laura Ashley smock, which spells the subservient woman locked in her place, is far more frightening than black, plastic boobs'. As a student, her non-conformism led to 'wildly theatrical outfits' and, amusingly, she admitted to Doreen Ehrlich that 'I tried to think Marks and Spencer but it always came out wrong' (*Contemporary Fashion*, 1995).

Storey has never been wary of man-made fabrics, being one of the first to experiment with the remarkable mono-filaments of the 1990s, including Courtauld's Tencel and ICI's Tactel. In 1993 she used the subtle sheen and permanent pleats of black acetate to accentuate the provocative nature of a body-hugging, clubland, 'Fortuny' sheath dress just 28 cms (11.25 ins) wide. A hefty, two-way zip bisects the dress in a suggestive manner and emphasizes its vertical linear movement.

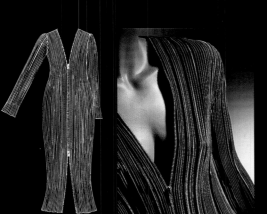 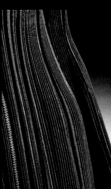 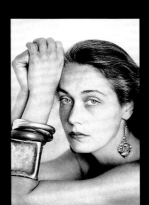

From left to right:
Line drawing, front of dress
Detail, V-shaped *décolletage*
Detail left hip and sleeve
Portrait of Helen Storey.
Courtesy of the designer

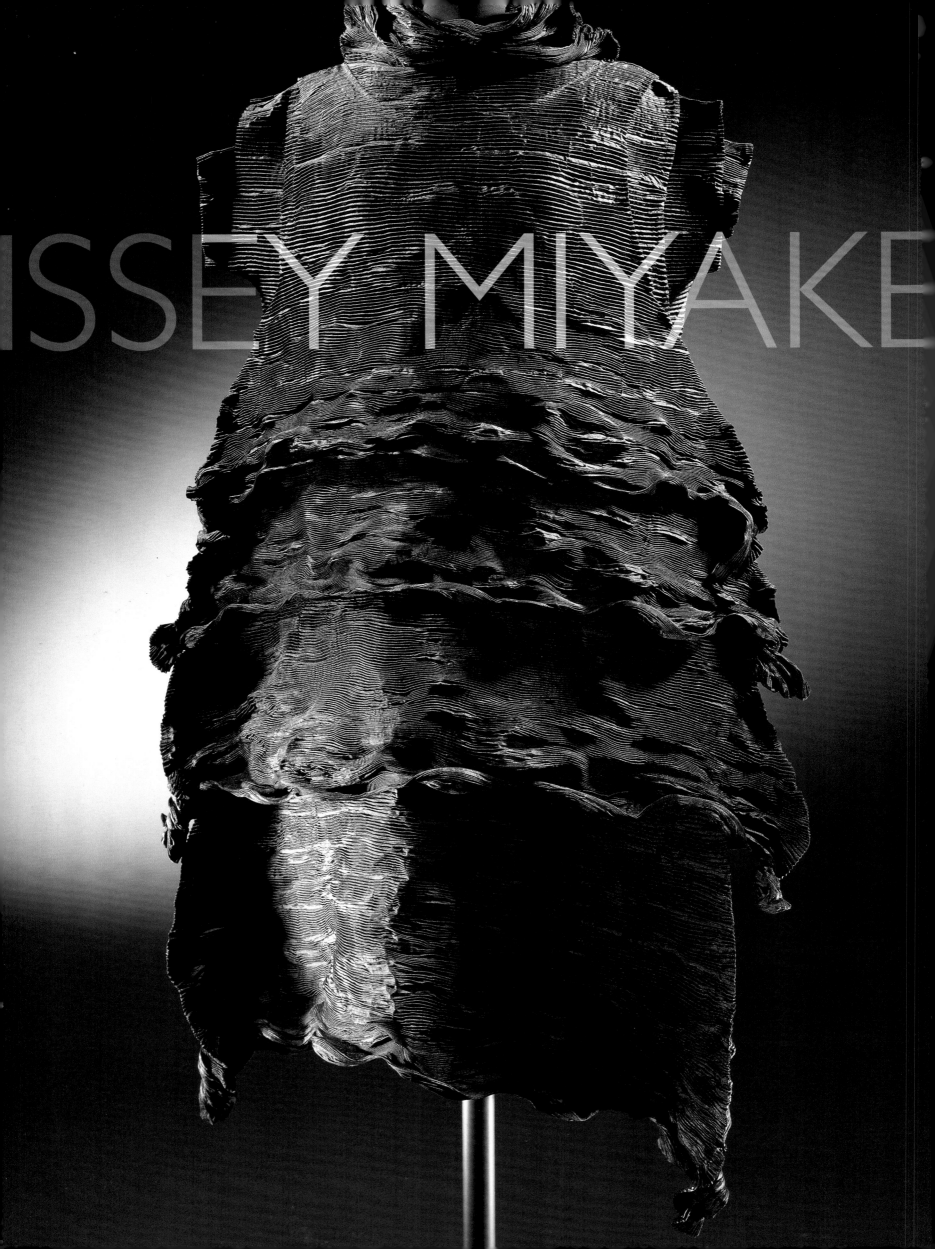

The 'Bouncing Dress',
Issey Miyake

Tokyo spring-summer 1993
Worn and lent by Jill Ritblat

The symbiotic relationship between clothes and movement has always been crucial to the art of designing and wearing dress. Adding a further dimension to this interdependence, black outlines and exaggerates all gestures, partially accounting for its popularity in the performing arts and the growth of its fashionableness in the twentieth century. With his imaginative experiments investigating form and technologically advanced fabrics, Issey Miyake (b. 1938) and his studio have transported dress into new realms. Miyake employs a palette of powerful, pure colours, but black and the neutrals are invariably present in his collections.

After studying graphic design in Tokyo, he trained at the Ecole de la Chambre Syndicale, Paris, before joining Guy Laroche, then Givenchy and afterwards Geoffrey Beene in New York. Returning to Japan, he opened the Issey Miyake Studio in 1970.

Movement is a major factor in Miyake's pursuit of the ultimate in functional clothing. Though amusingly named, the 'Bouncing Dress' is a serious and practical innovation, representing a key point Miyake had reached in spring-summer 1993 in his long-term exploration of the potential of pleating. The buoyant, pull-on dress has four layered parts of irregularly pleated polyester

seamed at the sides to create curvilinear hems twisted into 'horns' at the sides. When shown in Jill Ritblat's display 'One Woman's Wardrobe' in 1998 at the V&A, the dress provoked enormous interest and debate, its structure and texture being likened to geographical strata, ocean waves or the undulations of oyster shells. In Paris a similar dress was exhibited on a mechanical bouncing figure, inciting young visitors to join in the jumping. Motion contributes to the unique spirit of Miyake's designs; as this work reveals, even in the deepest black, they promote a 'sense of well being and joy in wearer and viewer alike' (Mark Holborn, *Issey Miyake*, 1995).

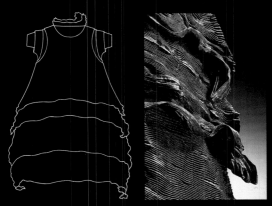
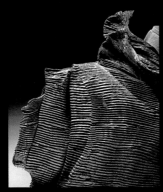

From left to right:
Line drawing, back
of dress
Detail, lower right side
Detail, right shoulder
and neckline

CHANEL

Suit, Karl Lagerfeld for Chanel

Paris spring-summer 1994
Given by the House of Chanel

After the death of Coco Chanel in 1971, the house of Chanel was no longer a leading player in Paris *haute couture*. Though it continued to provide a wealthy and ageing clientele with classics in the Chanel tradition, the demise of its charismatic founder robbed the business of its zest and clear direction. For twelve years unsuccessful attempts were made to revive the ailing operation, until in 1983 it once again became top international fashion news with Karl Lagerfeld's first collection for the label. Lagerfeld (b. 1938) has a profound appreciation of historical dress, which he combines with an astute understanding of contemporary movements in fashion. He carefully analysed and documented the components that had made Chanel a world

fashion leader then skilfully reworked and energized these elements for glamorous young customers at the cutting edge of style.

Initially Lagerfeld fused Chanel's hallmark designs with his own work in a subtle manner, but increasing familiarity with her techniques and favourite ploys prompted him to launch a new, brasher Chanel image for the 1980s and 1990s. At the same time he continued to produce elegant, understated Chanel designs to ensure the loyalty of long-term, less adventurous customers. Black had always been a recurring feature of Chanel's collections, and Lagerfeld ensured that it was a major part of the firm's rejuvenation. He created little black dresses with a difference, enriching them

with larger-than-life costume jewels and embroideries inspired by the Chanel archive. By just the right degree of exaggeration and change of balance, he transformed the Chanel look.

In luxurious black woollen bouclé, here Lagerfeld was faithful to the Chanel 1950s cardigan suit formula, with its edge-to-edge straight-cut jacket and easy-fitting, minimally flared skirt, but he broke the convention by replacing traditional silk trimming with the product of recent technology – bold extruded plastic braid.

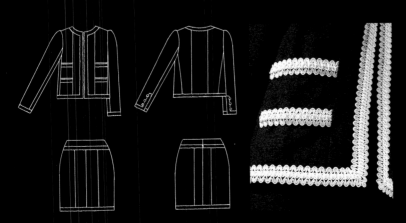

From left to right:
Line drawing, front of suit
Line drawing, back of suit
Detail, bottom left jacket

EAN MUIR

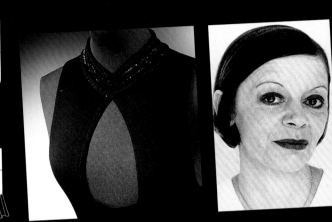

Jean Muir (1928-95) brought a discipline and a formality to dressmaking (she detested the word fashion) and approached colour with the same precision. Every season she composed her palette with enormous care to achieve a balanced range. Colour was critical to her: 'I'm a person who's totally affected by colour. I'm utterly miserable amongst what to me is bad colour' (Leeds City Art Galleries, *Jean Muir*, 1980). Though she frequently created with bright colours, she preferred subtle hues, cherished dark navy and regularly used black. The latter was ideal for her work, which married a 'no nonsense' factor to feminine grace and proved ideal for the working woman.

Self-trained, she had an exacting route to the top via Liberty's, Jacqmar, Jaeger and Jane and Jane before establishing her own company in 1966. Certain fabrics – woollen crêpe, supple suede and matt jersey – became her signature materials.

From Muir's last collection, this long, slender evening dress reveals her mastery of fine jersey, a fabric that is notoriously difficult to handle. Her intimate knowledge of the cloth enabled her to use it with complete confidence, taking advantage of its stretchy nature and good draping characteristics. Six panels make the svelte garment, which clings to the body down to knee level then flares out to

graze the floor
top stitched fo
an understated
the flowing co
keyhole neckli
sequinned sta
emphasize the
homage to M
included tribu
Liz Tilberis as
black dresses
Jean Muir litt
on gives one
and comfort

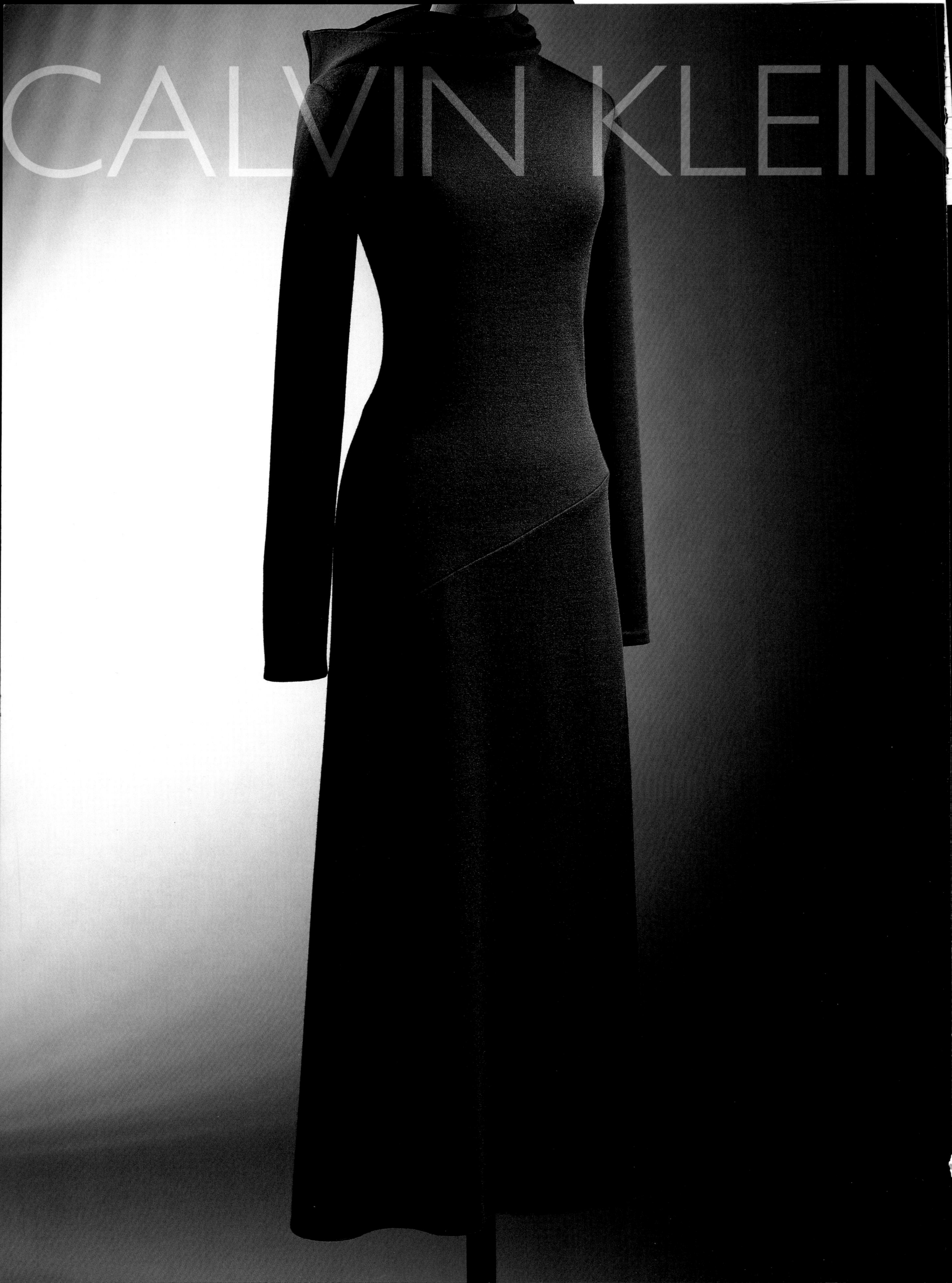
CALVIN KLEIN

'Bernadette', day dress, Calvin Klein

New York autumn-winter, 1996
Given by Calvin Klein

Svelte, simple and consummately elegant in supple black wool jersey, this day dress represents the belief in minimal aesthetics that Calvin Klein (b. 1942) has honoured since he began his ascent in the fashion world. A ruthlessly plain garment is not an easy design option. In order to succeed with such an idea, cut and construction have to be faultless, as no added frills or decoration are available to conceal any imperfections.

The smooth, body-hugging dress has a linear purity achieved by diagonal seaming that creates a long, lean torso above a gently flared skirt. The garment's covered-up look and demure hood have overtones of the cowled black habits worn for many centuries by the Benedictines or 'black monks'. Klein could have been describing this dress when, ten years after the foundation of his business, he told Bernadine Morris (*The Fashion Makers*, 1978): 'I don't like a lot of heaviness or bulk…I like clothes that slide when the body moves. They have to be easy and free, not stiff.' He asserted his faith in beautiful fabrics and his dislike of overdesigned, gimmicky clothes.

With an admirable discipline, Klein refused to be influenced by short-lived fads or way-out looks and, in luxurious textiles, he produced cleanly tailored clothes with subtle lines that evolved from collection to collection. The 'non-colours' were ideal for his classic designs; thus he regularly used black, white and grey, alone or in combination. Perceived as an American hero, Klein has been praised by his countrymen for his financial acumen, then berated for aggressive, unseemly marketing techniques. However, the same unswerving vision generated his controversial advertising campaigns, jeans and unisex underwear and this unpretentious little black dress.

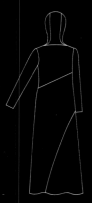
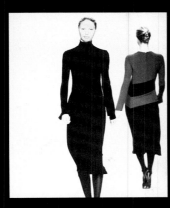
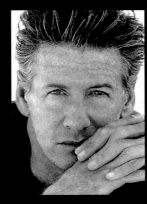

From left to right:
Line drawing, back of dress
Calvin Klein's new black
for autumn 1996,
a dark aubergine
dress on the catwalk
Portrait of Calvin Klein.
Courtesy of the designer

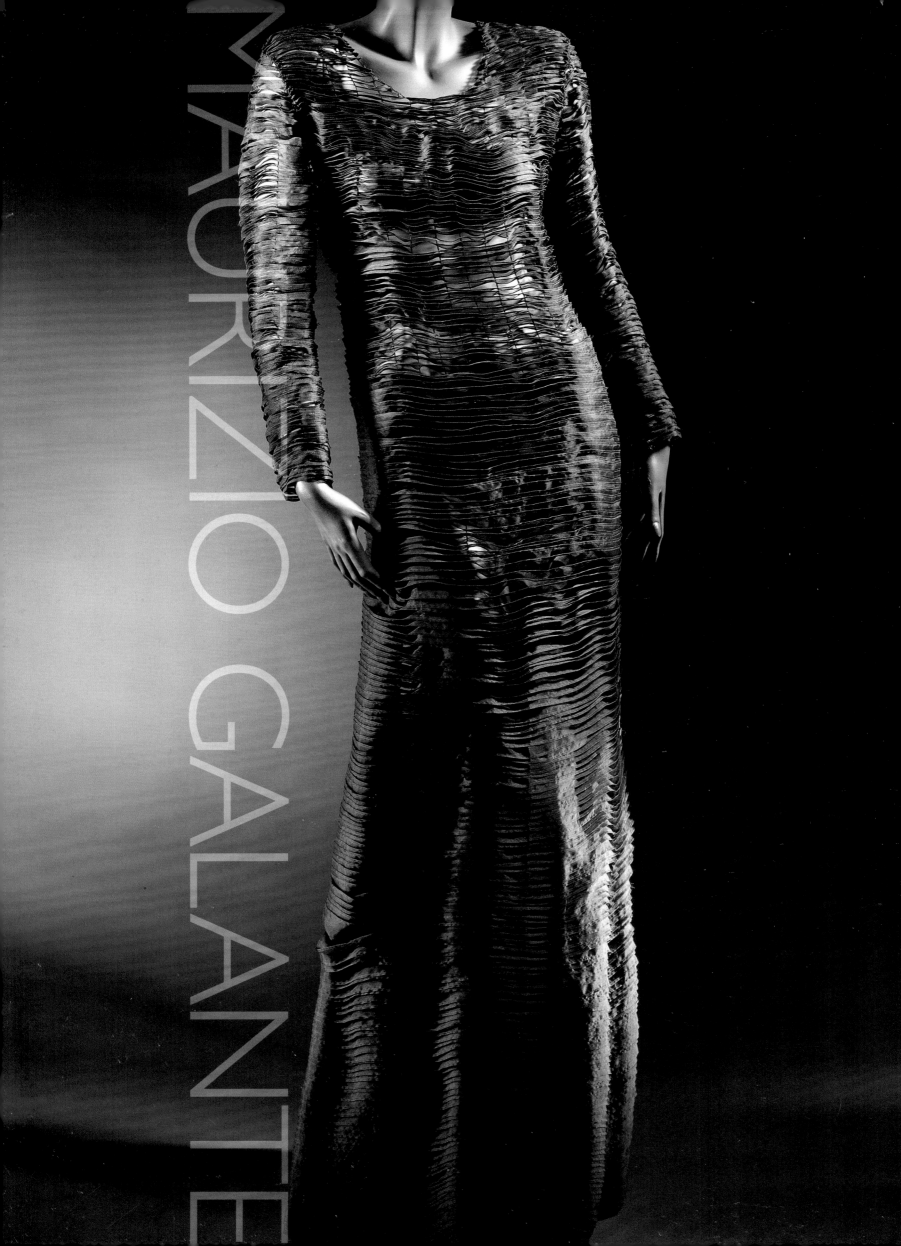

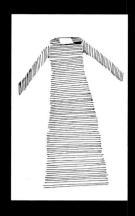 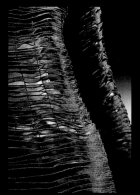 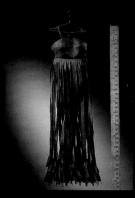

Evening gown, Maurizio Galante
Paris autumn-winter 1995-96
Given by Maurizio Galante

With his first collections in the early 1990s, Maurizio Galante (b. 1963) demonstrated how new, young talent constantly reinvigorates fashion. His complex, avant-garde designs are predicated upon the craft of couture – fine workmanship and close attention to infinitesimal details. Living in the country (he divides his time between France and Italy), Galante enjoys the colours of nature, preferring to compose each item in a single colour rather than in a melange of hues, which he feels are the cause of problems. Black occurs regularly in his work, and in 1995 black and white dominated his third season in Paris in a collection shown against a white voile curtain fluttering with black feathers. In addition to fashion he is passionate about plants, and his understanding of the growth and structure of botanical life informs his garment making.

Fine silks are painstakingly cut and assembled into multi-layered, petal-like configurations making 'dreamy organza dresses'. Organza has the exact amount of crispness required to retain the position of individual layers and the overall shape. Galante explores numerous possibilities – narrow, chevron panels are overlapped and curved to resemble leaf formations, and tiny strips are deployed vertically or horizontally to make skirts, bodices or entire gowns. Here hundreds of horizontal bands of silk organza, graduating from a width of 5 mm (0.19 in) at the shoulders to 5 cm (1.9 ins) at the hem, are held together by vertical lines of handworked buttonholing. The tube-like structure is shaped to accommodate the body's curves and, when taken off, the gown closes in the manner of a concertina.

The smallest black dress in the V&A is Maurizio Galante's limited edition, meticulously hand-made, 1997 Christmas card – a miniature evening dress just 35.6 cm (14 ins) high with a high-waisted bodice and laced back fastening; it has a long skirt of vertical organza strips, each terminating in a miniscule black lily.

Selected Book List

Accademia Valentino. *Valentino: Trent'anni di Magia*
   (Milan, Bompiani 1991)

Amies, Hardy. *Just So Far*
   (London, Collins 1954)

Amies, Hardy. *Still Here*
   (London, Weidenfeld & Nicolson 1984)

Anonymous. *Comments of a Countess*
   (London, Duckworth 1901)

Audsley, George Ashdown. *Colour in Dress*
   (London, Sampson, Low, Marston & Co 1912)

Ballard, Bettina. *In My Fashion*
   (London, Secker & Warburg 1960)

Balmain, Pierre. *My Years and Seasons*
   (London, Cassell 1964)

Baudot, François. *Yohji Yamamoto*
   (London, Thames & Hudson 1997)

Beaton, Cecil. *The Glass of Fashion*
   (London, Weidenfeld & Nicolson 1954)

Bender, Marilyn. *The Beautiful People*
   (New York, Coward-McCann 1967)

Bertin, Célia. *Paris à la Mode*
   (London, Victor Gollancz 1956)

Boehn Max von. *Modes and Manners*
   (3 vols) (London, Harrap 1932)

Carter, Ernestine. *With Tongue in Chic*
   (London, Michael Joseph 1974)

Carter, Ernestine. *Magic Names of Fashion*
   (London, Weidenfeld & Nicolson 1980)

Charles-Roux, Edmonde. *Chanel*
   (New York, Knopf 1975)

Charles-Roux, Edmonde. *Chanel and her World*
   (London, Weidenfeld & Nicolson 1981)

Chitty, Susan. *The Intelligent Woman's
   Guide to Good Taste* (London, MacGibbon
   & Kee 1958)

Coleman, EA. *The Genius of Charles James*,
   exhibition catalogue (New York, Holt, Rinehart
   and Winston for the Brooklyn Museum 1982)

Dariaux, GA. *Elegance*
   (London, Frederick Muller 1964)

Deslandres, Yvonne. *Paul Poiret*
   (London, Thames & Hudson 1987)

Diamonstein, Barbaralee. *Fashion: The Inside Story*
   (New York, Rizzoli 1985)

Dingwall, C and de la Haye, A. *Surfers, Soulies, Skinheads
   and Skaters* (London, V&A Publications 1996)

Dior, Christian. *Christian Dior's Little
   Dictionary of Fashion* (London, Cassell 1954)

Dior, Christian. *Talking about Fashion*
   (London, Hutchinson 1954)

Dior, Christian. *Dior by Dior*
   (London, Weidenfeld & Nicolson 1957)

Duras, M et al. *Yves Saint Laurent, Images
   of Design 1958-1988* (New York, Knopf 1988)

Etherington-Smith, M and Pilcher, J. *The IT Girls*
   (London, Hamish Hamilton 1986)

Etherington-Smith, M. *Yuki*
   (London, privately published 1998)

Fashion: An Anthology, exhibition catalogue
   (London, HMSO 1971)

Fischer-Mirkin, Toby. *Dress Code*
   (New York, Clarkson Potter 1995)

Forester, the Hon. Mrs CW. *Success Through Dress*
   (London, Duckworth 1925)

Fraser, Kennedy. *Scenes from the Fashionable World*
   (New York, Knopf 1987)

Fraser, Kennedy. *The Fashionable Mind: Reflections
   on Fashion 1970-1982* (New York, Nonpareil
   Books 1985)

Garland, Madge. *The Indecisive Decade*
   (London, Macdonald 1968)

Geffrye Museum. *Utility Fashion and Furniture
   1941-1951*, exhibition catalogue
   London 1974)

Gordon, Lady Duff. *Discretions and Indiscretions*
   (London, Jarrolds 1932)

Green, F and Quant, M. *Colour by Quant*
   (London, Octopus Books 1984)

Haedrich, Marcel. *Coco Chanel*
   (London, Robert Hale 1972)

Hartnell, Norman. *Silver and Gold*
   (London, Evans 1955)

Haye, Amy de la and Tobin, S. *Chanel: The Couturière
   at Work* (London, V&A Publications 1984)

Holborn, Mark. *Issey Miyake*
   (Cologne, Taschen 1995)

Howell, Georgina. *Sultans of Style*
   (London, Ebury Press 1990)

Hulanicki, Barbara. *From A to Biba*
   (London, Hutchinson 1983)

Jarman, Derek. *Chroma*
   (London, Century 1994)

Johnston, Lorraine (ed). *The Fashion Year*
   (London, Zomba Books 1985)

Join-Diéterle, Catherine. *Givenchy: 40 Years
   of Creation* (Paris, Editions Paris
   Musées 1991)

Jouve, Marie-Andrée and Demornex, J. *Balenciaga*
   (London, Thames & Hudson 1989)

Keen, Liane. *I Haven't a Thing to Wear*
   (London, Hodder & Stoughton 1965)

Keenan, Brigid. *Dior in Vogue*
   (London, Octopus Books 1981)

Kirke, Betty. *Madeleine Vionnet*
   (New York, Chronicle Books 1998)

Koren, Leonard. *New Fashion Japan*
   (Tokyo, Kodansha International 1984)

Latour, Amy. *Kings of Fashion*
   (London, Weidenfeld & Nicolson 1958)

Lee, Sarah Tomerlin. *American Fashion*
   (London, André Deutsch 1975)

Leeds City Art Galleries. *Jean Muir*,
   exhibition catalogue (Leeds 1980)

Lynam, Ruth (ed). *Paris Fashion*
   (London, Michael Joseph 1972)

McCardell, Claire. *What Shall I Wear?*
   (New York, Simon & Schuster 1956)

McCrum, Elizabeth. *Fabric and Form: Irish Fashion
   Since 1950* (Belfast, Sutton Publishing and
   Ulster Museum 1996)

Martin, Richard (ed). *Contemporary Fashion*
   (New York, St James Press 1995)

Martin, R and Koda, H. *Christian Dior*
   (New York, Metropolitan Museum 1996)

Menkes, Suzy. *The Windsor Style*
   (London, Grafton Books 1987)

Metropolitan Museum of Art.
Yves Saint Laurent, exhibition catalogue
(New York 1983)

Milbank, Caroline Rennolds. Couture
(London, Thames & Hudson 1985)

Milbank, Caroline Rennolds. New York Fashion
(New York, Abrams 1989)

Morris, Bernadine and Walz, B. The Fashion Makers
(New York, Random House 1978)

Moschino, Franco and Castelli, Lida. X Anni de Kaos!
1983-1993 (Milan, Edizioni Lybra Immagine 1993)

Mulvagh, Jane. Vogue History of 20th-Century Fashion
(London, Viking 1988)

Mulvagh, Jane. Vivienne Westwood: An
Unfashionable Life (London, HarperCollins 1998)

Musée de la Mode et du Costume de Ville de Paris.
Hommage à Schiaparelli, exhibition catalogue (Paris 1984)

Musée des Arts de la Mode.
Hommage à Christian Dior 1947-1957, exhibition
catalogue (Paris 1986)

Musée Historique des Tissus. Hommage à Balenciaga,
exhibition catalogue (Lyons 1985)

Museum of Costume, Bath and Brighton Museum.
Norman Hartnell, exhibition catalogue
(Haslemere, South Leigh Press, 1985)

O'Hara, Georgina. Dictionary of Fashion and
Fashion Designers (London, Thames & Hudson;
2nd ed. 1986)

Osma, Guillermo de. Fortuny: His Life and His Work
(London, Aurum Press 1980)

Page, Betty. On Fair Vanity
(London, Convoy Publications 1954)

Perschetz, Lois, W. The Designing Life
(New York, Fairchild Publications 1987)

Poiret, Paul. My First Fifty Years
(London, Victor Gollancz 1931)

Polan, Brenda (ed), The Fashion Year
(London, Zomba Books 1983)

Polan, Brenda. The Fashion Year
(London, Zomba Books 1984)

Post, Emily. Etiquette
(New York, Funk & Wagnalls 1922)

Quant, Mary. Quant by Quant
(London, Cassell 1966)

Rawsthorn, Alice. Yves Saint Laurent: A Biography
(London, HarperCollins 1996)

Remaury, Bruno. Dictionnaire de la Mode au
XXe Siècle (Paris, Editions du Regard 1994)

Rhodes, Zandra and Knight, A. The Art of Zandra
Rhodes (London, Jonathan Cape 1984)

Rykiel, Sonia. Et je la voudrais nue...
(Paris, Grasset 1979)

Rykiel, Sonia et al. Rykiel par Rykiel
(Paris, Editions Herscher 1985)

Savage, Jon. England's Dreaming: Sex Pistols and Punk
Rock (London, Faber & Faber 1991)

Schiaparelli, Elsa. Shocking Life
(London, JM Dent 1954)

Scott, Margaret. Late Gothic Europe
(London, Mills & Boon 1980)

Sladen, Christopher. The Conscription of Fashion
(Aldershot, Scolar Press 1995)

Steele, Valerie. Women of Fashion
(New York, Rizzoli 1991)

Steele, Valerie. Fifty Years of Fashion
(London, Yale University Press 1997)

Storey, Helen. Fighting Fashion
(London, Faber & Faber 1996)

Story, Margaret. How to Dress Well
(New York, Funk & Wagnalls 1924)

Sudjic, Deyan. Rei Kawakubo and
Comme des Garçons (London, Fourth Estate 1990)

Tobin, JJ (ed). Re-made in Japan
(New Haven and London, Yale University Press 1992)

Troubridge, Lady Laura. Memories and Reflections
(London, Heinemann 1925)

Vecchio, Walter and Riley, R. The Fashion Makers:
A Photographic Record (New York, Crown 1968)

White, Palmer. Paul Poiret
(London, Studio Vista 1973)

White, Palmer. Elsa Schiaparelli
(London, Aurum Press 1986)

White, Palmer. The Master Touch of Lesage
(Paris, Editions du Chêne 1987)

Wilson, Elizabeth. Adorned in Dreams
(London, Virago 1985)

Yoxall, HW. A Fashion of Life
(London, Heinemann 1966)

Concerning Black in Fashion

Berenson, Marisa. Dressing Up
(New York, Putnam's 1984), ch. 2

Buss, Chiara (ed). Silk and Colour
(Como, Ratti SpA 1997)

Harvey, John. Men in Black
(London, Reaktion Books 1995)

Hollander, Anne. Seeing Through Clothes
(University of California Press 1978), ch. 4

Edelman Holman, Amy. The Little Black Dress
(New York, Simon & Schuster 1997)

Martín i Ros, Rosa et al. El negre en el vestit,
exhibition catalogue (Barcelona, Museu Tèxtil I
D'Indumentària 1989)

Martin, Richard. 'A Note: Gianni Versace's
Anti-Bourgeois Little Black Dress (1994)',
Fashion Theory: The Journal of Dress, Body & Culture
(Oxford, Berg 1998), vol 2, issue 1

Mendes, Valerie. 'In Search of the Little Black Dress',
The V&A Album (London, De Montfort 1985)

Ribiero, Aileen. Ingres in Fashion
(New Haven and London, Yale University Press
1999), ch. 6

Sozzani, Franca et al. A Noir
(Paris, Editions Assouline 1998)

Taylor, Lou. Mourning Dress: A Costume and Social
History (London, Allen & Unwin 1983)

Glossary

Bandeau – from the French. A headband but also a general fashion term for various bands and band-like panels (sometimes stiffened).

Belstaff – English manufacturers of protective motorcycling clothes. They produced a popular, functional, long, belted jacket with numerous roomy pockets, a flap that passed between the legs and stud fastenings, in a black, wax-finished material. They also issued a 'Black Prince' suit.

Bias – direction running diagonally across the warp and weft of a fabric. To obtain the true bias, fabric should be folded at an angle of 45 degrees to the selvedges.

Bouclé – from the French for curled. Curly or looped yarn and also fabric (often knitted or woven wool) with a textured surface of loops or curls.

Bugle beads – small, cylindrical beads of glass, jet or composition.

Cambric – originally a plain weave linen (from Cambrai) but subsequently of linen or cotton with a low sheen on the right side. Produced in various qualities from fine to coarse.

Chenille yarn – from the French for caterpillar. A tufted, yarn of silk, cotton or wool and (in the twentieth century) of man-made fibres with a velvety, caterpillar-like pile.

Chiton – generic name for a classical Greek garment worn by both men and women. Rectangular in form, it varied in type as well as length, and various methods were employed to secure it around the body. It fell in graceful folds from the shoulders. Two broad categories were Doric and Ionic; the latter appears to have been made of linen with fine vertical crinkles.

Cloqué – French for blistered. A textured fabric (often in monochrome) with a raised (blistered) design achieved in the weave.

Crape – English spelling of crêpe, usually confined to fabric used for mourning.

Crêpe – plain weave fabric with an all-over crinkled texture (which can be subtle or bold) achieved by the use of alternate weft yarns that are tightly twisted in opposite directions (S spun and Z spun). When dyed, the fabric shrinks and the opposing twists cause the crinkled effect. A crêpe finish can also be achieved by chemical means, as well as by embossing.

Crêpe de Chine – French term. A lightweight, usually silk fabric (a type of crêpe) with a high weft and warp count, fine texture and subtle lustre. Originally woven in China, hence the name.

Crêpe romain – French term. A lightweight, matt crêpe (originally in silk) achieved by a particular configuration of warp and weft yarns that are tightly twisted in opposite directions.

Crin – French for horsehair; and also an abbreviated form of 'crinoline'. Originally a stiff, sized, fabric woven in horsehair and linen. Since World War II it has been made in nylon, has an open construction, comes in different widths and is sometimes tubular. Used for inner structures in dressmaking and millinery to give support and to stiffen.

Décolletage – from the French, indicating a low-cut neck.

Faille – slightly stiff fabric (originally in silk) with ribs across the width of the fabric, created by weft yarns that are heavier than the warp yarns. The rib is more pronounced than in poult but not as bold as in grosgrain.

Fluted – curves resembling flutes split longitudinally.

Gazar – created by the Swiss silk company Abraham & Cie for Balenciaga in 1958. A stiff fabric of silk which retains sculptural shapes.

Georgette – a plain weave, lightweight, sheer fabric woven in highly twisted warp and weft yarns.

Gimp – wire or cord covered with silk.

Grosgrain – from the French. Sturdy fabric (originally in silk) with pronounced ribs across the width of the fabric. It is similar to poult and faille but has the boldest rib.

Marquisette – from the French. Crisp, lightweight silk fabric.

Modesty – a decorative edging or detachable front to fill in a low neckline which would otherwise be unacceptably revealing.

Organdie – a very fine, crisp, transparent, plain weave cotton fabric in yarns with a high twist.

Organza – a very fine, crisp, transparent, plain weave silk fabric in yarns with a high twist.

Passementerie – French for trimmings. Decorative trimmings (in a variety of materials) of particularly ornate braids, gimp and beaded edgings.

Pelerine – French for a cape or a mantle.

Peter Pan collar – small, flat collar with rounded ends. Named after the leading character in JM Barrie's Peter Pan (the play was first performed in 1904).

Picot edged – from the French lace and needlework term. Fancy, machine sewn edging featuring little loops, often used on diaphanous fabrics to prevent fraying and as an attractive alternative to the comparative bulk of a conventional turned hem.

Poult – fabric (originally in silk) with ribs across the width of the fabric, created by weft yarns that are heavier than the warp yarns. Similar to faille and grosgrain but finer.

Rouleau – French for a roll. Tube of fabric or ribbon, sometimes exceedingly narrow, used to make fastenings (to be tied in bows); 'shoelace' straps; decorative trimming and piping.

Ruching – strips of fabric, lace or ribbon gathered as a dress trimming.

Scalloped – named after the shell fish. Edged or decorated with a continuous line of regular, semi-circular curves.

Shirring – parallel rows of gathers giving a ruffled appearance.

Slub – small, irregular bulge in yarn achieved in the process of spinning and (in the case of silk) throwing.

Soutache – from the French for braid. A narrow, round-edged braid (sometimes known as 'Russia') often used in decorative applied work for edgings or for loop fastenings.

Strass – a brilliant paste employed for imitation stones, developed (mid-eighteenth century) by and named after a jeweller to the French Court, Georges-Frédéric Strass. Used in costume jewellery and to decorate garments.

Taupe – French for mole. Term adopted by the trade to describe mole brown and give it a chic appeal.

Toile – French for unbleached linen. The pattern for a garment, usually in calico, which enables the designer to make changes and check fit before cutting out the final garment in expensive fabric. Toiles are also sold for copying, in limited editions or for mass production.

Trapunto – type of quilting in which the design is stitched in outline through two layers of fabric, then wadding is inserted through the back to bring the design into relief on the front.

Tree bark satin – heavily textured satin with striations resembling the bark of a tree.

Tulle – French for net (named after the town). Fine, small-meshed net originally of silk and subsequently of cotton or man-made fibres.

Voided velvet – velvet in which areas of tufted pile and flat (voided) areas without pile form the pattern.

Voile – French for veil. Plain weave, fine, semi-transparent fabric (of silk, cotton, rayon or wool) of high twisted yarns.

Volant – French dressmaking term for a shaped panel as well as a flounce.

Museum Numbers

Christian Dior, T. 461-1976, Frontispiece

Redfern, T. 32-1960, p.20

Lucile, Circ.645-1964, p.22

Mariano Fortuny, T.423-1976, p.24

Paul Poiret, T.338-1974, p.26

Chanel, T.86-1974, p.28

Jeanne Lanvin, T.334-1978, p.30

Drecoll, T. 394-1989, p.32

Madeleine Vionnet, T.89-1982, p.34

Anonymous, T.660-1996, p.36

Charles James, T.290-1978, p.38

Schiaparelli, T.394-1974, p.40

Schiaparelli, T.48-1965, p.42

Utility, T.60-1942, p.44

Molyneux, T.92-1982, p.46

Lucien Lelong, T. 296-1974, p.48

Christian Dior, T.116-B-1974, p.50

Matilda Etches, T.152&A-1973, p.52

Jean Dessès, T.113-1974, p.54

Claire McCardell, T.76&A-1978, p.56

Grès, T.263-1981, p.58

Norman Hartnell, T.238-1986, p.60

Michael, T.52:2-1997, p.62

Jean Dessès, T.104-1982, p.64

Christian Dior, T.118-1974, p.66

Balmain, T.51-1974, p.68

Balenciaga, T.234-1982 and T.124&A-1970, p.70

Balenciaga, T.334-1977, p.72

Dior (Yves Saint Laurent), T.125-1974, p.74

Galanos, T.218-1974, p.76

Balenciaga, T.22-1974, p.78

Lanvin-Castillo, T.52-1974, p.80

Hardy Amies, T.65-1988, p.82

Dior (Marc Bohan), T.139-1974, p.84

Mary Quant, T.52-1985, p.86

Biba, T.13-1982, p.88

Givenchy, T.232-1974, p.90

Valentino, T.443-1974, p.92

Courrèges, T.182-1990, p.94

Yuki, T. 264-1989, p.96

Vivienne Westwood and Malcolm McLaren, T.252&A-1989, p.98

Zandra Rhodes, T.66-1978, p.100

Swanky Modes, T.135-1983, p.102

Murray Arbeid, T.182-1980, p.104

Rei Kawakubo, Comme des Garçons, T.167&A-1985, p. 106

Donna Karan, T.100 and T.98 –1998, p.108

Yves Saint Laurent, T.332-1997, p.110

Alaïa, T.374&A-1985, p.112

Claude Montana, T.363-1989, p.114

Givenchy, T.318-1997, p.116

Yohji Yamamoto, T.27-1999 , p.118

Moschino, T.243-1989, p.120

Caroline Charles, T.250-1989, p.122

Giorgio Armani, T.154&A-1991, p.124

Anouska Hempel, T.111-1992, p.126

Helen Storey, T.210-1993, p.128

Issey Miyake, Loan, p.130

Karl Lagerfeld for Chanel, T.139 and T.140-1995, p.132

Jean Muir, T.218-1996, p.134

Calvin Klein, T.255-1997, p.136

Maurizio Galante, T.559-1997, p.138

Acknowledgements

Special thanks are extended to Sue Milner and Richard Davis who performed amazing feats of styling and photography with patience and good humour and to Leonie Davis for her commitment and lucid line drawings. I am deeply indebted to all those (designers, descendants and houses) who sanctioned this celebration of the creativity of fashion designers and makers. My secondment to the V&A Research Department provided the ideal environment for compiling this book. For their encouragement, practical help and information freely shared, I am particularly grateful to Linda Parry, Susan North, Amy de la Haye, Claire Wilcox, Avril Hart, Ngozi Ikoku and Helen Wilkinson of the Textiles and Dress Department; Paul Greenhalgh, Malcolm Baker, Jane Pavitt, Jane Buller, Clive Wainwright, Carolyn Sargentson, Ghislaine Wood, Greg Irvine and Gareth Williams of the Research Department; Mary Butler and Nicola Evans of V&A Publications; Moira Johnson, who edited the text and Valerie Chandler, who supplied the index; Lynda Hillyer and Audrey Hill of the Textiles Conservation Studio; Phillipa Glanville and Clare Phillips of the Metalwork Department; James Stevenson and Ken Jackson of the V&A Photographic Studio. In the same generous spirit, Charles Metcalfe (who suggested the title), Anthony del Tufo (the perfect intern), Jane Mulvagh, Jennifer Opie, Elizabeth McCrum, Leonora Curry Barden, Janet Skidmore, Shaun Cole, Marie Hélène Poix, Marie-Andrée Jouve, Rosa M Martín i Ros, Hannah Ford, Manny Silvermann, Mickey Riad, Peter Humm, Sarah Graham, Donald Miles, Roy Gamble, Roy Weightman, Edward Grafton, Marjorie Jones, Diane and Ernest Connell, Laurie Milner, Jaana Jätyri and Katie Swann gave of their time and knowledge. Thanks are also due to Soizic Pfaff of the Dior Archive and the librarians at Condé Nast Publications. To my husband Peter, for tolerating my fixation with black clothes and for steering me through – my eternal thanks.

Index

Alaïa, summer ensemble (1985) 16, 112-13
Amies, Hardy 45
    cocktail dress - 'Epigram' (1960) 82-3
Arbeid, Murray, evening dress (1978) 104-5
Armani, Giorgio, evening ensemble (1990) 124-5

Balenciaga 12, 63, 79, 91, 95
    day dress (1958) 70-71
    day dress - EISA label (1957) 70-71
    evening dress (1958) 72-3
    evening gown - 'Amphora' line (1960) 78-9
Ballard, Bettina 12, 39, 79, 81
ballooned skirts 59
Balmain, Pierre 47, 49, 111
    evening dress (1957) 1, 68-9
Beaton, Sir Cecil 14, 27, 35, 59, 75, 91
and Balenciaga 71, 72-3
Biba (Barbara Hulanicki) 14
    mini dress (1968) 88-9
Bohan, Marc, evening gown for Dior (1967) 84-5
bondage suits 16, 98-9
bouffant shapes 55, 58-9, 69

Castillo, Antonio del 81
Chanel 9, 10-11, 15, 19, 29, 133
    evening dress (c1922) 28-9
    suit (1994) designed by Karl Lagerfeld 132-3
Charles, Caroline, evening dress (1989) 122-3
cocktail dresses 13, 51, 83
Comme des Garçons (Rei Kawakubo) 16-18, 119
    ensemble (1982) 106-7
Courrèges, day dress (1972) 94-5
Creed, Charles: Utility design 45

Dariaux, Geneviève Antoine 13
Dessès, Jean 13
    day dress (c1955) 64-5
    evening gown (1948) 54-5
Dewsbury, Judy, Swanky Modes disco
    dress (1978) 16, 102-3
Diana, Princess of Wales: in black 18
Dietrich, Marlene 15, 105
Dior, Christian 7, 12, 13, 35, 49, 51, 61, 111
    afternoon dress - 'Maxim's' (1947) 50-51
    evening dress - 'Bal Masqué' (1958) designed by
        Saint Laurent 74-5
    evening gown (1967) designed by Marc Bohan 84-5
    evening gown - 'Soirée de Décembre (1955) 66-7
Donnellan, Michael: Michael suit 62-3
Drecoll, evening dress - 'Minuit Sonne' (1926) 32-3
Duff Gordon, Lady see Lucile

EISA: Balenciaga day dress (1957) 70-71
Elizabeth II, Queen: mourning clothes 61, 83
Etches, Matilda, evening ensemble (1947) 52-3
Evein, Bernard: Delphine Seyrig dress 15

fabrics: characteristics 8
    chiffon 51, 77
    crêpe 37, 43, 47, 49, 52-3
    jersey 16, 57, 89, 97, 135
    organza 139
    satin 37
    synthetics 16, 65, 129
    Lycra 16, 103
    polyester jersey 97
    Fath 13, 111, 117
    feathers 85, 91

Firbank, Heather 20-21
Ford, Tom 18
Fortuny, Mariano, evening gown (c1920) 24-5
    'Fortuny' sheath dress (Helen Storey) 129
Fox, Frederick (milliner) 105

Galanos (James Galanos), evening dress (1959) 76-7
Galante, Maurizio, evening gown (1995-96) 138-9
Gaultier, Jean Paul 121
Ginger Group: Mary Quant mini dress 86-7
Gish, Lilian 25
Givenchy 15, 91, 111, 131
    evening dress (1987) 116-7
    evening ensemble (1968) 90-91
Greco, Juliette 15
Grès, cocktail dress (c1950) 58-9

Hartnell, Norman 105
    evening gown (early 1950s) 60-1
Hayworth, Rita, in Gilda 15
Hempel, Anouska, evening gown - 'Marta' (1991) 126-7
Hepburn, Audrey, and Givenchy 15, 91
Herberfield, Melanie, Swanky Modes disco
    dress (1978) 16, 102-3
Hulanicki, Barbara (Biba) 14
    mini dress (1968) 88-9
Hurley, Elizabeth, 'safety pin' dress 16

James, Charles, evening gown (1936-37) 38-9

Karan, Donna, day dresses (1986-87) 108-9
Kawakubo, Rei (Comme des Garçons) 16-18, 119
    ensemble (1982) 106-7
Kennedy, Jacqueline (later Onassis) 9, 93
Klein, Calvin, day dress - 'Bernadette' (1996) 136-7

Lady in Black Fashions 13, 19
Lagerfeld, Karl, suit (1994) for Chanel 132-3
Lambert, Eleanor 77
Lanvin, Jeanne, evening dress (1922-23) 30-31
Lanvin-Castillo, evening gown (c1960) 80-81
Leigh, Vivien 53, 69
Lelong, Lucien 117
    evening gown (1946) 48-9
little black dress 7, 9, 10, 13-14, 47, 83, 105, 135
    and Chanel 10-11, 15, 29, 133
    most desirable characteristics 65
    Scarfe cartoon 18-19
Lord and Taylor: Drecoll 'Minuit Sonne' evening dress 32-3
Lucile (Lucy Wallace; Lady Duff Gordon) 10, 47
    dinner gown (1910-12) 22-3

McCardell, Claire, for Townley Frocks, day time
    ensemble (c1950) 56-7
McLaren, Malcolm, with Vivienne Westwood,
    bondage suit (1976) 98-9
Margaret, HRH Princess: Hartnell 60-1
Menkes, Suzy 17, 75, 97
Michael, suit (1954) 62-3
Miyake, Issey 16, 119
    the 'Bouncing Dress' (1993) 130-1
Molyneux 85
    afternoon dress (1946) 46-7
Montana, Claude, day dress (c1985) 114-5
Morton, Digby: Utility design 45
Moschino, Franco, evening dress (1988) 120-1
mourning clothes 7, 8, 9-10, 12, 21, 61
Mower, Sarah, rejected black 17

Muir, Jean, evening dress (1995) 134-5
Mulvagh, Jane 98-9, 117

New Look 51, 61

Onassis, Jacqueline, (earlier Kennedy) 9, 93

Parker Bowles, Camilla: Starzewski dress 19
Piaf, Edith, in black 15
Piguet, Robert 77, 85, 117
pleats 8, 13, 24-5, 39, 47, 53, 65, 69, 130-1
Poiret, Paul 39
    evening gown - 'Samovar' (1919-20) 26-7
punk clothes 16, 98-9, 100-101

Quant, Mary 14, 123
    mini dress (1967-68) 86-7
quilting 8, 52-3

Radziwill, Princess Stanislaus: Valentino 92-3
Redfern afternoon dress (1910-12) 20-21
Renouardt, Jane 31
Rhodes, Zandra 16
    evening dress (1977) 100-101
Rotten, Johnny: bondage suit 16, 98-9
Rykiel, Sonia: on black 19

'sack' dresses 71
Saint Laurent, Yves 17, 75
    evening dress (1985) 110-11
    evening dress - 'Bal Masqué' (1958) for Dior 74-5
Schiaparelli 11, 101, 117
    evening dress (1938) 40-41
    evening gown (1940) 42-3
Sex Pistols: bondage suit 16, 98-9
Seyrig, Delphine, in black 15
Starck, Philippe 19
Starzewski, Tomasz 19
Storey, Helen, sheath dress for clubwear (1993) 128-9
Swanky Modes, disco dress (1978) 16, 102-3

T-shirt dresses: Biba 89
Torimaru, Gnyuki (Yuki), evening dress (c1975) 96-7
Townley Frocks 56-7
Twiggy: in Biba 14

Utility day dress (1942) 44-5

Valentino, evening dress (1969) 92-3
Valois, Dame Ninette de 53
Vanian, Dave 16
Versace, Gianni 16, 121
Vionnet, Madeleine, evening gown (c1934) 34-5

Wallace, Lucy see Lucile
Walters, Willie, Swanky Modes disco dress (1978) 16, 102-3
Weinberg, Lady (Anouska Hempel), evening gown,
    'Marta' 126-7
Westwood, Vivienne 121
    bondage suit (with Malcolm McLaren; 1976) 98-9
Windsor, Duchess of: in black 74-5
Wolford: Philippe Starck's 'Starcknaked' 19
World War I and fashion 9, 10, 45
World War II and fashion 12, 44-5, 49, 51, 55

Yamamoto, Yohji 8, 16
    summer dress (1988-89) 118-9
Young, Esme, Swanky Modes disco dress (1978) 16, 102-3
Yuki (Gnyuki Torimaru), evening dress (1975) 96-7